DISCOURSES *of* EMPIRE

# PENN STATE STUDIES in ROMANCE LITERATURES

Editors   Frederick A. de Armas   Norris J. Lacy   Allan Stoekl

Refiguring the Hero:
From Peasant to Noble in
Lope de Vega and Calderón
by Dian Fox

Don Juan and the Point of Honor:
Seduction, Patriarchal Society,
and Literary Tradition
by James Mandrell

Narratives of Desire:
Nineteenth-Century Spanish
Fiction by Women
by Lou Charnon-Deutsch

Garcilaso de la Vega and the
Italian Renaissance
by Daniel L. Heiple

Allegories of Kingship:
Calderón and the
Anti-Machiavellian Tradition
by Stephen Rupp

Acts of Fiction:
Resistance and Resolution
from Sade to Baudelaire
by Scott Carpenter

Grotesque Purgatory:
A Study of Cervantes's *Don Quixote*, Part II
by Henry W. Sullivan

Spanish Comedies and Historical
Contexts in the 1620s
by William R. Blue

The Cultural Politics of *Tel Quel:*
Literature and the Left in the
Wake of Engagement
by Danielle Marx-Scouras

Madrid 1900:
The Capital as Cradle of
Literature and Culture
by Michael Ugarte

Ideologies of History in the
Spanish Golden Age
by Anthony J. Cascardi

Medieval Spanish Epic:
Mythic Roots and Ritual Language
by Thomas Montgomery

Unfinished Revolutions:
Legacies of Upheaval in
Modern French Culture
edited by Robert T. Denommé and
Roland H. Simon

Stages of Desire:
The Mythological Tradition in Classical
and Contemporary Spanish Theater
by Michael Kidd

Fictions of the Feminine in the
Nineteenth-Century Spanish Press
by Lou Charnon-Deutsch

The Novels and Plays of
Eduardo Manet:
An Adventure in Multiculturalism
by Phyllis Zatlin

Fernando de Rojas and the
Renaissance Vision: Phantasm,
Melancholy, and Didacticism in *Celestina*
by Ricardo Castells

The Poetics of Empire in the Indies:
Prophecy and Imitation in
*La Araucana* and *Os Lusíadas*
by James Nicolopulos

María de Zayas Tells Baroque Tales of Love
and the Cruelty of Men
by Margaret Greer

Vision, the Gaze, and the Function of the
Senses in *Celestina*
by James F. Burke

Adventures in Paradox:
Don Quixote and the Western Tradition
by Charles D. Presberg

# DISCOURSES of EMPIRE

*Counter-Epic Literature in Early Modern Spain*

BARBARA SIMERKA

*The Pennsylvania State University Press
University Park, Pennsylvania*

Publication of this book has been aided by a grant from the
Program for Cultural Cooperation Between Spain's Ministry of
Education and Culture and United States Universities.

Library of Congress Cataloging-in-Publication Data

Simerka, Barbara, 1957–
    Discourses of empire : counter-epic literature in early modern Spain /
Barbara Simerka.
       p.    cm. — (Penn State studies in Romance literatures)
    Includes bibliographical references and index.
    ISBN 0-271-02794-0 (cloth : alk. paper)
    1. Historical drama, Spanish—History and criticism.
    2. Spanish drama—Classical period, 1500–1700—History and criticism.
    3. Imperialism in literature.
    I. Title. II. Series.

PQ6121.H5 S56 2003
862'.051409358—dc21
2003004688

Copyright © 2003 The Pennsylvania State University
All rights reserved
Printed in the United States of America
Published by The Pennsylvania State University Press,
University Park, PA 16802-1003

It is the policy of The Pennsylvania State University Press to
use acid-free paper. Publications on uncoated stock satisfy the
minimum requirements of American National Standard for
Information Sciences—Permanence of Paper for Printed
Library Materials, ANSI Z39.48–1992.

CONTENTS

Preface and Acknowledgments   VII

*1*
Toward a Materialist Poetics of Counter-Epic Literature   1

*2*
"So That the Rulers Might Sleep Without Bad Dreams":
Imperial Ideology and Practices   15

*3*
Liminal Identity and Polyphonic Ideology in *Indiano* Drama   39

*4*
The Early Modern History Play as Counter-Epic Mode:
Cervantes's *La destrucción de Numancia* and Lope de
Vega's *Arauco domado*   77

*5*
The Novelistic History Play: Rojas Zorrilla's *Numancia* Diptych
and González de Bustos's *Los españoles en Chile*   129

*6*
"War and Lechery": *La gatomaquia* and the Burlesque Epic   161

*7*
Conclusions   181

Works Cited   203

Index   217

PREFACE AND ACKNOWLEDGMENTS

My interest in literary representations of discourses questioning militaristic and imperial ideologies began in 1992, as I battled conflicting desires to finish my dissertation and to become involved in the largely unreported peace movement that arose during "Operation Desert Storm," the first Persian Gulf conflict. My search to identify forms of anti-epic writing was accompanied by a growing awareness of the legacy of U.S. imperialist activity on nearly every continent since the end of World War II—information that generally goes unmentioned in major media but is well documented in the political and historical writings of Noam Chomsky and Howard Zinn, the political cartoons of Tom Tomorrow, and alternative publications such as *Z Magazine* and *The Nation*. Many thinkers who questioned previous manifestations of American hegemony supported the war in Afganistan, creating a sense of isolation for the small minority that continue to doubt. I count myself among them, even though I moved to New York just in time to witness the destruction of the Twin Towers, whose pillars of smoke could be seen from my living-room windows for several days after 9/11. I conclude this manuscript as we wage war on Iraq, despite worldwide protests, and I am grateful to be writing about a topic that is relevant to my pacifist convictions. It is important to state emphatically that I do not deceive myself concerning the material relevance of such academic endeavors. I do not contend that writing about counter-epic literatures constitutes any sort of meaningful form of political resistance. Yet all movements for change seek historical antecedents for current controversies, and it is my hope that the analysis of representations of an earlier phase and form of imperialism offered in this book may in some ways illuminate present concerns.

This work is the culmination of a decade of reading, thinking, and writing about the relationship between generic innovation and early modern literary representations of ideological issues. Earlier versions of several sections have been published previously. The exploration of genre theory and marxist criticism found in Chapter 1 was published previously in an article appearing in my anthology, *El arte nuevo de estudiar comedias*. The concept of a materialist poetics of reception was analyzed in an article on *El burlador de Sevilla* published in *Gestos*. Previous studies of *indiano* drama appeared in *Bulletin of the Comediantes* and *RLA,* and a preliminary comparison of Numancia and Arauco drama was offered in a *Cervantes* essay. All of those sections have been substantially reconsidered or recontextualized here. I should also note that all translations in this book are my own, unless otherwise indicated.

This enterprise has benefited from many supporters, including the readers and editors at Penn State Press, especially Laura Reed-Morrisson and Tim Holsopple, and the journals cited above. Participating in a 1995 NEH Summer Seminar on literary history at Princeton University, under the direction of Earl Miner, enabled me to benefit from both intellectual stimulation and magnificent library resources. The University of Texas at San Antonio provided grants for research time in the summers of 1997 and 2000 and support for research assistance from Shelley Dellert Davis, José Luis Ramírez, and Karina Stiles Cox. Three exemplary high school teachers—Mary Ann Hudnut, Nadine Dyer, and John Dempster—fostered my early interests in writing, literary criticism, and the Renaissance. Charles Fraker was an invaluable mentor during my undergraduate years. Although very little material from my dissertation appears in this essay, thesis directors James Parr and Nancy Vickers provided crucial encouragement and feedback during the earliest years of this project. James Parr has continued to be a valued mentor and friend and gave constructive advice about the final chapter. Frederick de Armas and Diana de Armas Wilson read numerous versions of the manuscript and offered important insights and references. Christopher Weimer's gift of *Stages of History* significantly strengthened my framework for the analysis of the Numancia and Arauco plays; his support, collaborations on conference panels and other projects, and friendship have also made a great contribution over the past decade. I owe a debt of gratitude and love to my parents, Charles and Dorothy Simerka, who expressed unconditional faith and support for my endeavors as a first-generation college student aspiring to become a scholar. I would especially like to acknowledge my husband, Steve Smith, who brought to my attention the progressive journalism that has been central to my intellectual development. His support over the years, ranging from several years as Mr. Mom to technical advice and neck rubs, has been a constant source of strength. The arrival on the scene seven years ago of my daughter, Rachel, undoubtedly delayed the completion of this project but enriched my life beyond measure. I thank her for her understanding about the evenings and weekends that were spent in front of the computer rather than in play.

# 1

## Toward a Materialist Poetics of Counter-Epic Literature

Discourses of empire appear in artistic, political, and theological writings of every genre in circulation in early modern Spain—from Lascasian critiques of forced conversion and genocide to the explications of Roman law by three generations of jurists who sought legal validation of Spain's right to the territory, labor, and mineral wealth of America, from Ercilla's poetic denunciation of Spanish military practices in Chile to hagiographic dramatizations of the lives of the *conquistadores* commissioned by their seventeenth-century progeny. This study focuses upon identifying and analyzing literary texts that represent and mediate discourses of imperialism in early modern Spain. It is not my purpose to argue that emergent and residual discourses posed significant material threats—"subversions"—to the prevailing system's order and stability. Rather, the goal of the materialist, "epochal" analysis of counter-epic texts offered here is to highlight the contestatory ideas against which hegemonic martial imperialist discourses defined and defended themselves—and thus to analyze the negotiation of imperial ideologies within texts that foreground the tensions produced by ideological confrontation. As Anthony Cascardi correctly observes, "What is 'ideological' about the historical role of literature in the Spanish Golden

Age is that it is not merely shaped by . . . tensions, but articulates a strongly inflected response to them."[1]

Many historians, including Anthony Pagden, John Lynch, J. H. Elliott, and Raffaele Puddu, have examined the relationship between unflattering early modern literary representations of European aristocracy and the social tensions that were produced by the shift from the warrior nobility of the feudal era to the courtiers of absolutist regimes. This modification of the nobility's role was frequently characterized as a loss of masculinity by those who opposed such changes (as well as by those who benefited from them). The critique of courtiers within counter-epic works gives rise to an interesting paradox, for those who do not fight are despised as feminine, while Romans, indigenous peoples, and Numantians are often coded as hypermasculine and thus barbaric. The rise of the merchant class as a significant competitor for economic power, while less pronounced in early-seventeenth-century Spain than in England or France, nonetheless constituted a related source of social instability and anxiety.[2]

Over the course of the sixteenth century, Spain experienced the dazzling heights of dominion over both a mineral-rich overseas colony and the Holy Roman Empire. It also endured a series of *fin-de-siècle* disasters associated with imperialism: the destruction of the Armada, a plunge in the quantity of metals flowing from the New World, and bankruptcy. As a result, the last decade of the century witnessed an intense debate over the relative advantages and liabilities of imperialist practice, a debate that continued well into the 1600s. There followed a period of retreat from imperialism under Philip III and Lerma, who sought to alleviate Spain's financial problems through truces with the Dutch, French, and English. This period of peace improved Spain's financial situation, but it also contributed to a sense of decline based upon nostalgia for the previous century's glory. For this reason (among others), Philip IV and Olivares did not renew the peace treaties when they expired. Instead, they embarked upon a series of relatively unsuccessful military ventures in the 1620s. The consequences of these ventures included not only a worsening of Spain's much-valued "reputation" but also the permanent loss of Portugal and the northern Protestant sections of the Netherlands known as the United Provinces—as well as twelve years of independence for Catalonia. Doubts about the validity

---

1. See Anthony J. Cascardi, *Ideologies of History in the Spanish Golden Age* (University Park: The Pennsylvania State University Press, 1997), 15.
2. Agostino Lombardo, "Fragments and Scraps: Shakespeare's *Troilus and Cressida*," in *The European Tragedy of Troilus*, ed. Piero Boitani (Oxford: Clarendon Press, 1989), 213.

of imperialism during this period extended to a questioning of involvement in European theaters of action and in the Americas, for defending Spain's trade monopoly with its colonies was a significant factor in many Continental conflicts. In addition to the pragmatic examination of the benefits and costs associated with the Christian imperial mission conducted by political and diplomatic figures as well as philosophers, the ethical dimensions of conquest sparked considerable discussion among theologians. Elliott notes that missionaries such as Antonio de Montesinos and his famous disciple, Bartolomé de Las Casas, who held Erasmian/Utopian views of the American indigenous population as an example of humankind's innate nobility prior to the debasements of civilization, "found it impossible to square the treatment that was being meted out to the natives with their own fundamental convictions about mankind."[3] This respect for the objects of conquest—though patronizing and Christocentric in its obsession with evangelization—is another important factor in the questioning of imperial warfare found in early modern representations of the battles at Numancia and at Arauco, Chile.

My exploration of the ideological tensions in early modern Spanish literature is consistent with contemporary practices in cultural studies. In a *Chronicle of Higher Education* article from February 2001 about the status of Golden Age Spanish literary study, Scott Heller states that "after years of notorious conservatism," Hispanists are "finally catching up" with the changes in methodology that marked a shift in English studies from analysis of the Renaissance from a humanist vantage point to interdisciplinary and postmodern explorations of "early modern" European culture.[4] In making this assertion about the novelty of such an approach, Heller overlooks a decade of important ideologically oriented studies of drama and prose by George Mariscal, Margaret Greer, Baltasar Fra Molinero, and William R. Blue, as well as anthologies edited by John Beverly, Mark Millington and Paul Julian Smith, and Marina Brownlee and Hans Ulrich Gumbrecht, to name just a few. His outline of current trends in early modern Hispanic studies, however, sketches the critical and theoretical landscape that this project seeks to explore and enhance. For example, my preference throughout for the term "early modern" rather than "Renaissance" or "Golden Age" Spain is intended, as Heller suggests, to reject traditional notions of sixteenth- and seventeenth-century Spanish society as a

---

3. J. H. Elliott, *Spain and Its World, 1500–1700* (New Haven: Yale University Press, 1989), 72.
4. Scott Heller, "The New Geography of Classical Spanish Literature," *Chronicle of Higher Education* 47, no. 21 (2 February 2001): A14.

monolithic and ideologically conservative entity. And, as many of the scholars Heller interviewed indicated, a deeper analysis of the diverse discourses circulating in early modern Spain is opening areas of investigation and providing new insights concerning canonical texts. My examination of several different forms of (mostly) noncanonical counter-epic writings can be viewed as part of this larger project.

I have chosen the label of "counter-epic" to describe these writings because they deploy a revisioning of epic values in order to examine a particular aspect of early modern martial aristocratic discourse.[5] The early modern Spanish counter-epic rewards careful analysis—and my study will take up several prevalent elements of baroque aesthetics, including the juxtaposition of numerous genres, the innovative "redeployment" of generic conventions (including generic parody), and the radical modification of traditional stock characters. But even as this study attends to the "formal" aspects of the counter-epic, it is also grounded in three materialist precepts. First, early modern Spanish culture was not uniquely monolithic and orthodox, but like all cultures, it contained residual and emergent discourses as a source of oppositional voices and ideologies. Second, the study of counter-epic literary representations can provide insights into one form of discursive mediation through which dominant military ideologies were examined and questioned. Third, the questioning of imperialist practice in counter-epic texts provides meaningful knowledge about the heterogeneity of early modern Spanish society. The following sections of this chapter will provide an overview of materialist poetic practice, and subsequent chapters will examine in detail the connections between specific instances of poetic innovation and imperialist ideologies.

## Materialist Poetics

Despite post-Soviet and post-structuralist declarations of the death of marxism,[6] Karl Marx's ideas concerning the nature of literary representation

---

5. Claudio Guillén cites the picaresque novel as an example of a counter-genre, the anti-romance, because the unheroic adventures of the *pícaro* function as the negative image of the chivalric hero and his martial achievements. See his *Literature as System: Essays Towards the Theory of Literary History* (Princeton: Princeton University Press, 1971). A similar inversion of heroic values expressed through redeployment of a conventional heroicizing genre is present in the body of early modern Spanish poetry and drama that deploys the epic as a counter-genre.

6. Like many critics who take a materialist approach to the study of culture, I do not capitalize adjectives such as marxist, gramscian, and so on (see Cary Nelson and Lawrence

continue to play an important role in the development of theories of textuality. By pointing out the class discourses that nineteenth-century theories of universal standards of beauty tried to suppress and by demonstrating that apparently "natural" standards of excellence are also the products of class ideology, Marx provided the foundation upon which scholars engaging with issues of gender and ethnicity could construct their own critiques of dominant aesthetic standards and canons.[7] "Cultural materialist" studies, however, have also identified several flaws in Marx's explanation of the role played by cultural productions—flaws that drastically undermine classic marxism's usefulness for the study of literary and other social practices.

The most troubling weakness in Marx's model of social and literary relations is the positing of a literature/society dualism, one that sets literature apart from other social activity. In *Marxism and Literature*, Raymond Williams identifies the source of this problem as the distinction Marx makes between a composer and a piano maker—and his subsequent supposition that aesthetic activity is not a part of material production.[8] This separation leads to Marx's construction of economic and social reality as a base, or referent, and aesthetic production as the superstructure that passively reflects that reality. There is a general consensus among critics and theorists who currently practice marxist-inspired materialist literary study that literature is a mode of production not different in kind from other social modes, one that takes an *active* role in the formation of social practices and discourses. Cascardi proposes such a stance when he describes the Golden Age literary text as "a social force, actively proposing solutions to historical conflicts" (*Ideologies*, 1).

Raymond Williams and Tony Bennett observe that the base itself is a process, an activity, rather than an object of study; it cannot, therefore, be the stable referent to which literature points (see Williams, *Marxism and Literature*, 96; Bennett, *Outside Literature*, 21). Williams asserts that monolithic views of the base fail to recognize the significance of competing discourses within a period and tend to grant significance only to expressions of the dominant voice (Williams, *Marxism and Literature*, 121–23). He advocates the practice of "epochal analysis"—the study of the relations between

---

Grossberg, eds., *Marxism and the Interpretation of Culture* [Urbana: University of Illinois Press, 1988], ix).

7. In *Outside Literature* (New York: Routledge, 1990), Tony Bennett identifies Marx's demystification of the bourgeois aesthetics of his era as particularly pertinent for contemporary criticism (32).

8. Raymond Williams, *Marxism and Literature* (New York: Oxford University Press, 1972), 95.

dominant, emergent, and residual formations—in order to provide a more comprehensive vision of the material forces that shape and are in turn shaped by cultural productions. Williams defines "residual" discourse as that which "has been effectively formed in the past, but it is still active in the cultural process, not only and often not at all as an element of the past, but as an effective element of the present. . . . It is crucial to distinguish this aspect of the residual, which may have an alternative or even oppositional relation to the dominant culture" (122). Emergent discourses do not always—or even often—consist of truly novel developments. According to Williams, they also involve a relation with the past, for at moments of "the default of a particular phase of a dominant culture there is then a reaching back to those meanings and values which were created in actual societies and actual situations in the past, and which still seem to have significance because they represent areas . . . which the dominant culture neglects, undervalues, opposes, represses, or even cannot recognize" (123–24).[9] A materialist reading of counter-epic texts reveals that the critiques of Spanish imperialist practice launched by Bartolomé de Las Casas, Juan Luis Vives, Furió Ceriol, and many others constitute a meaningful residual discourse as well as a source for the seventeenth century's emerging anti-imperialist discourses. Both aspects of this critique are relevant for studies of texts written during the century after the famous debates at Valladolid in 1550.

Scholars who practice materialist criticism usually do not foreground the stylistic and formal elements of texts. Louis Montrose describes his "cultural poetics" as a practice that replaces diachronic (stylistic) studies of literary texts with an analysis of "the synchronic text of a cultural system." Gregory Colomb characterizes an alternate "materialist poetics" as a practice that "redefines the notion of particulars, treating poetic particulars (words, images, figures) as parts of an intricate web connecting the social facts of persons and places to the 'prosaic' particulars of history."[10]

---

9. Materialist interpretive practices that grant significance to residual and emergent discourses are emphatically dismissed by New Historicist critics, who favor the Foucauldian analysis of cultural discourse and political power and who view literary representations of counter-hegemonic ideology as a tool used by dominant groups in order to consolidate their own power and legitimacy. See Bennett, *Outside Literature*, 19, and Williams, *Marxism and Literature*, 97; see also Jonathan Dollimore and Alan Sinfield, eds., *Political Shakespeare: New Essays in Cultural Materialism* (Manchester: Manchester University Press, 1985), viii, and Judith Newton and Deborah Rosenfelt, eds., *Feminist Criticism and Social Change* (New York: Methuen, 1985), xv.

10. Louis Montrose, "Professing the Renaissance: The Poetics and Politics of Culture," in *The New Historicism*, ed. H. Aram Veeser (New York: Routledge, 1989), 17; Gregory G. Colomb, *Designs on Truth: The Poetics of the Augustan Mock-Epic* (University Park: The Pennsylvania State

## Materialist Poetics of Character and Subjectivity

In early modern Spanish texts, the literary exploration of the "historical particular" of imperialism was not limited to representing actual warfare. The subgenre of *indiano* drama represents another aspect of military conquest: the role of the "colonial" subject at the imperial court. The term *indiano* is used by early modern dramatists to signify two types of individuals, both of pure European/Spanish blood: (1) men and women who were born in the New World and travel to Spain as young adults to find mates, and (2) men born in Spain who, lacking the monetary or social resources necessary to marry well in their youth, travel to the Indies to gain riches and return to Spain in middle age in order to "buy" a noble bride and access to higher levels of courtier society. The characters' social mobility constitutes a significant factor in the liminal status of *indianos* in these plays and is related to generalized early modern anxieties about the instability of identity and status. Indeed, anxiety about the transformative power of encounters with an "alien" culture plays an important role in all early modern European societies and the texts that represent them.[11] Counter-epics offer literary mediations of militant aristocratic values and intensively explore imperial policy, validating Cascardi's assertion that Golden Age texts serve to "sutur[e] together the various contradictions that in their contemporary world could be attributed to the conflicting value systems of class and caste" (*Ideologies*, 2).

Edith Villarino has identified more than two dozen plays with *indiano* characters.[12] Chapter 3 will focus upon four plays that feature the conflation of *villano* and *indiano* figures: Lope de Vega's *El sembrar en buena tierra (Cultivating in Good Soil)* and *El premio del bien hablar (Rewarded for Courtesy)*, Tirso de Molina's *La villana de Vallecas (The Provincial Woman from Vallecas)* and *La celosa de sí misma (Her Own Rival)*, and two Tirsian dramas with *indiano senex* characters, *Por el sótano y el torno (Through Nooks and Crannies)* and *Marta la piadosa (Pious Marta)*. The chapter highlights the multiple roles played by the liquid, monetary forms of wealth possessed by *indiano* characters. It will thus contribute to what Carroll Johnson has noted as a

---

University Press, 1992), xii. Colomb's model is equally useful for examining the "web" formed by the conjunction of baroque aesthetic practices and early modernity's social and political turmoil.

11. Walter Cohen, "The Uniqueness of the *Comedia*," in *Echoes and Inscriptions: Comparative Approaches to Early Modern Spanish Literatures*, ed. Barbara Simerka and Christopher B. Weimer (Lewisburg: Bucknell University Press, 2000), 26–28.

12. Edith Marta Villarino, "*El indiano*, un entremés de Lope de Vega," *Signos* 25, no. 31–32 (1992): 227–33.

frequently overlooked area of study: early modern Spanish textual representations of economic relations.[13]

## Materialist Poetics of Genre

In one of the four essays that constitute his *Anatomy of Criticism,* Northrop Frye creates a system that organizes all types of literature, from mythology to the modern anti-novel, according to several categories that simultaneously define and cut across generic boundaries. Fredric Jameson's marxist-inspired rejection of this system is based on objections to Frye's positing of an ahistorical, transcendent notion of literary types, one that fails to distinguish, for example, among medieval chivalric romances, Shakespeare's late plays (often referred to as romances), and the romantic historical novels of the nineteenth century. Jameson advocates the "historicization" of these differing works through an examination of which aspects of the contemporary social order are marginalized in each instance.[14] Shakespearean scholars were among the first to examine the relations between genre and political ideology from this standpoint. Stephen Greenblatt edited a special volume of *Genre* entitled *The Forms of Power and the Power of Forms* in 1982, and Jonathan Dollimore's *Radical Tragedy* (1984) examined the relationship between Jacobean tragic drama and the overthrow of the Stuart monarchy. These early studies of the relations between ideology and literary formation, however, analyzed the deployment of particular genres without a substantial reconsideration of New Critical definitions of those genres—or of the notion of "genre" itself.

A productive development within genre theory has been a turn away from New Critical visions of genre study as pigeonholing texts into static categories. The acceptance of new classes of writing also enables readers to revision the generic components of works already in the canon, as Wlad Godzich and Nicholas Spadaccini demonstrate in *Literature Among Discourses,* a work that examines the presence of cultural forms such as traditional proverbs, carnival festivals, and medieval religious drama in canonical early modern literature. The purpose of their volume is not "merely" to expand the canon; rather, it is to identify "the processes and mechanisms by which specific texts or classes of texts came to be differentiated from other discursive

---

13. Heller, "New Geography," A15; Carroll B. Johnson, *Cervantes and the Material World* (Urbana: University of Illinois Press, 2000), 5.
14. Fredric Jameson, *The Political Unconscious: Narrative as a Socially Symbolic Act* (Ithaca: Cornell University Press, 1981), 130–37, 110.

entities and given the label 'literature.'"¹⁵ In *Outside Literature*, Tony Bennett provides one of the most comprehensive theories of genre and ideology. His "sociology of genres," grounded in the conviction that literary studies are most valuable when literary texts cease to be considered a privileged and "unique" discourse, asserts that the task of genre study is not to define genres but rather "to examine the composition and functioning of generic systems" in order to define the boundaries that separate these systems in terms of "particular, socially circumscribed fields of textual uses and effects" (105, 112). Like Greenblatt and Dollimore, Bennett emphasizes the importance of studying literary texts in the context of other types of writing and other social processes, citing Leonard Tennenhouse's Shakespearean study, *Power on Display*, as a model. Bennett highlights the strengths of Tennenhouse's diachronic practice, in which dramatic representations of the monarchy are studied in the context of "royal speeches or proclamations, [of] ledger reports and parliamentary reports," so that "the organization of the system of generic differences—conceived as a differentiated field of social uses" may be achieved (110–11). (The social uses that Bennett lists include nation formation, class formation, and guides for rulers.) The materialist reformulation of genre study employed in my book's analysis of counter-epic poetics incorporates the interdisciplinary research and postmodern conceptions of textuality described here. At the same time, the book breaks new ground by reimagining the relationship between aesthetic analysis and ideological inquiry.

This study explores the redeployment of epic conventions and the creation of new literary forms within the context of early modern Spain's attempts to come to terms with the discrepancies between its imperial ideals and the changing economic and social realities of the late sixteenth and seventeenth centuries. Chapters 4 and 5 analyze the ways in which the

---

15. Wlad Godzich and Nicholas Spadaccini, *Literature Among Discourses* (Minneapolis: University of Minnesota Press, 1986), xiii. As Ralph Cohen observes, most current theory moves beyond the view "of genres as fixed to genre as process of change." John Snyder advocates the study of what genres do, rather than of what they are. Referring to Nietzsche's observation that only that which does not change can be defined, he suggests that genres be seen as "operational rather than essential," so that the most profitable study is of what genres have done "toward the political ends of victory, loss and stalemate." Snyder also suggests that genres themselves are ideological forces and that they constitute "incursions by texts into history." See Ralph Cohen, "Genre Theory, Literary History, and Historical Change," in *Theoretical Issues in Literary History*, ed. David Perkins (Cambridge: Harvard University Press, 1991), 86–87; John Snyder, *Prospects of Power: Tragedy, Satire, the Essay, and the Theory of Genre* (Lexington: The University Press of Kentucky, 1991), ix, 1–2, 205.

generically indeterminate anti-epic history play redeploys the themes, motifs, and aesthetic strategies of the martial literary tradition in order to evaluate the role of imperialist practices and discourses. Chapter 4 examines two plays, Lope de Vega's *Arauco domado (Arauco Conquered)* and *La destrucción de Numancia (The Destruction of Numancia)* by Cervantes. Chapter 5 analyzes three later revisions of those dramas: *Los españoles en Chile (Spaniards in Chile)*, by González de Bustos, and the Rojas Zorrilla diptych, *Numancia cercada (Numancia Under Siege)* and *Numancia destruida (Numancia Destroyed)*. These counter-epic texts represent two key moments of imperial conquest and dramatize military and imperialist issues in a serious tone, exploring imperial expansion's troublesome consequences for the colonizing civilization as well as for its victims.[16]

Chapters 6 and 7 analyze the burlesque epic mode found in Lope's *La gatomaquia (Battle of the Cats)*, Scarron's *Virgile travesti (Virgil Travestied)*, Shakespeare's *Troilus and Cressida*, and two sonnets by Francisco Quevedo that parody the *Aeneid* and *Poem of the Cid*. The burlesque form of counter-epic discourse combines parody and satire in its humorously deprecatory representations of military heroes and battles. These chapters foreground the ways in which burlesque epic texts emphasize the commercial aspects of life to undermine literary idealizations of military and heroic activity.

Considering two critically marginalized early modern genres—the *indiano comedia* and the burlesque epic—as well as the less canonical "late baroque" works of Rojas Zorrilla and González de Bustos does not simply expand the canon by including texts that problematize military heroism and imperialism. And I do not seek to draw ahistorical parallels between contemporary peace movements and the antiwar factions of Hapsburg Spain. Instead, this study demonstrates the significant contribution of innovative generic deployments to the representation of discourses in discord. As Ralph Cohen observes, genre study is central to the recent opening of the canon to writers previously marginalized due to gender, sexual preference, race, or class—and, I would add, due to their representation of ideologies at odds with the hierarchical norms of later ages. An awareness that such marginalized texts were ignored because they "did not fit a conception of education aimed at preparing white males for advancing in

---

16. They also offer dramatizations of national history similar to those found in Shakespeare's *Henriad*. Phyllis Rackin's *Stages of History: Shakespeare's English Chronicles* (Ithaca: Cornell University Press, 1990) provides insights into the ideological and generic features of the English history play that are central to my analysis of the generic and discursive indeterminacy found in counter-epic history plays representing Numancia and Arauco materials.

social and economic hierarchies" contributes to a more complex understanding of the ways in which the categorization of cultural forms helps shape our perceptions of the world ("Genre Theory," 90).

## Materialist Poetics of Reception

The recognition of heterodox cultural practices is also relevant to a revisioning of early modern reader/audience response. Rather than seeking to establish a univocal reaction to orthodox or transgressive elements within counter-epic texts, I would argue that reception, like production, is significantly influenced by the competition among discourses.[17] Thus, in describing the variety of discourses concerning imperialism available to those who wrote about this topic, I am at the same time seeking to delineate expanded parameters of audience response. In fact, critical awareness of discourse-bound heterodoxy in the reception of plays or texts is at least as significant as recognizing its impact on production. I will not seek to identify a single ideology in any counter-epic text, for, as post-humanist criticism has shown, even if authorial intention can be "discovered," texts are notoriously slippery.

Reception theory can be said to have its origins in Aristotle's notion of catharsis as the socially beneficial response to the suffering of the tragic hero. Hans Robert Jauss and Wolfgang Iser have developed notions of reader response that center on the reader's previous textual experiences. Although the foci and purposes of their projects differ, both agree that the reader's text-based "horizon of expectations" or "repertoire" is the factor that most strongly determines the reception of a new work. Readers will not produce a cacophony of idiosyncratic textual readings because all readers respond to a text, which itself defines and sets the parameters of what can be read.[18] Stanley Fish challenges the notion that the stable nature of texts is the factor that limits interpretive divergence. He argues instead that responses do not vary widely because all reading practices are formed by "interpretive communities" that perform two functions: to educate readers

---

17. The following exploration of materialist reception appeared previously, in a different context, in my article "The Demystification of Providential Ideology: Skepticism and Unbelief in *El burlador de Sevilla*," *Gestos* 23 (April 1997): 38–66.

18. Hans Robert Jauss, "Literary History as a Challenge to Literary Theory," in *New Directions in Literary History*, ed. Ralph Cohen (Baltimore: The Johns Hopkins University Press, 1974), 18, 23; Wolfgang Iser, *The Implied Reader: Patterns of Communication in Prose Fiction from Bunyan to Beckett* (Baltimore: The Johns Hopkins University Press, 1978), 205, 230.

and to monitor scholarly practices.[19] The models of these three theorists share the assumption that the reception of a text is first and foremost an aesthetic experience, as can be seen in their explanations both of stability of response and of the way in which the reception of a text changes over time.

For Jauss, "literary" texts are distinguished from "popular" ones by virtue of their success in shattering the reader's horizon of expectations through innovations in form and style. As new literary works modify this horizon, they also enable the reader to modify his or her vision of literary history and to see older works in a new light ("Literary History," 18–19). Because Iser focuses on the reading process—the gap-filling activities that constitute the mode of interaction between text and reader—his explanation of critical revisions emphasizes the change in the reading process that arose in response to modern works that require a more demanding "structuring activity" (*Implied Reader*, 205). Fish, on the other hand, highlights the importance of professional critical activity for changing responses to texts. He identifies archeological findings (new evidence about an author or a genre, for instance) and new theoretical paradigms as the most significant factors for producing changes in the way works are taught (*Text*, 364). According to Fish, responses to all subsequent works will be guided by the interpretive strategies learned in the classroom; reader response is thus determined by the norms of the interpretive community. All three of these theorists seem to exclude history in their explanations of literary history and to posit a monolithic reading experience, as critics have pointed out.[20] I would like to suggest that Raymond Williams's concept of discursive competition—that is, the contest among dominant, emergent, and residual formations—can serve as a corrective for both of these weaknesses and can provide the basis for a more historicized theory of response.

As I have noted, the "base" (to use an old marxist term in a non-marxist sense) inferred by Iser, Fish, and Jauss as the factor that limits the possibilities of reception is almost entirely literary. There are few, if any, references to the nonacademic experiences that might affect response. (This is due in part to the specter of entropy raised by critics of reader-oriented theories, who wrongly supposed that response theory sought to study the individual reader, a person whose horizon was based on a unique combination of psy-

---

19. Stanley Fish, *Is There a Text in This Class?* (Cambridge: Harvard University Press, 1980), 338–46.
20. Robert C. Holub, *Reception Theory: A Critical Introduction* (New York: Methuen, 1984), 99; Catherine Gallagher, "Re-covering the Social in Recent Literary Theory," *Diacritics* 4, no. 2 (1982): 41.

chological factors. Despite their misunderstanding of the work of response theory, these critics successfully influenced the development of monolithic reception theories.) By introducing Williams's "epochal analysis" into the study of how responses to cultural phenomena vary, it is possible to historicize the reader or spectator and also to account for a limited plurality of responses as the result of sympathy for and awareness of residual or emergent discourses. In addition, the expanded "horizon" or "repertoire" of the respondent will include the significant nonliterary discourses in circulation, and the "interpretive community" can be reformulated to take into consideration the "ideological community." A materialist theory of reception will thus delineate the nonliterary elements of the cultural formations mediated in a text and analyze the dominant, residual, and emergent versions of those formations in order to describe the oppositional as well as affirmative responses available to the contemporary reader or spectator, supplementing the approaches advocated by Jauss, Iser, and Fish.

A materialist approach to reception study may help overcome one further weakness in Iser's and Jauss's conceptions of the reading process. Both of these German thinkers were heavily influenced by the Russian Formalist conception of defamiliarization, or estrangement. A reading model that privileges astonished awareness of a previously unrecognized convention—whether literary or sociohistorical—and imagines a dramatic shift in the perception of the world as the ideal response takes for granted a reader who is, in marxist terminology, blinded by a false ideology. And Jonathan Culler's observation about Fish's model of interpretive cruxes is also relevant here: he writes that Fish's description of his own reading process must be false, for if he continued to read each new poem according to his original horizon of expectations, then he learned nothing from the reading process.[21] Similarly, a respondent may reevaluate her belief system and adopt some aspect of an emergent or residual formation, or she may reject the insights offered and continue to affirm the dominant discourses. A respondent cannot be continually shocked by defamiliarization into repeated "naive" or "virginal" rejections of the status quo. The defamiliarization model totally ignores the respondent who has already questioned hegemonic formations and therefore cannot even begin to account for that respondent's reception of the representation of an oppositional discourse. In my analysis of counter-epic texts, reader response will be envisioned along

---

21. Jonathan Culler, "Stanley Fish and the Righting of the Reader," *Diacritics* 5, no. 1 (1975): 31.

a continuum similar to that formed by the range from Lascasian to Sepulvedan positionalities described in Chapter 2, with counter-hegemonic response seen as a valid position rather than as a rare exception or even an impossibility.

## Conclusion

Here, I have sketched an outline of the dynamics between counter-epic poetic practice and cultural inscriptions of imperialist ideology. I should also note that gender study is a crucial component of every chapter in this book. In this, I have benefited from the scholarly efforts of other Hispanists attuned to gender, including Malveena McKendrick's early study of gender dynamics and the important contributions of anthologies of feminist studies edited by Valerie Hegstrom and Amy Williamsen, Anita Stoll and Dawn Smith, and the critical editions of women writers produced by Electa Arenal, Stacey Schlau, Teresa Soufas, and others. (The translations of early modern women writers by H. Patsy Boyer and others have also enabled feminist scholars in many fields to gain knowledge of and appreciation for early modern peninsular negotiations of gender roles.) My study does not incorporate female writers, for I am aware of no woman-authored counter-epic text. But in the counter-epic's scrutiny of aristocratic and martial values, deviations from supposed medieval norms are often represented as a degraded, effeminate "decline" from a previous idealized masculinity. In addition, certain subgenres, particularly the burlesque epic and the late baroque history play, utilize female characters as scapegoats for social instability and corruption.

These counter-epic texts take on new life and new forms of signification when studied in the context of recent critical examinations of the consequences of imperialism represented in early modern poetry. David Quint's *Epic and Empire* offers a comprehensive examination of the questioning of martial discourse in a variety of sixteenth-century "epics of losers," including d'Aubigné's *Les Tragiques (The Tragic Ones)* and Ercilla's *Araucana*. In addition, scholarship among Hispanists has provided extensive insights into colonial discourses within Ercilla's and Pedro de Oña's poetic narratives of the conquest of Chile, a useful context from which to reexamine dramatizations of the conquests of Arauco and Numancia. Such disparate yet related elements conjoin in this study to form a materialist poetics of the conflicting representations of imperial ideologies in early modern Spanish counter-epic texts.

# 2

## "So That the Rulers Might Sleep Without Bad Dreams"
### Imperial Ideology and Practices

As Philip Mason has observed, imperialist societies require an ideology that permits both the colonizer and the colonized to accept imperial power relations as the natural order—an ideology that provides restful nights for the rulers.[1] Conventional analyses of early modern Spanish society and its cultural formations interpret the post-Tridentine period as an era characterized by a monolithic, universal affirmation of Spain's role as the "Defender of the Catholic Faith." Historian Raffaele Puddu's viewpoint, similar to that of José Antonio Maravall, allows no room for dissent. Puddu asserts, "el espiritú público castellano se caracterizaba por el respeto a las tradiciones, la ortodoxia, y el principio de autoridad" (the public spirit of Castile was characterized by respect for tradition, orthodoxy, and the principle of authority) and that "la cultura era utilizada como sostén del absolutismo y de la Contrarreforma" (culture was used to support absolutism and the Counter-Reformation).[2] Contemporary cultural critics have undermined such visions of historical periods as monolithic entities and have reformulated the process of cultural inquiry to include the study of oppositional discourses—not only in order to argue that "radical" texts sometimes

---

1. Philip Mason, *A Matter of Honour: An Account of the Indian Army* (London: Cape, 1974).
2. Raffaele Puddu, *El soldado gentilhombre* (Barcelona: Argos Vergara, 1986), 11.

constituted a significant threat to dominant political formations but also, and more importantly, to gain a fuller understanding of the historical and cultural processes through which hegemonies constitute and defend themselves. This study of counter-epic literary reinscriptions of imperialist discourse can thus be seen as an attempt to identify the poetic and dramatic modes through which a *de*naturalization of early modern Spain's hierarchical and imperial power relations was given voice.³ In this chapter, I will focus upon the political, juridical, and theological contexts in which counter-epic examinations of imperial practice circulated.

Literary critics have begun to trace the relationship between negative early modern literary representations of European aristocracy and imperialism and the shift from the warrior nobility of the feudal era to the effeminate courtiers of absolutist regimes. In Hapsburg Spain, as in early modern England and France, advances in military technology during the fifteenth and sixteenth centuries led to a transformation of the function of the nobility from a feudal warrior class to the "service" aristocracy of the court—and to discourses that characterized this new form of nobility as feminized.⁴ At the opposite pole, commentators also criticized the excess desire for glory that prompted unwise military actions. Juan Luis Vives specifically linked heroic narrative and the negative aspects of Spanish imperialism, blaming the exaltation of martial values in epic and romance for the illegitimate wars of conquest engaged in by contemporary military leaders to win glory.⁵ Although the emerging merchant class posed less of a threat in Spain than in other parts of Europe, it produced additional opportunities and anxieties connected to imperialism's commercial dimensions (Lombardo, "Fragments and Scraps," 213). A related but unique element of early modern Spanish history is the social instability created by wealthy *indianos*, whether *criollos* or *peninsulares*, who returned to Spain after long, profitable sojourns in the New World. These *peruleros* upset the mercantilist colonial economy (upon which all of Spain's imperial ventures depended for financial support) by their economic activities in Seville, by engaging in direct trade both with Spanish producers and with other European countries, and by flooding the Spanish economy with silver.⁶

3. Jan P. Nederveen Pieterse, *Empire and Emancipation: Power and Liberation on a World Scale* (New York: Praeger, 1989), 252.
4. Larry Clarke, "'Mars His Heart Enflamed with Venus': Ideology and Eros in Shakespeare's *Troilus and Cressida*," *Modern Language Quarterly* 50, no. 3 (1989): 211.
5. David Quint, *Epic and Empire* (Princeton: Princeton University Press, 1993), 5.
6. John Lynch, *Spain Under the Habsburgs*, 2d ed. (Oxford: Oxford University Press, 1981), 2:214.

Throughout Spain's "Golden Age," an extended debate was waged not only among political advisors and secretaries, jurists, and theologians but also among poets, dramatists, and novelists concerning the legality, morality, and relative advantages and liabilities of imperialist practices.[7] This chapter, after providing an overview of imperial activity during the reigns of Philip II, Philip III, and Philip IV, will utilize recent historical studies to examine several strands of imperialist thought, including (1) the role of Rome in the early modern Spanish political *imaginaire;* (2) jurist debates concerning the right to travel and colonize, the validity of the papal bulls granting dominion over the Americas to Spain and Portugal, the definition of a just war of conquest, the right to utilize indigenous labor, and the benefits and liabilities associated with ruling a large empire; (3) theological debates concerning the moral and ethical dimensions of colonization; (4) the critique of the role of grandee "warlords" within military memoirs written by the new class of professional soldiers that emerged in the sixteenth century; and (5) the role of political factionalism in determining military and diplomatic policy.

## An Overview of Spanish Imperialism, 1559–1665

When Philip II ascended to the throne of Spain, he inherited both a vast empire and empire-sized problems, including a severe shortage of the capital necessary to finance continued dominance of far-flung territories and resistance to direct Spanish rule or a Spanish-dominated European empire among Protestants in the Low Countries and in England (where Philip served as Prince Consort to Queen Mary), Republican sympathizers in the Kingdom of Naples, and indigenous rebels in South America, including the Araucanians and the heirs to the Incan throne. Even fellow Catholics in the papal states and France posed potential threats.[8] In addition, this was a period in which the forces of Islam, embodied in the Ottoman Empire, constituted a potentially serious risk for the Mediterranean coast of Philip's dominions (Pagden, *Spanish Imperialism*, 6).

---

7. J. H. Elliott, *Imperial Spain: 1469–1716* (New York: Pelican, 1963), 26.
8. Anthony Pagden, *Spanish Imperialism and the Political Imagination: Studies in European and Spanish-American Social and Political Theory, 1513–1830* (New Haven: Yale University Press, 1990), 40–41, 92; Carlos Javier de Morales, "Francisco de Eraso y los Ebolistas," in *La corte de Felipe II*, ed. José Martínez Millán (Madrid: Alianza, 1984), 123–26; Lynch, *Spain Under the Habsburgs*, 1:142, 288–300, 350–53; Ricardo Ferrando Keun, *Y así nació la frontera* (Santiago: Antártica), 11–12.

After riots erupted in 1566 in the Netherlands, Philip II replaced moderate regent Margaret of Parma—who advocated negotiation with the coalition of noble and middle-class adherents of various strands of Protestantism—with the aggressively militant duke of Alba. Alba responded to the crisis by imprisoning and then executing two of the aristocratic leaders of the revolt, the counts of Egmont and Hornes; heightening Inquisitorial activity in the region; and attempting to levy taxes upon the nobility and merchants. After eight years of failure either to subdue the entire region or to reincorporate the northern provinces of Holland and Zeeland through authoritarian and militaristic policies, Alba was replaced in 1574 by a moderate, Luis de Requesens. His attempts to achieve a diplomatic peace were seriously undermined by the 1576 sack of Antwerp at the hands of imperial soldiers whose salaries were long overdue (this was the most serious of more than forty mutinies of imperial troops that occurred throughout the Low Countries between 1507 and 1607—an enduring cause of tension in the dominated areas). This sack produced, in turn, major uprisings throughout the Low Countries. In 1578, after Don John of Austria also failed to restore order, Philip finally turned to Alexander Farnese, the Duke of Parma (and son of Margaret of Parma). John Lynch considers Farnese the most successful of the Spanish governor generals of the northern provinces. Through a combination of negotiation and intense, brutal siege warfare, Farnese was able to reestablish control over all areas except for Holland, Zeeland, and Utrecht; these three declared independence, joined together as the United Provinces, and soon rivaled Antwerp as the financial center of northern Europe. As part of Philip II's decision to make peace throughout Europe at the end of his reign, the king arranged a marriage between his daughter, Isabella, and the next governor general of the Netherlands, the Archduke Albert of Austria. Moreover, he granted limited autonomy to the area—an arrangement that did not succeed in reintegrating the United Provinces into the Spanish empire (Lynch, *Spain Under the Habsburgs*, 1:288–307).

After the death of Queen Mary, the ascension of Elizabeth I to the British throne and her subsequent rejection of Philip as a spouse set the stage for continually escalating tension between England and Spain during the final two decades of Philip's rule. Traditional explanations for this conflict emphasize religious differences, though contemporary historians and thinkers have turned to financial considerations.[9] Without a doubt, Spain's

---

9. Antonio Domínguez Ortiz, *The Golden Age of Spain, 1516–1659*, trans. James Casey

overseas and Continental dominions were a critical factor in this discord, as England employed piracy, illegal trade, and financial and tactical support of the rebellious United Provinces to alter the balance of power in early modern Europe (1:316, 331–36). Although plans for an Armada to attack England had been discussed throughout the 1580s, Sir Francis Drake's 1587 attack on Cádiz and his destruction of the New Spain fleet that lay at port there played a decisive role in the move to amass a flotilla in 1588. Bad weather played a large part in the defeat of the Armada, but the enterprise was doomed from the outset: the portion of the Iberian fleet assembled by Farnese in the Netherlands needed protection in order to cross the English Channel, and this northern fleet needed to be positioned at a deep-water port so that the larger vessels from the Lisbon-based fleet could get close enough to protect the smaller ships. Philip failed, however, to provide the financing for the expedition necessary to acquire a deep-water port (1:335–38). Although the Spanish navy recovered relatively quickly from the loss of the Armada in material terms and even launched a second Armada in 1596, a large part of that Armada consisted of escort ships redeployed from the Atlantic trade route, and interruptions in the shipping of silver from America certainly factored into the bankruptcies at the end of Philip II's reign (1:349–50).

In the early 1590s, while still at war with the Dutch and the English (and while Ercilla was composing the third volume of his counter-epic account of Spanish defeats in Chile), Philip II decided to pursue the throne of France after the murder of Henry III. This unsuccessful military effort failed to bring an additional crown to the Spanish dominion, and it caused further loss of territory in the Netherlands, territory that was seized by the United Provinces rebels while Governor General Farnese pursued Philip's French dreams (1:350–55). There followed a period of retreat from imperialism under Philip III and Lerma, supported by active diplomacy on the part of the Netherlands regent, Archduke Albert, as Spain sought to alleviate its financial problems through truces with the Dutch as well as with France (1598) and England (1604). The Twelve-Year Truce with the Netherlands, signed in 1609, revealed the complete debacle of a half-century of armed conflict, for the United Provinces made no concessions concerning tolerance toward the minority Catholic population (2:15, 42–43). This peace, however, did not extend to the Americas. The anxieties raised by continued failure to conquer the Araucanian population fully manifested themselves

---

(New York: Basic Books, 1971), 6; Lynch, *Spain Under the Habsburgs*, 1:314.

in the creation of a special subcommittee within the Council of the Indies in 1600—*la junta de guerra de Indias* (2:23-23).

The period of relative calm that lasted nearly two decades did produce the desired improvement in Spain's financial situation, but nostalgia for the perceived glory days of the previous century contributed to a sense of *declinación* (Elliott, *Spain and Its World*, 116-23). For this reason among others, including a lack of enthusiasm for extending the treaties with the Dutch, English, and French, Philip IV and Olivares allowed the peace treaties to expire and initiated several military ventures in the 1620s. The capture of Breda constitutes the high point of this phase of military activity. Soon after Velázquez painted his triumphal commemoration of the event, however, Breda again revolted successfully. Olivares also dedicated three years and significant resources to an unsuccessful effort to gain control of the Duchy of Mantua at the end of that decade. In the 1630s, Spain's commitments to the western portion of the Hapsburg Empire led to unproductive involvement in the Thirty Years' War. To finance these costly military engagements, Philip IV was forced to convene the provincial *cortes* in an effort to obtain additional revenues. Olivares took the unusual step of suggesting new forms of taxation aimed at the nobility and the clergy, such as taxes on the sale of offices or on the value of property owned, but the *cortes'* hierarchical structure prevented acceptance of these proposals. The revenue was derived instead from the customary practice of taxing basic necessities, thus targeting the "have-nots" rather than the "haves" (Lynch, *Spain Under the Habsburgs*, 2:98). Olivares also failed to obtain support for his "union of Arms" plan, whereby each province and imperial territory would contribute troops or monies to the empire's defense (2:105-6). When Olivares decided that Catalonia would serve as the base for attacks launched against France in the 1639 and 1640 phases of the Thirty Years' War, forcing those in the region to provide support in the form of billets for imperial troops, a peasant uprising against the abuses of the billeted soldiers led to a more general revolt (2:113). The negative consequences of Philip IV and Olivares's imperial adventures thus included not only the decay of Spain's *fama* but also twelve years of independence for Catalonia, the loss of Portugal (which took advantage of the Catalan revolt to declare its own independence in 1640), and permanent independence for the United Provinces with the treaty of 1648 (Elliott, *Spain and Its World*, 116-23). Incapable of learning a lesson from these setbacks, Philip IV pursued unattainable imperial aims to the very end of his reign. In 1659, for example, he signed the declaration of peace ending the Thirty

Years' War in order to concentrate all his energies on an unsuccessful attempt to reconquer Portugal (Lynch, *Spain Under the Habsburgs*, 2:133).

Spain's overseas colonies, though geographically distant, were nonetheless strategically enmeshed with its European possessions. On the one hand, New World precious metals constituted between 10 and 20 percent of the crown's revenues during the sixteenth and early seventeenth centuries and thus contributed crucial economic support for Continental military activity. On the other hand, issues related to Spain's control of the wealth of its colonies were a primary element in Iberian hostilities with the English and Dutch, who engaged in piracy and illegal trade. Thus, ironically, American silver was needed to finance the wars waged in order to assure Spain's continued monopolization of American minerals and trade (1:137, 179). Over the course of the seventeenth century, the economic benefits derived from the American colonies declined significantly. By the 1630s, the veins of silver that could be extracted easily and cheaply were exhausted, and access to the mercury needed for more elaborate and expensive extraction processes was limited (2:87). A shortage of low-cost labor had also become a serious problem, as indigenous populations were decimated through disease, overwork, and the hazardous conditions under which mining was practiced. Imported African slaves proved unsuitable due to their inability to withstand mountain climates as well as their refusal to perform the actual labor (2:224–25). The colonies deviated further and further from the mercantile colonial economic model as they ceased to provide a significant export market. In addition to the direct economic action of *criollos* in Europe and the illicit trade activity with other European countries, the rise of productive economic activity and intra-colonial trade in the Americas also played a key role. By the late sixteenth century, the colonies had already created their own shipbuilding industry and were cultivating and trading among themselves many of the staple agricultural products previously imported from Spain. In the following decades, trade in luxury products such as tropical fruits, coffee, sugar, and *cacao* began. The colonies thus absorbed more and more of the dwindling quantity of the mineral wealth extracted rather than sending it to Spain in exchange for peninsular products (2:191–215). Even as he advocated military activity on multiple fronts in Europe, then, Olivares came to think of America as a "poisoned chalice" (Elliott, *Spain and Its World*, 25–26).

Ricardo Ferrando Keun's *Y así nació la frontera (The Birth of the Frontier)* provides valuable insights into the Spanish efforts to conquer southern Chile during this period. The uprising against Valdivia, which led to the naming of García Hurtado de Mendoza as head of the forces sent to repacify the area (and sets the stage for the events dramatized in Arauco plays), is attributed to "la destrucción de sus viviendas [de los indígenes] y sus siembras y cosechas, el trabajo obligado y abusivo, . . . el robo de sus bienes, el maltrato, cosas concretas que les hacen reaccionar" (the destruction of the indigenous people's livelihoods and crops, abusive forced labor, . . . theft of their possessions, mistreatment, material events that caused them to react) (11–12). Thus, Keun rejects psychohistorical explanations of unusual Araucanian ferocity and love of liberty in favor of documenting oppressive lived experience and investigating exactly what material circumstances replaced the prior autonomy enjoyed by the native peoples (12). As Luis Galdames notes in his *History of Chile*, the moment of victory celebrated in the Arauco plays was quite short-lived; although the marquis of Cañete left Chile in 1561, convinced that the area was completely conquered, "he had scarcely left the country" when successful revolt began to unravel the dominion he had established.[10] Keun adds that throughout the early modern period, attempts to pacify Chile were hampered by the crown's failure to provide adequate manpower and resources, the rapid indigenous assimilation of European military strategies, the Dutch incursions along the Chilean coast, and, in some cases, the help of Spaniards who defected to the indigenous cause or of Spanish treaty violations (123–30). The viceroys of Peru described expeditions to Chile as highly unpopular assignments. The marquis of Cañete wrote in 1593 that the colonial troops, "ante esta posibilidad, prefería[n] ir a 'galeras'" (rather than this posting, preferred to serve on galley ships); in 1600, being named governor of Chile was termed "el mayor sacrificio que podía pedirse a un hombre" (the greatest sacrifice that could be asked of a man) (120, 134). In 1601, Spanish efforts in Chile were bolstered for the first time by the naming of a military leader of significant renown who had proven himself in the European theater and who was given the troops and other resources requested. Alonso de Ribera chose the Biobío River, just south of Araucanian territory, as the border of the lands he would seek to pacify and defend. Control of the Araucanian region was thus a high priority during the period when the plays about the marquis of Cañete were written (139–51). The importance of this boundary can be seen in the specific reference found in *Arauco domado:* when Don García sallies forth from the fort at Penco to engage the Araucanians,

---

10. Luis Galdames, *A History of Chile*, trans. and ed. Isaac Joslin Cox (New York: Russell and Russell, 1964), 86.

"al río Biobío / [que] valerosamente marcha" (he heads valorously for the Biobío River) (*AD* II, 155).¹¹ The continued resistance of native Chilean peoples, like that of the Dutch Protestants, led to a series of debates during the seventeenth century over the relative merits of all-out war and negotiated truces as well as over the proper treatment of conquered peoples (Keun, *Y así nació la frontera*, 200–22). Enslavement of the indigenous peoples captured during rebellions was a particularly contentious issue, with royal proclamations permitting the practice alternating with truce periods during which enslavement was outlawed (204–12).

## Rome and the Spanish Political *Imaginaire*

The epic provided the artistic form against which early modern Spanish poets and playwrights developed counter-generic modes in order to interrogate imperial policy. Their selection of the literary form most closely associated with Greco-Roman cultural dominance demonstrates the continuing importance of classical literary forms in the early modern period. Thomas Greene describes the literary mimesis found in counter-generic texts, which "expose the vulnerability of the subtext," as a "dialectical" imitation emphasizing both the similarities and the disparities between two distinct "*mundi significantes.*"¹² The dialectical imitations of epic ideology and form found in the history plays of Cervantes, Rojas Zorrilla, Lope de Vega, and González de Bustos are used to delineate both the parallels and the distinctions among "civilized" and "barbaric" societies in a manner that destabilizes the hierarchical value system justifying Spain's colonial and imperial enterprises.

Frederick de Armas traces the link between cultural representation and political praxis when he notes that in Cervantes's *Numancia*, "classical views of cosmology, heroism and empire serve to evaluate a present in which Spain wishes to carry the mantle of imperial authority."¹³ The accomplishments of the classical world preoccupied and shaped all fields of scholarly endeavor in early modern Europe. In his introduction to *Lords of All the*

---

11. References to *Arauco domado* (abbreviated as AD) include act and page numbers; there is no standard edition with scene and line numbers for this work.

12. Thomas Greene, *The Light in Troy: Imitation and Discovery in Renaissance Poetry* (New Haven: Yale University Press, 1982), 45–46.

13. Frederick de Armas, *Cervantes, Raphael, and the Classics* (Cambridge: Cambridge University Press, 1998), xii.

*World*, historian Anthony Pagden notes that the Roman Empire "has always had a unique place in the political imagination of western Europe. Not only was it believed to have been the largest and most powerful political community on earth, it had also been endowed by a series of writers with a distinct, sometimes divinely inspired, purpose."[14] In early modern European constructions of Rome, the glorification of armed conquest was central to the notion of Roman grandeur (64). Not surprisingly, then, when sixteenth-century thinkers began "to ask themselves what sort of thing an empire was, what it should be, and whether or not it could be justified," they drew heavily upon Rome's military legacy as well as its literary, legal, and philosophical traditions (12). Likewise, when court historiographers sought to create an "official history" of the Spanish Empire, they demonstrated parallels between Roman and Iberian expansionist practice to legitimize Spanish dominion in the Americas (32). Pagden identifies two of Charles V's courtiers, the chancellor Mercurio de Gattinara and the historian Pedro de Mexía, as the principal figures in the construction of Charles as a new Constantine and of his dominion as the sole modern remnant of and heir to the Roman legacy. In this scenario, Spain's Christian mission is construed as the equivalent of the Roman desire to bring *pietas* (civic virtue) to an uncivil "Other" (40–43, 44). For historiographers, jurists, and poets alike, the Roman Empire served as the touchstone against which contemporary events and discourses were evaluated.

### JURIDICAL JUSTIFICATIONS OF IMPERIAL EXPANSION

Historians describe Philip II as a "stickler for the law" when deciding royal policies. Proliferating efforts to justify the American imperial enterprise through legal arguments—arguments based upon a sometimes contradictory combination of biblical and Roman precepts—should therefore be seen as a sincere rather than cynical attempt to guarantee Spain's role as "guardian of universal Christendom" (Lynch, *Spain Under the Habsburgs*, 1:360; Pagden, *Spanish Imperialism*, 6). The *juntas* assembled at various times throughout the sixteenth century to debate colonial practices can be seen as a related phenomenon, one belonging to "a tradition of ritual legitimization that the Castilian crown had, since the late middle ages, regularly

---

14. Anthony Pagden, *Lords of All the World: Ideologies of Empire in Spain, Britain, and France, c. 1500–c. 1800* (New Haven: Yale University Press, 1995), 11.

enacted when confronted by uncertain moral issues" (Pagden, *Spanish Imperialism*, 5). As Pagden shows in *Spanish Imperialism and the Political Imagination,* "this habit of seeking political legitimation ensured the existence of a lively and by no means uncritical inquiry into the behavior of the state" (6). The primary topics of legal inquiry, as noted above, included the right to impose civilization and Christianity upon primitive groups, the right to the labor of indigenous peoples, the definition of a just war of conquest, dominion over lands not ruled by Christians as guaranteed in the Papal Bulls of Donation, the right to the wealth of the conquered territory, and the relative pragmatic merits of expansionist and isolationist policy. Serious doubts concerning imperial policy were voiced throughout the early modern period in the *juntas* convoked by Ferdinand, Charles V, and Philip II and in other bodies where policy was debated. Francisco de Vitoria himself noted, however, that the conclusions of these royal advisors were often necessarily ignored by monarchs who "think from hand to mouth"—that is, who make decisions based upon pragmatic reality rather than lofty idealism (Pagden, *Spanish Imperialism*, 5). Even as he raised moral and legal objections to Spain's occupation of the Americas, Vitoria conceded that the logical conclusion of his arguments, Spanish withdrawal from these territories, would be "intolerable in practice" (32). Nonetheless, evidence of the continuing strong interest in specific legal and moral questions that the debates provoked emerges in the Numancia and Arauco plays, which utilize the terminology and frameworks described in this section in their scrutiny of the imperial enterprise.

Edward Said notes that the doctrine of the beneficent civilizing of barbarous peoples is ubiquitous in European colonial writings of all eras.[15] In a chapter aptly entitled "Dispossessing the Barbarian," Pagden points out that Spanish justifications of the conquest of the Americas were based upon the Roman legal theory of *dominium*—the natural rights of human beings to control their bodies, labor, property, and freedom (*Spanish Imperialism*, 15). Roman jurists validated the empire's right to conquer any people who did not exercise *dominium* through the structures of a functional "civil" society. The Roman definition of civil society, though, emphasized the delineation of private property rights and consequently excluded most of the groups found in the Americas (31). Early in the sixteenth century, Juan López de Palacios Rubios and Matías de Paz used this argument to assuage doubts raised by Antonio de Montesinos concerning Spanish

---

15. Edward Said, *Culture and Imperialism* (New York: Random House, 1993), xi.

activity in Hispaniola. Later in the century, Juan Ginés de Sepúlveda put forth the most extreme versions of this argument to be found in early modern Spain: his *dominium*-based justifications of colonialism argued that natural law "grants *dominium* to all those who are civilized beings over all those who are not" (14–15, 27–29). Vázquez de Menchaca, one of Philip II's principal advisors at the final Council of Trent, affirmed the European right to exercise cultural rather than political *dominium* over members of barbarous groups. This distinction appears meaningless, however, in that he advocates no significant change in the material condition of the dominated groups (Pagden, *Lords,* 60). Although Vasco de Quiroga, the bishop of Michoacan, has been considered a progressive force due to his Utopian community projects, his writings advocated benevolent conquest in order to eradicate the "tyranny" and "disorder" found in native political systems (Pagden, *Spanish Imperialism,* 26). Pagden reports that critics of this line of thought, including Francisco de Vitoria and the other members of the "School of Salamanca," held that even though indigenous civilizations were very different from European civil societies, they did constitute "recognizable political communities," and therefore "the conquest of America could be made legitimate only by demonstrating that the native population had forfeited [their natural rights—*dominium*] by their own actions" (15, 17). Vitoria and Domingo de Soto delineated an alternate view of the native population: neither beasts nor irrational humans, indigenous people were similar to children and thus in need of a guide to hold *dominium* for them until such time as they could mature and exercise their own rights appropriately. This form of *dominium* exercised on behalf of another was known as *dominium directum* (17, 20). Here, Soto's and Vitoria's reasoning (although grounded in different political terminology) ultimately produces a similar justification of imperial conquest as an act of "charity" that will benefit the less-developed conquered peoples (20). Consideration of the relative barbarity and civility of the vanquished group is central to the representation of imperial practice in the Numancia and Arauco plays.

The issue of Spain's right to benefit from the labor of the indigenous inhabitants of America, as exercised through the *encomienda* system, also produced controversy. Antonio de Montesino's 1511 attack on the behavior of Spanish colonists emphasized the "cruel and horrible servitude" that they forced upon the natives of Hispaniola (14). Sepúlveda and Vasco de Quiroga were the strongest supporters of the *encomienda* system of labor exploitation, using the Roman interpretation of *dominium* and Ciceronian and Aristotelian notions of essential biological inferiority in their assertions that the indigenous groups fell into the category of pre-rational or morally inferior peoples deemed to be merely "humanoid" and thus "natural slaves" (Pagden, *Spanish Imperialism*, 17–21, 25–30; *Lords*, 19–22). Scholastic thinkers such as Soto, Vitoria, Juan de la Peña, and Melchor Cano rejected both Roman and Aristotelian versions of the "natural slave" theory. Critique of the Spanish exploitation of native labor can be seen in literary treatments of the Arauco material, including Pedro de Oña's reinscription of the Ercillan epic poem and Gaspar de Ávila's *El gobernador prudente (The Prudent Governor)*.[16] The emphasis upon the vast fortunes of the protagonists of *indiano* plays, in conjunction with the scrutiny of their role in court society, may also be interpreted as an indirect reference to the unjust treatment of American inhabitants, a crucial element in the acquisition of *indiano* wealth.

Debates concerning the Spaniard's right to exploit the mineral wealth in the lands previously controlled by indigenous peoples also incorporated Roman theories of *dominium*. In response to the denial of any form of Spanish *dominium* over the American territories or population as articulated by the School of Salamanca, Quiroga and Sepúlveda asserted that because none of the indigenous civilizations organized their political structures or their codes concerning property ownership in a civilized manner, and because they lacked a monetary economy, they did not exercise the true form of *dominium* that would prevent conquest or appropriation (Pagden, *Spanish Imperialism*, 26–29). In addition, Sepúlveda cited Augustine's arguments validating the Roman appropriation of Egyptian wealth, arguing that the native peoples, like the Egyptians, forfeited the rights to their metals because they used them for idolatry rather than for commercial purposes. Sepúlveda concluded that the unused or abused Indian wealth could rightfully be claimed by the Europeans because it still constituted "a common part of Adam's patrimony to which the Spaniards had a high moral claim by having traded metals which were useless in the ancient Indian world, for such useful things as iron, European agricultural techniques, horses, donkeys, pigs, sheep, and so on" (29). These debates took place in the 1550s and were considered to be of mere "antiquarian interest" by the time of Antonio León Pinelo's 1630 justification of Spanish imperial practice: Pinelo cited the fact of occupation and the belief on the part of the

---

16. William Mejías López, "Testimonio juridico de Alonso de Ercilla: Desafios, poder temporal regio y estado araucano," *Revista de Estudios Hispánicos* 21 (1994): 78; Melchora Romanos, "La construcción del personaje de Caupolicán en el teatro del Siglo de Oro," *Filología* 26, no. 1–2 (1993): 201.

original settlers in the validity of the Papal Bulls of Donation to silence any remaining objections to the colonial project (34). The repeated references, however, to the incredible estates of *indiano* protagonists and the dramatized debate over their suitability as spouses for peninsular noblewomen give evidence of a continuing preoccupation with the advantages and the problems associated with this new source of wealth—as well as an unabated awareness of the human suffering and questionable ethics associated with the appropriation of the indigenous *dominium*. The debates of the 1550s can thus be understood as a residual discourse, one that provided a source of oppositional thought for later considerations of the imperial enterprise and for the seventeenth-century manifestations of Lascasian thought.

The "just war" theories of Vitoria, Soto, and others developed from their need to justify Spanish conquest, sovereignty, and *dominium* despite having denied Europeans the right to conquer indigenous civilizations due to their lack of civility. These theories were based in part upon Cicero's *Republic* and Augustine's *City of God* (Pagden, *Lords,* 52, 96–98). Tzvetan Todorov writes that Palacios Rubio's 1514 *Requerimiento* constitutes the first effort to frame the conquest in just war terminology: if the indigenous people are offered the opportunity to "cooperate" with the invaders but refuse, then enslavement is morally defensible. He points out that this document embodies the paradox that haunts the legitimacy of Christian empire, for "Christianity is an egalitarian religion; yet, in its name, men are reduced to slavery."[17] Sebastián Fox Morcillo, a major critic of military solutions to the problems in Flanders, sanctioned war to secure peace or to enlarge the "republic."[18] Vitoria, Luis Molina, and Francisco Suárez agreed that extension of empire and personal profit were not sufficient justifications for war—but that just wars could be waged in the defense of innocent indigenous peoples against uncivil neighbors and in order to guarantee the right to try to convert the native population.[19] Praise for García de Mendoza's (temporary) success in reconquering, for Philip and God, the Chilean territory lost by Valdivia can be found in several of the Arauco plays; the figures who utter prophecies concerning the future Spanish empire found in

---

17. Tzvetan Todorov, *The Conquest of America,* trans. Richard Howard (New York: Harper and Row, 1984), 147.

18. Angelo J. Di Salvo, "Spanish Guides to Princes and the Political Theories in *Don Quijote,*" *Cervantes* 9, no. 2 (1989): 51, 57.

19. Bernice Hamilton, *Political Thought in Sixteenth-Century Spain* (Oxford: Oxford University Press, 1963), 142.

Cervantes's and Rojas Zorrillas's *Numancia* plays also present the expansion of the nation in a positive manner, although other parts of the plays render this affirmation doubtful.

Ferdinand and Isabella grounded the legitimacy of the conquest of America upon Alexander VI's Papal Bulls of Donation of 1493, which confirmed Spain's right to colonize territories found in the Atlantic not already ruled by a Christian sovereign and to evangelize the peoples encountered there. By the mid-sixteenth century, however, relations between the Vatican and the Spanish crown had deteriorated, which led theorists to ignore the papal "plenitude of power" doctrine when constructing arguments in defense of imperial practice. Royal advisors were no longer willing to acknowledge the Pope's authority in secular political matters (Pagden, *Spanish Imperialism*, 14). Still, papal validation of missionary endeavors continued to be cited in legal and literary writings as a legitimate motive for conquest, and this argument can be found in Lope's Arauco play.

Spanish thinkers also debated imperial practice from a pragmatic point of view, examining the relative benefits and liabilities to be derived from possessing vast expanses of territory. Pagden notes that in opposition to the supporters of imperialism, who often grounded their support by referring to the *Reconquista* tradition, Spain also possessed "a powerful, and no less popular tradition of isolationism, in terms of which a king's first and sole duty was to his subjects. Any attempt to enhance his reputation by foreign wars which could bring his subjects no immediate and appreciable benefit was a violation of the contract by which he held his crown" (6). Here again Roman thought and policy exerted considerable influence. Soto and other jurists who defended Spain's right to its European territories but not to overseas conquests cited the geographical boundaries of the Roman Empire as the natural limits for any successor nation (Pagden, *Lords*, 53). Diego Covarrubias and Vázquez de Menchaca, following Roman *Lex Rhodia*, argued that an overextended empire cannot provide all its citizens the good government and civil society that are among the prime justifications for empire, and they contended that the attempt to do so weakens the seat of the empire as well as distant dominions. They also believed that empires should be limited to peoples who share similar customs, for true community cannot be formed among highly disparate constituencies (50–61). Pagden credits Vázquez de Menchaca with shifting the terms of imperial debate from an exploration of legal and theological issues to "a concern with the calculation of purely human benefits" (62). In addition, Diego Saavedra Fajardo anticipated the economic theories of Adam Smith when he asserted that the circulation of large quantities of mineral wealth is harmful to a nation's economy—which is why God buried gold and silver in the bowels of the earth, where it would not be easily accessible (69). The *indiano* plays do not directly rehearse these arguments over the pragmatic concerns associated with ruling a vast empire. The representation of the *indiano* character and his wealth as a potentially destabilizing social force, however, can be seen as a contribution to the debates over the possible negative effects of the colonial enterprise upon the home metropolis. In these explorations of the possible harm the imperial enterprise may visit upon the colonial power, early modern counter-epic literature differs greatly from the nineteenth-century texts studied by Edward Said, where, he asserts, the passing references to the British and French empires are essentially hegemonic: the purpose of such references, he argues, "is not to raise more questions, nor to disturb or otherwise preoccupy attention, but to keep the empire more or less in place" (*Culture and Imperialism,* 74). Despite the differences in how these metropolitan literatures mediated colonization, Said's insights into the functions of nineteenth-century texts are equally relevant for analyzing those of the seventeenth century.

## Lascasian Critiques of Conquest

For Franciscan and Dominican missionaries influenced by Erasmian and Utopian thought, the American indigenous population exemplified the innate nobility of humankind prior to civilization's debasements. Antonio de Montesinos and Bartolomé de Las Casas emphasized the contradiction between Spanish claims to a superior civilization and its uncivilized treatment of native peoples (Elliott, *Imperial Spain,* 72). This paradox is best expressed in Las Casas's metaphoric juxtaposition of the indigenous peoples of Hispaniola as gentle lambs slaughtered by the Spaniards "como lobos y tigres y leones cruelísimos" (like the cruelest wolves, tigers, and lions).[20] Early modern anti-imperialist discourse of Spain and the Americas, which has come to be known as Lascasian, rejects the belief that a "forced introduction into 'civility' was legitimate as the preliminary and necessary condition of voluntary conversion" (Pagden, *Lords,* 31). Indeed, Las Casas described the conquerors as the group lacking civility: he

---

20. Bartolomé de Las Casas, *Brevísima relación de la destrucción de Indias,* ed. Manuel Ballasteros Gaibrois (Madrid: Fundación Universitaria Española, 1977), 3.

observed that their gluttony caused the indigenous people to starve, while their lasciviousness destroyed the honor of native families (*Brevísima relación*, 5–6).

Regular, supervised labor was seen by Europeans as a key ingredient of the civilizing process, for idleness was considered a root cause of uncivil social practices. Las Casas, however, condemned the *encomienda* system's treatment of natives as exploitation, "oprimiéndolos con la más dura, horrible, y áspera servidumbre en que jamás bestias ni hombres pudieran ser puestas" (oppressing them with the harshest, most horrible and severe servitude that has ever been imposed upon human or beast) (4). He describes with great sympathy the men, women, and children who perished from overwork in gold mines and agricultural fields (11–12). In order to evoke the sympathy of the reader, Las Casas employs a particular form of pathetic representation that is also seen in the Cervantes *Numancia* play: violent aggression interfering with the process of a mother nursing her offspring. In the Cervantine drama, siege warfare brings starvation, so that mothers no longer produce milk; in this history, Las Casas asserts that in addition to denying sustenance to *encomienda* laborers, the Spaniards appropriated for themselves "la leche de las tetas [de] las madres paridas" (milk from the breasts of women who have just given birth) (13). Contemporary historiography has made us aware of the differences between early modern and present-day standards of accuracy and have cast doubt upon the complete veracity of Las Casas's histories. There is no denying, however, the clear intent to produce documents that would modify Spanish attitudes and material practices in the Americas. In fact, awareness that Las Casas did exaggerate and employ literary techniques to influence his readers strengthens the arguments of those who study the history of negative representations of warfare. To describe the enemy as one who does not respect the sanctity of the newborn babe is to question his humanity in a way that justifies all forms of violent retribution.[21] It is thus particularly significant that Las Casas launches this dehumanizing accusation against his own countrymen and that dramatizations of broken families are ubiquitous in Arauco and Numancia plays.

Las Casas also uses legal terminology as he justifies indigenous attacks upon the Spaniards as self-defense, asserting that "nunca los indios de todas las Indias hicieron mal alguno a cristianos; antes los tuvieron por venidos

---

21. Fabricated stories in 1991 similarly accused Iraqi soldiers of stealing incubators from Kuwaiti nurseries.

del cielo, hasta que primero muchas veces habían recibido de ellos muchos males, robos, violencias" (the indigenous peoples of the Indies never caused harm to any Christian, but believed them to be sent from heaven, until after they had experienced their many cruelties, thefts, and violent assaults) (5). Further, "los indios tuvieron siempre justísima guerra contra los cristianos" (the indigenous peoples always had most just cause for their wars against the Christians), but the Spaniards, to the contrary, "nunca tuvieron justa contra los indios" (never had just cause to attack the indigenous peoples) (12). Las Casas characterized the indigenous contact with Spaniards as a wholly negative experience, for in every part of the New World, the Christians "siempre hicieron en los indios todas las crueldades dichas y matanzas y tiranías y opresiones" (always committed all the previously mentioned cruelties, killings, tyrannies, and oppressions) (14). Again, the representation of Spaniards always committing all of the atrocities described is ideologically significant, if exaggerated.

Unlike Vitoria or Soto, in his late writings Las Casas was willing to advocate major policy changes based upon moral considerations. He put forward the form of international interaction practiced by the Portuguese in India as the preferred colonial model. In Las Casas's idyllic scheme, all of the lands would be returned to indigenous control, restitution would be made for illegal appropriations of labor and minerals, and only a very small number of soldiers would be deployed—for the purpose of protecting missionaries, not for acquiring and defending colonial territory. The Spaniards would then pursue "licit trade rather than illicit occupation."[22]

William Mejías López has shown that some aspects of Lascasian discourse continued to exert influence into the seventeenth century, as seen in the writings of Diego de Medellín, bishop of Santiago de Chile, who criticized *encomienda* labor as a cruel abuse and who earned sympathy for his viewpoint through his portraits of the indignities heaped upon women, children, and elderly and handicapped persons forced to perform labor beyond their capacities ("Testimonio juridico," 88). Like Las Casas, Medellín also blamed Spanish mistreatment of the natives as the just cause for continued resistance by the Chilean native peoples (89). Mejías López provides an extensive bibliography of a strong Lascasian tradition in seventeenth-century Lima (93). Although Las Casas himself came to question his focus upon indigenous assimilation and moved toward a more relativist

---

22. Pagden, *Spanish Imperialism*, 32–33; quotation from Todorov, *Conquest of America*, 192–93.

position in his later writings, pointing out that some European customs appear barbaric to indigenous groups, "Lascasian" discourse generally continued to emphasize assimilability as the primary virtue of the native American and conversion as the ultimate goal (Todorov, *Conquest of America*, 165–92).

## THE PROFESSIONAL SOLDIER

Raffaele Puddu cites correspondence from two royal advisors, Ramón de Ezquerra and Gutiérrez de los Riós, to support his contention that when Philip II began to bestow *hábitos* in the military orders to aristocrats (who themselves had no combat experience) as a reward for bureaucratic service or financial support, it was seen as a significant factor in the decline in the quality of leadership and thus undermined the effectiveness of military actions (Puddu, *Soldado gentilhombre*, 148, 162). Puddu's study, though flawed in its conception of the monolithic nature of early modern Spanish society, provides valuable information about the prestige of the Spanish military and aristocracy in the wake of the emergence of a new "professional soldier" class in the sixteenth century. It also illuminates a little-known popular literary genre—the memoirs of these professional soldiers. Puddu explains that throughout the Middle Ages, prohibitions on the bearing of arms among "commoners" fundamentally marked the boundary between nobles and plebians. He attributes the shift in this policy in the sixteenth century to the ever-escalating need for troops in an imperial regime. Changes in military practice resulting from the technologizing of warfare (which eliminated "heroic" epic contests between individuals at the same time that it augmented casualties) may well have reduced the number of aristocrats willing to participate in military action.

Puddu views the change in recruiting policies as a vehicle through which professional soldiers came to view themselves as honorary members of the aristocracy and thus as a force that "contribuía a consolidar el respeto por las órdenes privilegiadas y la devoción a la corona" (contributed to the consolidation of respect for the privileges of rank and of devotion to the crown) (11). Other critics have indicated that this change in the role of the aristocracy within the military also contributed to a decrease in status for a nobility that no longer distinguished itself through service to its country. Puddu concedes that of the career options presented in the popular *dicho*—"o Iglesia, o Mar o Casa Real" (Church, Military, or Palace)—court service was not as highly esteemed as military action: "es preciso señalar que las alternativas apuntadas en el celebre refrán no deben considerarse equivalentes . . . el servicio armado del rey goza de un prestigio muy superior al que se adquiere en las filas de la burocracia" (I must emphasize that the three alternatives indicated in the famous refrain should not be considered as equals . . . armed service was awarded far more prestige than bureaucratic duties) (148–49). Thus, at the same time that theologians and jurists debated the ethical and legal validity of imperial warfare, the changing profile of the Spanish soldier also gave rise to contradictory notions concerning aristocracy and warfare, notions that were given voice in the popular memoirs.

The memoirs of Ramón de Ezquerra, Jerónimo de Urrea, Marcos de Isaba, Francisco Verdugo, and Martín de Eguiluz strongly protested the awarding of officer commissions to noblemen on the basis of social hierarchy rather than prior martial experience and the marginalizing of men who deserved commissions because of long years of effective service. These memoirs also attributed military defeats to the inept leadership of decadent grandees who preferred courtly frivolities to the glories of the battlefield, thus repeating a common negative stereotype of the era that is central to counter-epic discourses. Puddu asserts that this critique, like the representation of the Duke and Duchess in Book 2 of *Don Quijote*, is aimed at a small minority within the upper levels of society; it does not constitute an antiaristocratic discourse so much as an attempt to restore traditional medieval aristocratic practices and values (160). (Literary critics have made similar assertions concerning the ideological dimension of Arauco and Numancia dramas and burlesque epic poetry.) The soldiers' memoirs call for aristocratic and military reform and can be seen as simultaneously oppositional and conservative in nature. They criticize the contemporary incarnation of the aristocratic order, but they also affirm the underlying institution of social hierarchy in its ideal form.

Puddu's analysis of *armas y letras* pamphlets of the period indicates an additional contradiction. He points to Don Quijote's famous after-dinner speech, as well as the support for combat expressed in the *armas y letras* treatises of Bernardino de Mendoza, Francisco de Valdés, and Martín de Eguiluz, to argue that military action retained significant prestige. Despite the growing participation of commoners, "la convicción de que las armas enoblecen al hombre ocupa un lugar de primera importancia en el ideario español" (the conviction that bearing arms ennobles men is at the forefront of the Spanish *idearium*) (151). According to Puddu, then, the ideal of bearing arms in support of Spanish imperial glory continued to win approval, but the actual military strategies chosen and implemented generated significant controversy and discord both within the ranks of career soldiers and among those who read their memoirs.

## POLITICAL FACTIONS AND IMPERIAL POLICY

Recent historical inquiry into the role of political factionalism in Spain's imperial policies has produced new insights into anti-imperialist and pacifist sentiments during the reign of Philip II. According to the traditional interpretation put forward by J. H. Elliott, Gregorio Marañón, and others, based upon the sixteenth-century observations of Leopold von Ranke, this factionalism constituted a clear-cut ideological schism. The group headed by the duke of Alba was characterized as strongly nationalist, favoring an aggressive military approach both abroad and in Castile's relations with the other Spanish provinces. The opposing group, led by Philip's *privado* (personal and political advisor) Ruy Gómez de Silva, prince of Eboli, was seen as proto-pacifist, as indicated by the support of the more moderate tactics developed by Furió Ceriol, who advocated negotiating with the Netherlands and preserving the rights of the individual provinces.[23] Lynch argues that this bipolar analysis of the Ebolists as doves and the Alvists as warmongers is incomplete. While Eboli favored negotiations with the Netherlands, his motivation was to free up resources and troops for launching an attack on England—a goal that Alba did not support (*Spain Under the Habsburgs*, 1:202). Lynch attributes Alba's reluctance to attack England to the economic hardships that would result from closing the English Channel to imperial trade (1:311–12). In his biography of Ruy Gómez de Silva, James Boyden relates the disagreements over military policy to a caste-based competition between the two primary rivals for influence over Philip. Alba, head of one of the foremost grandee households of Spain, presented himself as an exemplar of the feudal warrior aristocracy and considered the role of primary advisor to be his entitlement because of merit and blood (Boyden, *Courtier and King*, 96–98). Gómez de Silva, from a minor family of the Portuguese nobility, acquired his position as *privado* as a result of the personal ties he formed with the young prince after having been brought into the royal household by Philip's Portuguese mother. Alba

---

23. James Boyden, *The Courtier and the King* (Berkeley and Los Angeles: University of California Press, 1995), 93–94; Elliott, *Spain and Its World*, 261–64.

and his supporters were deeply offended by the favors showered upon a member of a lower social order. Boyden, citing a letter written by Venetian ambassador Antonio Tiepolo, argues that Eboli's pacifism was purely pragmatic, an attempt to dilute the influence of Alba and other grandee "warlords" by limiting military engagements: "in peacetime Ruy Gómez de Silva could exercise preponderant influence on his King, in wartime he could not" (105). Boyden mentions the personal friendships that Eboli made with the Dutch nobility as an additional factor in his advocacy of diplomatic solutions. Carlos Morales explains this pro-Dutch sentiment as a result of Eboli's alliance with Francisco de Eraso, one of Charles V's key advisors in Brussels, who was also an advocate of moderation with the Dutch rebels because of the long history of cordial relations during Charles's reign (Morales, "Francisco de Eraso," 130). José Martínez Millán offers two further explanations for the factionalism. He posits that Philip's sister, Juana of Austria, who served as regent during the waning years of Charles V's reign, acted as the true "catalyst" for the Ebolists. He attributes the success of Juana and Eboli to the strength of the Portuguese faction brought to the Castilian court by Philip's mother. Naturally, the Portuguese group would favor regional autonomy rather than a centralizing imperial strategy. In this scenario, the rivalry between the two groups predated Philip's rule and had its roots in the rivalries among Charles V's advisors. Alba's aggressive militarism thus derived from his role as the champion of a party that favored the primacy of Castilian interests within the empire.[24] Martínez Millán also points to religious differences between the two groups that were relevant to foreign policy. He notes that the most prominent advocates of diplomatic solutions, including Princess Juana, Eboli, Margaret of Parma, and Margaret's son, Alexander Farnese, had been raised within the reformist Jesuitical tradition, and their view of relations between Spain and Rome differed greatly from the views of Alba and his more traditional Castilian supporters (88–92).

These explorations of the sixteenth century's political factionalism point to personal, religious, regional, and caste conflicts rather than "pure" ideological discord as the basis for disagreement among political advisors. Diverse motivations among the partisans strengthens, rather than weakens, my central thesis. The wide variety of attitudes toward imperialist military activity and the warrior aristocracy expressed in counter-epic texts of the early modern period were intended to be (and were read as) contributions

---

24. José Martínez Millán, "Familia real y grupos políticos: La princesa Doña Juana de Austria," in *La corte de Felipe II*, ed. Martínez Millán, 88–89.

to a lively public debate concerning Spain's imperial project. Political factionalism and the controversies concerning the legal, theological, and military aspects of imperial ideology and practice constitute a polyphonic, contradictory, and contested discursive *tabla* upon which poetic and dramatic writers inscribed their counter-epic meditations.

3

LIMINAL IDENTITY AND POLYPHONIC IDEOLOGY
IN *INDIANO* DRAMA

The celebration (or condemnation) of the quincentennial anniversary of the first European encounter with America gave rise to a reconsideration of Columbus's legacy and a much-needed examination of the *comedia*'s representation of the New World and its inhabitants. This examination, however, tended to focus on the Spanish presence in the Americas and on the peoples encountered there. Comparatively little critical attention has been granted to the effects of the colonial enterprise as mediated in peninsular Spanish cultural productions, even though a significant number of Golden Age dramas feature an *indiano* character who plays a crucial role in the *dénouement* of the action that takes place in Spain.[1] In his study of the role of this character in Tirsian drama, Alfonso Urtiaga distinguishes between *indianos*, who were born in Spain, spent time in the Americas, and then returned to Spain to seek a position in court society, and *criollos*, who were born in

I would like to thank participants in the AHCT listserve who suggested relevant *indiano* plays, especially Charles Ganelin, Bob Blue, Alix Ingber, and Valerie Hegstrom.
 1. See also my earlier studies of *indiano* drama, "The *Indiano* as Liminal Figure in the Drama of Tirso and His Contemporaries," *Bulletin of the Comediantes* 47, no. 2 (1995), and "The Indiano Senex as Subaltern Figure in Tirso's *Marta la piadosa* and *Por el sótano y el torno*," *Romance Language Annual* 11 (1999). This chapter recontextualizes and expands significantly upon the ideas offered in those two articles.

Mexico or Peru. In the plays themselves, though, the epithet *indiano* is used to refer to both groups of people, and this chapter follows their lead, for it is not the birthplace of the characters but their acquisition of wealth in the New World that marks them as Other. An important factor noted by George Mariscal is the typically "nonaristocratic" social category from which the *indiano* emerged.[2] Edith Villarino writes that more than thirty Siglo de Oro dramas portray *indiano* figures. This chapter limits its focus to two representative and easily accessible works by Lope de Vega—*El sembrar en buena tierra (Cultivating in Good Soil)* and *El premio del bien hablar (Rewarded for Courtesy)*—and four by Tirso de Molina. The Tirsian works are *La villana de Vallecas (The Provincial Woman from Vallecas)*, *La celosa de sí misma (Her Own Rival)*, *Marta la piadosa (Pious Marta)*, and *Por el sótano y el torno (Through Nooks and Crannies)*. All six feature an *indiano* protagonist who seeks to marry a peninsular Spaniard as part of the process of being accepted into court society.

Early modern Spanish plays that foreground *indiano* characters as protagonists can be viewed as counter-epic texts, even though they neither directly address or represent imperialist military activity nor serve as reinscriptions of classical epic plots and stylistics. Instead, they offer insights into an alternative subgenre through which the early modern stage mediated the Spanish colonial enterprise. *Indiano* drama addresses the issue of empire through its representation of colonialization's consequences for the early modern Spanish "metropolis." Many of the debates concerning imperial ideology and practice waged in the sixteenth century focused upon issues that are directly relevant to the real-life *indiano*, including doubts about the morality of Spanish appropriations of indigenous minerals and labor (as voiced by Las Casas, Soto, Vitoria, and others) and pragmatic considerations of the relative benefits and drawbacks associated with obtaining, ruling, and defending an extensive empire, expressed most strongly by Vázquez de Menchaca.

This examination of dramatic representations of the dynamics between peninsular metropolis and American colony is grounded in the insights offered by Edward Said's *Culture and Imperialism*. Said's study addresses the overlooked significance of the colonial· issues present in nineteenth- and twentieth-century European texts whose plots do not directly take up imperialist expansion. His readings of the novels of Kipling, Austen, Sartre,

---

2. George Mariscal, "Can Cultural Studies Speak Spanish?" in *English Studies/Culture Studies: Institutionalizing Dissent*, ed. Isaiah Smithson and Nancy Ruff (Urbana: University of Illinois Press, 1994), 69.

and others point out the way the colonial experience—and contact with the "native"—marks the modern European experience and its cultural productions. In both *Orientalism* and *Culture and Imperialism,* Said argues that colonial discourse is not a neutral description of observed phenomena; instead, it creates realities through "a body of theory and practice in which, for many generations, there has been a considerable material investment."[3] In these two books, Said documents how western Europe's identity and economy have depended historically upon the distinctions it established between Western and non-Western, metropolitan and colonial. *Culture and Imperialism* documents how the novel mediated the creation of alterities that accompanied the colonial enterprises launched after the Americas obtained their freedom. Said claims that the representation of this "second wave" of colonialism is particularly noteworthy for its "unique coherence and special cultural centrality," and he limits his study to texts that mediate this second wave (*Culture and Imperialism,* xxii). I would like to suggest that his model of inquiry into identity production within imperial metropolitan societies also provides a useful paradigm for analyzing counter-epic discourses in early modern literature. My own study of the representation of the *indiano* in seventeenth-century Spanish drama highlights an overlooked form of the cultural mediation of imperial practice.

## Ethnicity and Identity

One significant factor in the representation of indianos is related to early modern anxieties concerning the instability and flexibility of identity. Mariscal writes that in Spain, "for the governing elites intent upon maintaining the myth of a traditional and homogenous society the othering of all returnees through writing and theatrical practice was a symptom of the anxiety produced by the unforeseen creations of a new world-system."[4] Stephen Greenblatt writes about a more general European context in his assertion that "Renaissance self-fashioning . . . occurs at the point of encounter between an authority and an alien . . . any achieved identity always contains within itself the signs of its own subversion or loss."[5] Thus,

---

3. Edward W. Said, *Orientalism* (New York: Random House, 1979), 6.
4. George Mariscal, "The Figure of the *Indiano* in Early Modern Spanish Culture," *Journal of Spanish Cultural Studies* 2 (2001): 56.
5. Stephen Greenblatt, *Renaissance Self-Fashioning: From More to Shakespeare* (Chicago: University of Chicago Press, 1980), 9.

one potential outcome of encounters with other cultures is apostasy. Greenblatt provides an Iberian example in his analysis of Diaz del Castillo's story of Gonzalo Guerrero.[6] This seaman was washed ashore on the Yucatán coast; when contacted eight years later by Cortés, he declined to rejoin his compatriots because of his attachment to his privileged status among the indigenous people and his devotion to his native wife and children. In comparing this metamorphosis to that described by Edmund Spenser in his *View of the Present State of Ireland*, which analyzes English colonizers of that Celtic island, Greenblatt notes that fears of linguistic betrayal, the subversive attractions of foreign women, and miscegenation are at the heart of early modern notions of mutable identity (*Renaissance Self-Fashioning*, 184–85).

Sylvia Molloy presents a case study of a more direct example of altered identity, one documented in the *Naufragios* written by Alvar Núñez Cabeza de Vaca in the sixteenth century. This first-person narrative confirms Europe's preoccupations about the contagion of otherness, for after spending several years living in close proximity to Amerindians and adopting their lifestyle, the *conquistador* no longer feels comfortable wearing Spanish garb and sleeping in a bed.[7] Molloy notes that this undeniable personal transformation is particularly striking in the passage that describes indigenous encounters with different groups of Christians: the explorer writes that he could not convince the natives with whom he and his men had been living that "éramos de los otros cristianos" (we were Christians like those others) (448–49). Molloy categorizes this modified perception as "la alteración de los espacios fundamentales del reconocimiento, las nuevas líneas que configuran al yo entre otros vueltos semejantes o entre semejantes vueltos diferentes" (an alteration of the fundamental aspects of recognition, the new lines that delineate a self that has become like the other, that among its peers now appears as other) (447). For the colonizer society, this form of transformation— "aindiado pero no indio, hispanohablante pero no español" (indianized but not indigenous, Spanish-speaking but not Spanish)—constituted an intolerable form of hybridity (ibid.). None of the plays studied here represents the *indiano* as a hybrid figure. It is important to recognize, however, that such anxiety about the transformative power of encounters with an "alien" culture (to use Greenblatt's

---

6. Stephen Greenblatt, *Marvelous Possessions: The Wonder of the New World* (Oxford: Clarendon Press, 1991), 140–41.
7. Sylvia Molloy, "Alteridad y reconocimiento en los *Naufragios* de Alvar Nuñez Cabeza de Vaca," *Nueva Revista de Filología Hispánica* 35, no. 2 (1987): 448.

term) plays an important role in the liminal status of *indiano* people and dramatic characters.

In the small body of critical writings concerning *indiano* characters, no consensus exists to describe how they are represented. The most comprehensive study is Alfonso Urtiaga's *El indiano en la dramática de Tirso de Molina*. Urtiaga asserts that Tirso's representation of these characters is generally positive, in keeping with "la conocida insistencia por parte de Tirso en presentarnos como héroes a personajes que tratan de hacerse meritorios por sus propias obras" (Tirso's well-known propensity to create protagonists whose merit derives from their actions).[8] Anita Stoll points out that in the court of Philip IV, the definition of nobility was a source of debate, with opinion divided between those who emphasized lineage and those who focused on character and deeds. For Stoll, *indiano* characters function as stock characters who embody the debate over the conflicting ideals of nobility. Gareth Davies makes a connection between provincials and *indianos* as outside observers of the morals and mores of the capital city who "carry the banner of non-metropolitan superiority."[9] Mariscal characterizes the *indiano* as a literary and social figure who challenges the contemporary notion of social evolution in the early modern period as an orderly and gradual transition from hereditary aristocracy to bourgeois capitalist: the *indiano* "participates in both types of behavior simultaneously, and thus crosses easily between the twin poles of traditional opposition" ("Figure," 59). In fact, the *indiano*, as a liminal figure, plays all of the roles these critics identify.

Glen Dille emphasizes all the negative aspects of the Spanish view of the *indiano*. In an MLA paper, he called the Americas "a dumping ground and refuge for societies' dregs"; this sentence was not included in the published article. Dille's published essay does retain his assertion that Spaniards were "underwhelmed" by the American conquest, and explains this purported lack of interest as a "European perception of the Indies as too remote and too exotic to imagine." Dille cites the small number of plays that take place in the New World—only fourteen out of a corpus of hundreds—as proof that Spain was not much impressed with the Spaniards who undertook the

---

8. Alfonso Urtiaga, *El indiano en la dramática de Tirso de Molina* (Madrid: n.p., 1965), 9.
9. Anita K. Stoll, "The Dual Levels of Antonio Hurtado de Mendoza's *Cada loco con su tema*," *Bulletin of the Comediantes* 44, no. 1 (1992): 73, 74; Gareth A. Davies, "The Country Cousin at Court: A Study of Antonio de Mendoza's *Cada loco con su tema* and Manuel Bretón de los Herreros' *El pelo de la dehesa*," in *Leeds Papers on Hispanic Drama*, ed. Margaret A. Rees (Leeds: Trinity and All Saints College and Simbaprint, 1991), 54.

conquest, and not much impressed with what they found.[10] Dille is correct that *comedias* addressing American issues reveal a complex set of anxieties regarding the effects of the imperial project on the colonizing society. That said, his dismissal of the importance of the tensions produced by the overseas venture for the metropolitan society and his failure to take into account the representation of *indiano* characters hints at precisely the limited, Eurocentric perspective criticized by Said. Analyzing a representative sample of *indiano* dramas will demonstrate that Spaniards were indeed interested in those who traveled to or were born in the newly encountered territories and their unfamiliar experiences. One indication of this interest is that in many of the plays cited in this study, the *indianos* use New World vocabulary to describe the exotic foods, fauna, and geography of the Americas. Dramatists assumed that their audiences would be familiar with these new words and places—or, at the least, curious about them (see *La villana de Vallecas* I.4 and II.9; *La celosa de sí misma* II.10; *Marta la piadosa* I.8).

The most prominent trend I have identified in the plays under consideration is the liminality by which the *indiano* characters are marked. Their complex representation operates at three levels. They are marginalized as subaltern, Americanized figures, yet they are incorporated into the dominant culture through conflation with stock characters. These stock characters, however, also constitute marginalized or ridiculed groups. Gayatri Chakravorty Spivak concurs with Said's analysis of colonial power relations in her observation that "in most analyses of third world [*sic*] or postcolonial texts and peoples, the European vantage point," as narrativized by "the law, political economy and ideology," consistently marks the colonial subject as Other.[11] Spivak cites Pierre Macherey's contention that a less oppressive form of intellectual inquiry would foreground the examination of what a text does not or cannot say as she advocates her central thesis that "subalterns"—peoples marginalized by a combination of factors, including imperial power relations, race, class, ethnicity, and gender—cannot speak authentically in the voices granted to them by Western cultural productions (286, 294–96, 308). James T. Abraham has applied Spivak's notion of the silenced subaltern to the representation of Native American female characters in *Amazonas en las Indias* from Tirso's Pizarro trilogy. Abraham

---

10. Glen F. Dille, "America Tamed: Lope's *Arauco domado*," in *New Historicism and the Comedia: Poetics, Politics, and Praxis*, ed. José A. Madrigal (Boulder: Society of Spanish and Spanish-American Studies, University of Colorado, 1997), 111–14.

11. Gayatri Chakravorty Spivak, "Can the Subaltern Speak?" in *Marxism and the Interpretation of Culture*, ed. Nelson and Grossberg, 271, 281.

writes, "In this case, the playwright draws from classical mythology and popular legend to cast the 'new' beings that inhabit unknown lands into an already familiar mold: the myth of the Amazon. Ultimately, while on the surface allowing the subaltern to speak, the play actually reflects the West's tendency to speak for and marginalize the other, while maintaining its place as Subject."[12] A similar projection of European myths of Amazonia onto colonial females emerges in the 1582 diary of Richard Madox. In the diary, Madox recounts a tale of warring African women told to him by a Portuguese trader (see Greenblatt, *Renaissance Self-Fashioning*, 181). (Like the Diaz del Castillo story of Guerrero, these narrations tend to be—indeed, they must be—second- or third-hand information.) The conflation of new forms of alterity with extant literary models of marginalized, exotic, or alien identities, as deployed by Lope and Tirso, is a common cultural practice through which dominant groups delineate the border between insider and outsider, subject and subaltern.

The *indiano* characters depicted by Tirso and Lope suffer a similar fate. Like the Amazonas, they, too, are forced into familiar molds. These figures are silenced through conflation with two stock comic characters: the *villano*, or provincial nobleman, and the *senex amans*, the antagonist in May-December romances. Even though the use of these stock characters does not produce uniformly negative portrayals of the *indiano*, it does perpetuate the European propensity to appropriate the voices of its marginalized peoples. Many practitioners of postcolonial theory, including Stephen Greenblatt, have observed that colonizing societies tend to describe indigenous societies as a mirror of Western myths of otherness.[13] In this context, examining the conflation of *indianos* and the *senex* and *villano* stock characters can provide additional insight into the early modern strategies of marginalization that contribute to the liminal status of the *indiano*. Mariscal identifies a related form of conflation in his analysis of the "collapse" of *indianos* with *conversos*, another "residual" marginal group: "if the aristocratic imagination converted the *indiano* into a *converso*, it was because the dominant discursive formation was ill-equipped to construct figures produced by the new world situation and made visible through the process of transatlantic exchange" ("Figure," 57).

12. James T. Abraham, "The Other Speaks: Tirso de Molina's *Amazonas en las Indias*," in *El arte nuevo de estudiar comedias*, ed. Simerka, 148.
13. Stephen Greenblatt, *Shakespearean Negotiations: The Circulation of Social Energy in Renaissance England* (Berkeley and Los Angeles: University of California Press, 1989), 26–27.

An illustrative example of Spain's vision of the colonial space as itself subaltern can be seen in Lope de Vega's *La noche de San Juan (Midsummer Night)*. In Act I, an *indiano*'s description of Peru highlights four of the common American motifs of the period (*NSJ* I.ix). The first is of Lima as a great city, "el mejor / fruto de española empresa . . . que no lima de Valencias, / que no le hacen competencias / Nápoles y Pausilipos" (the best fruit of the Spanish empire . . . that does not bow to Valenica, that is not overshadowed by Naples or Pausilipos). The mines of Potosí, source of the wealth that is central to *indiano* social mobility, are described as "el milagro / mayor de la Naturaleza, / cuyas entrañas y centro / son una imagen de plata" (the greatest miracle of Nature, its core and center is the very image of silver). Possession of such a vast territory is also of paramount importance for the role Spain plays in European geopolitics: "es, por las Indias, el rey / enviado de los otros reyes" (our king is envied by other kings because of the Indies). Finally, the tropical splendor of the region evokes comparisons to Eden: "que del mundo en cuanto trata / fueron el Adán y Eva" (this world is like that of Adam and Eve). Even in this glowing tribute, America cannot be described as a new entity, cannot be given its own voice. Rather, its status derives from similarities to known locations and familiar mythography.

## Stock Characters and Subjectivity

In the plays under consideration here, the *indiano* character is conflated with the *villano*—the *comedia* character of minor noble lineage, rural or provincial habitation, and empty pockets—who serves as the counterpoint to the figure of the *cortesano*. (Although I have not chosen a colloquial variant for *villano* in translating titles, the connotations of the period are similar to those for the contemporary term "hick," designating an unworldly rural figure.) The comedies that foreground this strategy include Tirso de Molina's *La celosa de sí misma* and *La villana de Valleca* and Lope de Vega's *El premio del bien hablar* and *El sembrar en buena tierra*. The virtuous rural character that critiques wicked city ways has a very ancient textual lineage. In *The Country and the City*, Raymond Williams analyzes a trajectory from Virgil's *Georgics* to Renaissance pastoral poetry to the novels of Thomas Hardy (and, I would add, to the 1960s television program *Green Acres*), all of which offer both a nostalgic lament for a tranquil rural way of life that has been suddenly and recently endangered along with a critique of contemporaneous urban "progress."[14] Williams does not present his history of the representation of nostalgia for rural life in order to assert that this topic is universal, timeless, or archetypal; instead, he argues that a full comprehension of the theme's development requires an investigation into the particular material circumstances of each manifestation (12). He also points out that the first examples of this theme appear in conjunction with the imperialist phase of Roman history and that tensions between city and country are most likely to surface at moments of pivotal economic transition (48–49). Both of these observations are relevant to an explanation of the rise of the discourses of *menosprecio de corte y alabanza de aldea* (contempt for court and praise for rural life) in early modern Spain, which appear not only in Antonio de Guevara's 1593 essay of that title and in literary texts of all genres, but also, as Augustin Redondo shows, in a wide variety of other writings. These include Spain's first agricultural treatise, an early sixteenth-century text by Gabriel Alonso de Herrera that complains of *hidalgos* abandoning fertile land to obtain a better life at court or in the Indies, and legal and political documents seeking to alleviate grain shortages.[15] Another of Guevara's essays, *El villano del Danubio (The Provincial from the Danube)*, explicitly reveals the tensions between the traditional values of rural communities and the erosion of those traditions in the wake of (Roman) imperialist practices.[16]

Representation of the problematic relations between urban and rural values is not univocal, however; several critics have noted that texts incorporating the *menosprecio de corte y alabanza de aldea* theme often subvert that dichotomy by revealing the similarities in rural and urban modes of life or by emphasizing the negative aspects of provincial life.[17] This duality is present in some of the works that I will study and is a significant factor in the status of the *indiano* who identifies with provincial rather than courtier norms. An additional complicating factor is that the conflation of the *indiano*

---

14. Raymond Williams, *The Country and the City* (New York: Oxford University Press, 1973), 9–11.
15. Augustin Redondo, "Du 'Beatus Ille' horacien au 'Mépris de la cour et éloge de la vie rustique d'Antonio Guevara'," in *L'Humanisme dans les lettres espagnoles*, ed. Augustin Redondo (Paris: Vrin, 1979), 255, 258–59.
16. Carmen R. Rabell, "'Menosprecio de corte y alabanza de aldea': ¿Crítica lascasiana, propaganda imperialista o 'Best-Seller'?" in *Actas Irvine-92, Asociación Internacional de Hispanistas*, vol. 3, ed. Juan Villegas (Irvine: University of California, 1994), 247.
17. J. F. G. Gornall, "Gongora's *Soledades:* 'Alabanza de aldea' without 'Menosprecio de corte'?" *Bulletin of Hispanic Studies* 59, no. 1 (1982): 25; Williams, *The Country and the City*, 52; Rabell, "'Menosprecio de corte,'" 245.

and the *villano* involves a significant paradox. As Redondo and Carmen Rabell both assert, in "Menosprecio de corte y alabanza de aldea," Guevara's primary goal is to denounce the role that money plays in urban social mobility—and thus Guevara is in a sense deprecating the role the *indiano* would come to play in Spanish society in the following century (see Redondo, "Du 'Beatus Ille' horacien," 262; Rabell, "'Menosprecio de corte,'" 249). In plays that subordinate the *indiano* outsider to the *villano* outsider as represented by Guevara and others, the *indiano* is frequently made to give voice to the sentiments of the *villano*. Ironically, this "ventriloquism" delegitimates the *indiano*'s own mode of social advancement and forces him to repeat the discourses that stigmatize him. (Such a situation epitomizes the lack of voice Spivak posits for the subaltern.)

The links between imperial expansion and the large-scale urbanization of Spain in the sixteenth century are documented well in Elliott's *Imperial Spain*, although the book itself does not explore the connections. The four key factors Elliott identifies in the relationship among rapid urban expansion, significant depopulation of rural areas, and Spain's internationalist agenda are (1) the preferential treatment granted to the international wool trade and sheep grazing over agricultural production, (2) the conquest of the Americas and the resultant changes in the Spanish economy, (3) the need for a bureaucracy to govern the far-flung Hapsburg territories acquired when Charles I ascended to the imperial throne, and (4) the dramatic rise of taxes on production in order to pay for imperial projects in Europe and America. In the plays under consideration here, emphasis falls upon the second factor mentioned above. The notorious wealth of the *indianos* in search of noble peninsular spouses is the primary source of dramatic conflict.

## Staging the *Indiano*

Lope de Vega's *El premio del bien hablar* is typical of *indiano* plays that foreground the *menosprecio de corte* theme in order to subordinate the outsider status of the *indiano* character to that of the *villano*. These plays incorporate four primary elements. First, a wealthy *indiano/a* who seeks to marry a *cortesano/a* is the protagonist; she or he is often referred to as simply "*indiano/a*" and frequently laments that prospective spouses are interested only in his or her money. Second, this character is surrounded by a cast of male and female *cortesanos* who serve as negative foils through their displays of greed, infidelity, and deceptive behaviors. Third, there are repeated evocations of the negative stereotypes of court life found in *beatus ille* writings: rapid change, a fast pace of life, sexual decadence, and criminal activity. Fourth, there are frequent specific numerical references to the amounts of all the characters' incomes, dowries, and pocket money.

In *El premio del bien hablar*, *indiano* siblings Leonarda and Feliciano have come to Madrid to marry. In the opening scene, Leonarda complains that all the men in the city, including her fiancé, Don Pedro, display more interest in her fortune than in the attractive figure her maid compliments. Feliciano echoes this concern in a later scene:

> Como yo pienso Leonarda,
> que mi dinero pretenden,
> guardo el alma y doy la bolsa
> que es lo que ellas apetecen.
>
> (*PBH* I.xi)[18]

(As I see it, Leonarda, since it is my money they desire, I guard my heart, and give of my purse, which is what they lust after.)

This negative impression is confirmed when Don Juan, who has already been identified as a *forastero*, or outsider, takes refuge with Leonarda. Juan is being pursued because he criticized a man who was speaking openly of marrying his brother to an *indiana* for her dowry and who disparaged the family's Vizcayan provenance and ill-gotten wealth—a speech act that led to involvement in a duel (*PBH* I.iii). Leonarda recognizes that the man in question is Diego, her betrothed's brother, and she defends the worth of her family by pointing to her father's ancestry:

> Es de mi padre el solar
> el más noble de Vizcaya
> que a las Indias venga o vaya,
> ¿qué honor le puede quitar?
> Si le ha enriquecido el mar,
> no implica ser caballero.
>
> (*PBH* I.iii)

---

18. *References to El premio del bien hablar, La villana de Vallecas, El sembrar en buena tierra,* and *Marta la piadosa* (abbreviated *PBH, VV, SBT,* and *MP,* respectively) include act and scene numbers; there are no standard editions with line numbers for these works.

(My father is of the most noble Vizcayan lineage that has ever gone or will ever go to the Indies, so how can his honor be questioned? Although his journey has enriched him, that does not endanger his noble status.)

Here, family honor is validated precisely through subordinating American experiences to provincial heritage, a move that simultaneously affirms and denigrates the status of the *indiano*. Leonarda continues to demonstrate both pride and anxiety concerning her lineage when she instructs her servant to give Don Juan a document to prove that "tengo/sangre de un señor de España" (I have the blood of a Spanish gentleman) (*PBH* I. vi). When Feliciano meets Don Juan's sister, Angela, he too is quick to mention his peninsular origins: "[t]engo sangre de Vizcaya" (I have Vizcayan blood) (*PBH* I.viii).

Feliciano unwittingly expresses contempt for courtier discourse as well as ridicule of *indianos* when, upon hearing of the duel, he asserts that Diego would speak ill only of *"ruin gente"* (lowly people), not knowing that his own family had been slandered (*PBH* I.iv). In the following scene, Leonarda's father, Don Antonio, continues the process that will establish the boundary between corrupt urbanites and virtuous *villanos* by blaming Feliciano's current misdeeds on the bad influence of his son's new friends and by praising the outsider for speaking in defense of women (*PBH* I.v). Pedro (who is also Feliciano's best friend) tries to assure his prospective father-in-law that he has no interest in Leonarda's dowry: "[s]i llevo en mi Leonarda tal tesoro, / ¿no me basta saber que es prenda mía?" (If my Leonarda is herself a treasure, isn't it enough for me to know that this gem is mine?) (*PBH* II.vii). The audience, however, who has already heard otherwise, can now add hypocrisy to the list of this *cortesano*'s defects.

The life story of the *forastero*, Don Juan, provides an extra dimension to this drama's examination of *indianos* and court life (*PBH* I.iii). In recounting his biography to Leonarda, he explains that he and his sister, descendants of the count of Aranda, are about to set sail for the Indies in order to escape imprisonment for engaging in a duel. Like the duel he waged with Don Diego, the earlier battle also concerned defending female honor against a man who spoke badly of women (in this play, Lope emphasizes disrespect for women as a *cortesano* vice). This brief narration illuminates the *indiano* condition by offering an honorable scenario for departure to the colonial territory, yet as in the case of Leonarda and Feliciano's assertions of Vizcayan blood, it grounds and thus subordinates *indiano* merit in peninsular history and bloodlines. Don Juan's critique of the ungallant speech of courtiers also constitutes an essential element of his status as an outsider in Seville, where the drama takes place. Through her marriage to such an outsider, Leonarda reinforces the conflation of *indiano* and *villano*. In this scenario, she validates the *alabanza de aldea* theme, but she also helps mark both groups as marginal and subaltern.

Similarly, in Tirso's *La celosa de sí misma,* both the *indiana* bride, Magdalena, and the mandated bridegroom, Melchor, are outsiders at court. Melchor has just arrived in Madrid from León; Magdalena's father has arranged his daughter's marriage to this provincial nobleman because "maridos cortesanos / son traviesos y livianos" (courtier husbands are treacherous and frivolous) (*CSM* I.ii.203–4). Melchor's *gracioso,* Ventura, criticizes the capital city in the opening lines of the play, reiterating the conventional negative ideas of city life: "todo lo nuevo aplace" (novelty prevails); "se vive de prisa" (life is fast-paced); "se vende el amor / a varas, medida y peso" (love is for sale or trade); "vienes pollo; / y temo . . . / que te pelen ocasiones; / que aun gallos con espolones / salen sin cresta ni plumas" (you arrive as a pullet, and I'm afraid you'll be swindled . . . even roosters end up without crests or feathers) (*CSM* I.i.5, 29, 35–36, 52–56). Melchor confirms this vision of urban ways at the end of Act II. When it seems that his marriage plans have fallen through, he immediately declares his intent to abandon the "laberintos" (mazes) of life in Madrid and return to León (*CSM* II.xiii.1073–82). Ventura points out that his initial prophecy concerning the fate of newcomers at court has come true: "entran como tú, brillantes, y salen almas del limbo" (they arrive, like you, resplendent, and end up as souls in limbo) (*CSM* II.xiii.1083–85).

The newly arrived *indiano* Jerónimo emphasizes another negative stereotype of urban life, the lack of community: "no da / lugar aun de conocerse / los vecinos, ni poderse / hablar" (there is no way to even get to know your neighbors, nor to be able to speak to one another). His courtier neighbor dedicates nearly sixty verses to this subject (*CSM* I.ii.116–75). Magdalena confirms the idea of lasciviousness at court as she begins to worry that her fiancé might be "mudable y liviano" (fickle and venal) because he fell in love with a woman at first sight in church. She includes "cortesano" among the negative adjectives (*CSM* II.i.54–56). Later, when Sebastián reveals that Melchor fell in love the very instant he arrived in the capital and that he would have broken his promise to meet Magdalena if he had not encountered her host on the street, Alonso sums up the negative influence attributed to urban centers. He observes that this behavior is no surprise, for "Esta Corte / es todo engaños y hechizos" (this court is nothing but deceptions and spells) (*CSM* II.x.895–96).

All of the preceding comments are archetypal in the sense that they could apply to any of the manifestations of rural/urban tension cited by Williams. Ventura, however, introduces the more specific subject of the way in which American fortunes serve to reinforce the greed of spendthrift courtiers. He asserts that it is a foregone conclusion that Magdalena will be considered beautiful at court, because

> ¿Cuándo has visto tú oro feo?
> Con seiscientos mil ducados
> de dote, ¿qué Elena en Grecia
> . . . . . . . . .
> se le compara?
>
> (*CSM* I.i.96–99)

(When has gold ever looked ugly? With such a large dowry, how could Helen of Troy rival her?)

Melchor distinguishes himself as an outsider who adheres to a different set of values when he replies, "aunque el dinero es hermoso, / yo no tengo de casarme, / si no fuere con belleza / y virtud" (although money is attractive, I will marry only a woman who is beautiful and virtuous) (*CSM* I.i.103–6). Initially, Melchor's reluctance to marry for money and his provincial origins mark him as an outsider in Madrid and as a voice of *villano* superiority. Melchor's emphasis on marrying for sentimental rather than financial considerations soon comes to be a mark of eccentricity rather than virtue, though, because he falls in love with a veiled woman based on seeing only her beautiful white hand, and later, her eyes. His subsequent failures to recognize those eyes and that hand—the veiled woman is, of course, the *indiana* woman his father had chosen for him—emphasize Melchor's impractical and fanciful nature. That said, after his first meeting with his official fiancée, Melchor reveals a practical streak; he concedes that if the veiled woman turns out to be unattractive, he will wed Magdalena, "que, si no es hermosa, es rica" (for, if she is not beautiful, at least she is rich) (*CSM* II.ii.196). But he also insists that if the veiled woman's face is as pretty as her hand, he will marry her even if she is poor. His fantasy of life with this bride is a compendium of *beatus ille* conceits. With her at his side, he will live "en quieta vida, / al yugo de amor atado, / daré dueño a mi familia, /

señora a mi herencia corta, / y a mi padre nuera e hija" (a peaceful life, bound by love; I will give my family a leader, my estate a mistress, and my father a daughter-in-law and daughter) (*CSM* II.ii.204–8).

Melchor's status as virtuous *villano* is further undermined in Act III, when another of the *damas* in this play adapts the veiled-woman disguise in order to trick Melchor into marriage. He doesn't even notice that the eyes he sees today are blue, while those he saw previously were dark; his valet points out the discrepancy, but Melchor pays no attention (*CSM* III.viii). When the "real" veiled woman arrives, Melchor is incapable of distinguishing which of the two is the woman for whom he is willing to reject the *indiano* fortune. Both women produce convincing evidence, and Melchor is forced to ask his valet's opinion (*CSM* III.ix). In this context, his continual rejection of a marriage of convenience—going so far as to claim that he would not marry the *indiana* "si despojara / al Potosí de sus pesos" (if she controlled all the riches of Potosí)—cannot be seen as providing an alternate role model to the courtier contemplating marriage to an *indiano* out of greed (*CSM* III.vii.410–11). As noted earlier, texts that feature the *menosprecio de corte y alabanza de aldea* theme often incorporate a dualistic vision of both courtier and *villano*. In *La celosa de sí misma*, the provincial Melchor manifests a complex mixture of idealism and ignorance that problematizes his status.

The primary *cortesano* figure in this work is Sebastián, who seeks to break up the marriage between Magdalena and Melchor. His multifaceted strategy reveals his adherence to the corrupt values associated with urban life. First, he appeals to the assumed greed of the bride and her family:

> mi calidad y mi hacienda
> bastarán a persuadirla.
> Viejo es su padre. ¿Quién duda
> que su edad será avarienta?
> Seis mil ducados de renta,
> si el oro todo lo muda,
> y el hábito que ya espero,
> ¿qué cosa no alcanzarán?
>
> (*CSM* II.vii.625–32)

(My status and fortune will suffice to persuade her. Her father is elderly; who can doubt that he will be greedy in his old age? With an annual income of six thousand ducats—for gold transforms everything—and the title I expect to obtain, how can anyone resist?)

When his sister, who has fallen in love with Melchor, replies that his competitor is "muy galán" (very gallant), Sebastián assures her, "pero más lo es el dinero" (money is even more so) (*CSM* II.vii.634–35). Next, he plans to say that Magdalena cannot marry Melchor because she had already promised to marry him. Finding witnesses to lie for him will be no problem, because "tiene en sus calles / todos los vicios Madrid" (every vice that exists can be found in Madrid's streets) (*CSM* II.vii.644–45). Even though his machinations are ultimately unsuccessful, they nevertheless reinforce many negative stereotypes of the courtier. Sebastián's stated motivation for marrying Magdalena, however, is the standard one for the period and the genre; he claims to have fallen in love with her beauty and never speaks of a desire for her fortune. In this regard, he is a far more complex character than Pedro, the *cortesano* figure in *El premio del bien hablar,* who is motivated solely by greed. In place of a simple conflation of virtuous *indiano* and *villano* in opposition to vice-ridden courtier, *La celosa de sí misma* presents an intricate matrix of character types—urban, provincial, and "foreign"—whose diverse interactions contribute to the changing hierarchies of early modern Spanish society. Nonetheless, in Tirso's *La celosa de sí misma* (as in Lope's *El premio del bien hablar*), the marriage between *indiano* and provincial characters helps maintain the delineation of both groups as Other, and the emphasis throughout the play upon the variety of destabilizing social consequences presented by marriages to *indianos* serves to reinforce the group's outsider status. (The *indiano* Jerónimo's role is further marginalized by his lowly final status. He serves as the compensatory groom for the woman who wanted to marry Melchor.)

Tirso's *La villana de Vallecas* also presents a diverse and complex scrutiny of the roles of *indianos, villanos,* and *cortesanos* within court society. Redondo has pointed out that critiques of urbanizing societies often idealize rural traditions as the valued relics of a prior golden age ("Du 'Beatus Ille' horacien," 254). The *dama,* Serafina, is a courtier who has just been betrothed to Don Pedro, the Mexican-born son of her father's childhood friend. The opening scene, however, takes place in Valencia, and features two secondary characters, Don Vicente and his sister, Violante. Violante is present only in the letter she leaves for her brother informing him that she has been dishonored by a *madrileño* and thus must retire to a convent. In reality, Violante disguises herself as an ordinary *labradora* and travels to court to restore her honor. She expresses a much more positive opinion of urban values than is usual in *indiano* plays:

En Madrid hay tribunales
para todos . . .
. . . . . . . .
Yo espero en Dios que ha de ser
madre Madrid de mi honor.

(*VV* I.ix)

(In Madrid there are courts to right every wrong. . . . I hope to God that Madrid will be the mother of my honor.)

(In fact, Violante herself will be the mother of her own honor: she orchestrates the restitution of her honor nearly single-handedly.) Earlier in the first act, as Pedro and Agudo, his servant, travel upon the road to Madrid, their conversation features a more typical condemnation of their destination. The *indiano* refers to the capital as a "golfo de damas" (full of ladies); Agudo modifies this to "antes golfo de las yeguas" (rather, full of mares) and adds that despite her name, his bride cannot possibly be a "Serafín" (angel) (*VV* I.iv). The two men recount a litany of stereotypes that combines *menosprecio de corte* with elegiac references to a previous gilded era. Pedro denounces both the times and the capital in his observation that

[n]o son los hombres de ahora
de tan sanas intenciones,
. . . . . . . .
. . . aun de la más honrada,
sacan falsas consecuencias

(*VV* I.iv)

(Men today do not have such good intentions . . . they malign even the most honorable woman.)

These characterizations are confirmed when the man with whom Pedro shares his dinner, Don Gabriel, later reveals himself to be the man who deceived Violante and who then arranges to switch suitcases with the wealthy *indiano*. The fact that this disreputable man is both a *madrileño* and a soldier who had been serving in the imperial army in Flanders amplifies the scrutiny of imperialism's negative impact on Spanish society.

The two plot lines converge as Violante encounters Pedro in Madrid just at the moment he discovers that he has the wrong suitcase and thus does not have the letters of introduction—nor, more crucially, the money and jewels—that are the "testigos" (proofs) of his identity (*VV* I.x). This episode points to a problem raised in several of the *indiano* plays: the instability of the social identity of a character who arrives from a distant and unknown place, seeking to be accepted into the closed and knowable world of the court. The remainder of the play dramatizes Pedro's efforts to prove his identity in time to outwit Gabriel, who tries to take advantage of the fact that no one in Madrid has ever seen the *indiano* in order to usurp his bride as well as his luggage. Violante's participation in these efforts, attempting to marry the man who dishonored her, contributes to the multiple stigmatization of the *cortesano* Gabriel as thief, liar, and seducer.

The ultimate target of critique in this play is not so much any particular individual as it is the courtly system of values that rewards greed and selfishness. As his initial exultation at the contents of Pedro's bags subsides, Gabriel notes that the treasures "a pensamientos crueles me inclinan" (evoke cruel thoughts) (*VV* II.i). His valet points out that Madrid is nothing like Valencia, birthplace of El Cid and the virtuous Violante; rather, it is a "cátedra de socarrones" (cathedral of scoundrels) where "viven todos / de industria, y hasta los lodos / cubren aquí su malicia" (everyone lives by artifice . . . even the mud covers its true nature) (*VV* II.i). In his rejection of Pedro's claim to his own name, Don Gómez, Serafina's father, blames this perceived deception on the urban ambience: "la corte os ocasiona / y sus enredos a usar / marañas con que engañar" (the court and its webs of deceit inspire you to use intrigues to fool people) (*VV* II.ix). Pedro, stung by this humiliating rejection, recalls that Spanish courtiers whom he had previously met in Mexico had described the court as a locus of "dobleces y engaños" (duplicity and deceits) and then likens the city to the deadly "laberintos de Creta" (labyrinths of Crete) (*VV* II.xv). In a scene where Violante pretends to be Don Pedro's fiancée, newly arrived from Mexico, she offers a fresh metaphor to convey the outsider's impression of Madrid: "confusa Babel" (confusing Babel) (*VV* III.iii). And when Gabriel finally begins to feel remorse for robbing Pedro—as a gentleman, he may steal a woman but not a "hacienda" (inheritance)—his valet attempts to dissuade him, focusing on the fact that his current favorable situation is entirely dependent on the ill-gotten gains:

> tu amor, cuyo decoro
> sólo ha estribado hasta ahora
> en la hacienda que trujiste

> pues por las joyas que diste
> a tu serafín te adora
> y así, en faltando las galas,
> dará a tus favores fin.
>
> (*VV* III.v)

(Your love is founded solely upon the fortune that you brought, for your angel loves you for the jewels you gave her. If you lack this wealth, you will lose her favor.)

Gabriel's ultimate decision to return a large portion of Pedro's fortune indicates a complexity of character similar to that demonstrated by Sebastián in *La celosa de sí misma*.

Although Serafina has been delighted with the prospect of marrying her generous *indiano* groom, the moment she hears (through Violante's machinations) that he has brought a woman with him from Mexico, she immediately believes the rumor and blames this infidelity on his American heritage: "[r]azón el que afirma tiene / que cuanto de Indias nos viene / es bueno si no los hombres" (those who say that everything from the Indies is good, except the men, are correct) (*VV* III.xi). Of course, *comedia* convention requires that characters involved in courtship immediately believe all such negative reports about their prospective mates. Such misunderstandings are a primary engine of comic emplotment. Still, Serafina's reaction emphasizes one of the many forms of oppression of the subaltern figure—the tendency to attribute all character flaws of a particular individual to inherent defects of the group to which she or he belongs and to view those defects as justification for denying that group access to power.

When Pedro's true identity is finally revealed and his fortune is restored, Serafina happily accepts him as her spouse. Even in this moment of comic *anagnorisis* and reintegration, however, economic vocabulary dominates, as we have seen. Serafina pledges her devotion with the promise "pagaros con el alma" (to pay you with my soul), to which Pedro replies, "Si me amáis, ¿qué mayor paga?" (if you love me, there is no greater recompense) (*VV* III.xxii). This play graphically represents the conflict between greed and contempt for alterity that marks the interactions between peninsular and colonial societies. The liminal status of the American outsider is particularly highlighted in *La villana de Vallecas* through the trials suffered by Pedro, because his identity and thus his social position are shown to be extremely tenuous.

Lope's *El sembrar en buena tierra* presents the most incriminating view of the court, dramatizing the most vociferous critiques and the most dastardly *cortesanos*. In the opening scene, Don Félix arrives from Lima in order to pursue his *hábito*. His valet expresses fear that courtiers "le sabrán limar el oro / de las Indias de Occidente" (will know how to extract his West Indian gold) (*SBT* I.i). (Note the play on words of Lima, the city, and "limar," "to steal.") In this play, much of the condemnation of urban life focuses on the female courtier. Florencio, who is Félix's guide in Madrid, asserts that although there are some good women there, most care more about their clothing than anything else (*SBT* I.ii). Women are represented as even more alien than native Americans: Florencio claims that the extravagant fashions *cortesanas* now wear "da[n] risa a mil naciones / que llaman bárbaras" (provoke laughter in a thousand so-called barbaric nations) (*SBT* I.ii). Like Pedro and Agudo in *La villana de Vallecas*, Florencio combines *menosprecio de corte* with nostalgia for an earlier and better society, asserting that "antiguamente, [las cortesanas] querían / su marido e hijos" (in the past, court women loved their husbands and children) (*SBT* I.ii). Félix's father inscribes similar warnings in the letter that accompanies the money he sends his son. He writes, "huye de los peligros cortesanos / que ponen a los pies las ocasiones / para empeñar el alma con las manos" (avoid dangerous courtiers, who will seize the opportunity to tarnish your soul) (*SBT* I.xi).

Félix embodies the naive, generous *indiano*. The way in which he is treated by the other characters divides the court into two distinct groups: the worldly denizens of the capital, whose goal is to acquire as much of Félix's fortune for themselves as possible, and the virtuous characters who esteem him for his "agradable persona" (good character) and help him when his finances suffer a temporary reversal (*SBT* I.iv). Doña Prudencia and her maid, Inés, fall into the former category. Prudencia reveals herself as an avaricious pragmatist when she ridicules men's use of Petrarchan poetic conventions to win her favor as a poor substitute for expensive gifts: "porque no tienen qué dar, / poder desa suerte hablar" (when they have nothing but words to give, they speak in this way). She indicates that she expects better from an *indiano* suitor (*SBT* I.ii). Florencio comments that this remark proves one of the few certainties in life:

> que sepa una mujer
> cómo ha de sacar dinero . . .
> en que no es mucho aprender
> una sola cosa, pues ellas

no saben más de engañar,
y si dan en estudiar,
desde que nacen doncellas
hasta que mueren sin don,
esta ciencia o este vicio,
y tienen tanto ejercicio,
¿sabránlo con perfección?

(*SBT* I.ii)

(The one thing women know is how to get money . . . since it is not hard to learn to do one thing well, they are experts at deception, and if they study anything from cradle to death it is this science or vice. Since they have so much practice, how could they know it less than perfectly?)

Florencio is proven correct when Félix rejects the list of clothing items that Prudencia has requested, saying that "un amante verdadero" (a sincere lover) buys fine jewelry. Not surprisingly, Prudencia just happens to have an item in mind, and she also manipulates Félix into offering to buy her a coach (*SBT* I.vii). By the beginning of Act II, she has coerced Félix into spending all the money his father sent to him on gifts for her. He has even exhausted all his credit. At this point, Prudencia's maids foreshadow their mistress's rejection of the now-impoverished *galán*. Félix complains that "como ya a las criadas / de Prudencia no les doy, / como en su desgracia estoy, / son conmigo malcriadas" (since I no longer have anything to give Prudencia's maids, I am in disgrace with them and they are rude to me) (*SBT* II.ii). Although Prudencia has indeed lost interest, when they meet by chance in front of a store, she accepts the money Félix offers her so that she can have a shopping spree. She adds insult to injury with the comment, "porque veáis que os estimo, / acepto el ofrecimiento" (so that you will see how much I care for you, I accept your gift) (*SBT* II.vi). Prudencia's character flaws are not limited to greed. When she learns that Alonso (Celia's fiancé) has arrived at court, she and her maid set up a plan to attract Alonso's attention out of sheer spite: "Yo le daría un pesar [a Celia]" (I want to create trouble for her) (*SBT* I.vi). In the final scene of the play, after having already told Félix that she will marry Alonso because of her uncertainty about the size of the estate Félix would inherit, Prudencia attempts in vain to win him back, because the inheritance turns out to be enormous. Félix rejects her with the observation that "a quien pobre me desprecia, / no es justo quererla rico" (it would be wrong to love someone now that I'm rich, if she despised me when I was poor) (*SBT* III.xvi). Thus, the story of Prudencia and Félix can on one level be reduced to a morality play in which *indiano* Virtue triumphs and *cortesana* Greed is disappointed.

Celia's fiancé, Alonso, is the epitome of the greed and lust associated with the *cortesano*. In courting Prudencia, he assuages her objections that he is already engaged to Celia with the suave assurance that

> El alma ya vos sabís
> que tiene capacidad
> de cualquier infinidad,
> y que en ella estar podéis,
> aunque Celia viva en ella.
>
> (*SBT* I.x)

(You know that the heart has an infinite capacity, so there is room for both you and Celia there.)

Further, in order to be able to marry Prudencia without losing the inheritance linked to marrying Celia, he schemes to find a way to make Celia break the engagement, so that she rather than he will have to forfeit the dowry (*SBT* II.iii). Like Prudencia, Alonso remains a pragmatist throughout the drama. When Prudencia tells him that she has decided to marry Félix to obtain a larger fortune, Alonso expresses understanding and then sets his sights on Félix's sister, Ana, who has just arrived in Madrid with an impressive dowry (*SBT* III.xi).

By contrast, Celia and her maid, Elena, embody the woman of yesteryear invoked by Florencio. One of the proofs of this perfection is Celia's ability to value Félix for himself and not for his fortune. When Celia learns that Félix is courting Prudencia, she expresses sympathy: "un mancebo de tan generosas prendas / haya tropezado en Scila" (such a nice young man has encountered such an awful trap) (*SBT* I.xiii). After quarreling with her fiancé over his excessive jealousy, Celia describes her ideal mate to her maid: "a la traza de este *indiano:* / blandura, palabras tiernas, / aquel semblante agradable / y aquella humildad compuesta" (just like that *indiano*, with his gentility, tender words, attractive face, and even-tempered humility) (*SBT* I.xiv). Celia's generosity is also noteworthy; she buys the small diamond Félix needs to pawn for a much larger price than his servant specified, spurring Galindo to observe that she is like a man in this display of "virtud liberal" (great generosity) (*SBT* II.vi). In addition, she provides three thousand *reales* so that Félix will not be thrown in jail for an overdue loan, a gesture Florencio terms "piadosa acción" (merciful action) (*SBT* II.x), and she also donates the funds necessary for Florencio to sail to Peru to settle Félix's estate, which leads Galindo to call her "un angel" (*SBT* II.xii). And in contrast to Prudencia and Alonso, who select their mates on the basis of economic rather than emotional factors, Celia declares that she is willing to marry Félix, even if his only "hacienda" (inheritance) is his "talle y discreción" (figure and discretion), because "no hay oro en el mundo / como un alma bien templado" (no fortune is more valuable than a temperate character) (*SBT* III.iv). Thus, even when she learns that she and Alonso cannot legally divide their inheritance and that unless she marries Alonso she will lose the dowry her father left, she insists that "los gustos son . . . la cosa más fuerte" (personal desire is the most important factor) (*SBT* III.v).

Similarly, although Florencio had warned Félix to be careful with his spending, this loyal friend is unstintingly generous with the scarce resources he has when Félix runs out of money. Florencio sells the few pieces of jewelry he has and even takes money from his parents to help his friend (*SBT* II.i). His loyalty to Félix is so great that when Félix's father dies in Lima, Florencio agrees to undertake the arduous sea journey to America to act as his friend's estate executor so that Félix can remain in Madrid, near his beloved (*SBT* II.x).

In the final act of the play, Félix validates the faith Florencio and Celia demonstrate in him. The play's title, *El sembrar en buena tierra*, is used as a metaphor on several occasions in reference to the change of heart that Félix undergoes: he forgets about Prudencia in response to the seeds of kindness and generosity that Celia has planted in the "fertile soil" of his basic good nature. Florencio also reaps the appropriate reward for his constancy. Félix correctly spurns Alonso's offer to marry his sister because "fue a las Indias Florencio . . . y es bien pagarle el viaje" (Florencio went to the Indies . . . it is only right to reward him for his journey). Further, "el partir con los amigos / fué siempre ley de nobleza" (sharing good fortune with friends has always been the basis of nobility) (*SBT* III.xvi). Félix's model comportment in the last act proves that he possesses all of the qualities associated with the ideal of the courtier. As we have seen, however, most of the play's characters cannot look beyond stereotypes and persist in seeing Félix and his sister merely as sources of wealth.

In *El sembrar en buena tierra*, evocations of the *menosprecio de corte* theme serve to separate the characters into two camps: *cortesanos* versus those who possess true nobility of spirit, whether *madrileño* or *indiano*. Those who adhere to the traditional virtues harvest the largest rewards, but no serious punishment befalls those who value wealth above all else, for Prudencia and Alonso will share the smaller but still sizable inheritance that Celia has forfeited to marry Félix. In addition, the last-minute attempts by Prudencia and Alonso to marry one of the *indiano* siblings demonstrate that the influence of the prevailing courtly atmosphere is so strong that most individuals will not (indeed cannot) learn the moral lesson that other characters have illustrated. Although individual peninsular characters are capable of choosing mates on the basis of character rather than fortune, such figures are the exception rather than the rule—as the extravagant adjectives applied to Celia make clear. For early modern Spanish society as a whole, *indianos* constitute liminal or even subaltern figures who are grudgingly incorporated into court society for the sake of material benefit but remain excluded from participation in and formation of the discourses and ideologies that determine their identity.

Spanish dramatists did not limit themselves to a single aesthetic strategy for representing the *indiano*. The marginalization of the *indiano* characters in these plays derives from their conflation not only with the *villano* but also with another stock dramatic figure, the *senex amans*. The elderly *indiano* wishing to obtain a young wife is a particularly problematic figure: he upsets the stability of court hierarchies because he shares with eligible young men the possession of wealth and the assurance that he has no previous (legitimate) heir, but his physical attributes coincide with the figure of the *senex*. Joost Daalder notes that in tragic drama, such as Seneca's *Troades* and *Oedipus*, the *senex* figure is represented as a source of moral authority and wisdom.[19] In comic drama, however, the elderly normally function as targets of satire on the basis of an inappropriate "geriatric sexuality" that elicits "gerontophobia."[20] Robert Magnan observes that in classical and medieval writings, human life is strictly divided into *juventus, senescentus,* and *senectus,* with each stage possessing rigidly defined behaviors and attitudes.[21] The young peninsular rival of the *indiano senex* in *Marta la*

---

19. Joost Daalder, "The Role of 'Senex' in Kyd's *The Spanish Tragedy*," *Comparative Drama* 20, no. 3 (1986): 248.

20. José I. Suárez, "Characterization of the Elderly in Vicentine Drama," *South Atlantic Review* 62, no. 1 (1996): 38; Richard Freedman, "Sufficiently Decayed: Gerontophobia in English Literature," in *Aging and the Elderly: Humanistic Perspectives in Gerontology,* ed. Stuart F. Spicker et al. (Atlantic Highlands, N.J.: Humanities Press, 1978), 50.

21. Robert Magnan, "Sex and Senescence in Medieval Literature," in *Aging in Literature,* ed.

*piadosa* emphasizes the manner in which an American fortune enables an old man to transgress the boundaries that separate the passion of youth from the sterility of old age:

> Dichoso es el interés
> del oro, pues de mi tío
> estiman el casto amor
> en más que el juvenil mío
> ¡Ay dinero encantador!
> ¡Qué grande es tu señorío!
>
> (*MP* I.viii)

(The influence of money is great, for they value my uncle's impotent love more than my youthful vigor. Oh, the enchantment of money! How immense is your domain!)

Wido Hempel points out a series of *refranes* from medieval and Golden Age Spanish texts that characterize sexual desire on the part of the aged as "algo censurable, pernicioso, vergonzoso, ridículo" (something that is contemptible, pernicious, shameful, ridiculous), citing Cervantine characters such as *el viejo celoso* and even Don Quijote as examples.[22] The amorous *senex* is thus conventionally represented as an object of contempt for attempting to participate in the activities reserved for a different age group (Suárez, "Elderly in Vicentine Drama," 39).

In his Freudian reading of the negative representation of the *senex*, Laurence Porter points out that ambivalent literary treatments of this character type are linked to psychological ambivalence toward all father figures, particularly in situations where there is rivalry for a love object. This observation is relevant to *Marta la piadosa*, where the *indiano* captain is in competition with his nephew. Although Porter refers specifically to the Dostoevskian corpus, his assertion that it is rare to find an elderly male character who is "wise, nurturing and a sexual being all at once" applies equally to the *comedia*.[23] Suárez notes correctly that readers of the post–Civil

---

Laurel Porter and Laurence M. Porter (Troy, Mich.: International Book Publishers, 1984), 13–30.

22. Wido Hempel, "El viejo y el amor: Apuntes sobre un motivo en la literatura española de Cervantes a García Lorca," in *Actas del VIII Congreso de la Asociación Internacional de Hispanistas*, vol. 1, ed. David A. Kossoff et al. (Madrid: Istmo, 1986), 693.

23. Laurence M. Porter, "Farce and Idealization: Dostoevsky's Ambivalence Toward Aging," in *Aging in Literature*, ed. Porter and Porter, 86–87, 88.

Rights era cannot expect early modern writers and audiences to conform to contemporary sensibilities concerning "historically disadvantaged" groups—such as the old or the *indiano* (41). Attempting to delineate the way in which particular historical moments are marked by their boundaries and their criteria for social inclusion or exclusion, however, is a worthy scholarly endeavor.

Tirso's *Por el sótano y el torno* provides a typical example of the monologic representation of an old *indiano* as an undesirable mate—and hence a marginal figure. The wealth of the elderly captain in this text is the primary basis for his claim to a young bride and acceptance into court society. The servant who describes Jusepa's engagement explains that her older, widowed sister, Bernarda, has arranged for her sibling to wed "setenta años, dorados" (seventy gilded years) and declares that this fiancé is so old, he must be "hermano del Cid" (the Cid's brother) (*MP* I.iii). The captain's age is referred to on many occasions. He is "nuestro setentón" (the guy in his seventies) (*MP* I.iii) and "un viejo remozado" (a rejuvenated old man) (*MP* I.xv), so near death that "ya sus vísperas publica" (his obituary is already prepared) (*MP* II.i). These characterizations correspond to the criteria described above for the satiric and marginalizing treatment of the amorous *senex*.

The primary arguments against "May-December weddings" in this text emphasize the inability of the elderly to stimulate desire and produce offspring. There are frequent references to the physical inadequacies of old age, beginning with the servant's observation that "a la niña le pesa / mezclar con su sangre fría / la de edad tan floreciente" (the young girl hates to mix with his cold blood that of her blooming youth) (*MP* I.iii). Jusepa laments that marriage to "quien no puede ser padre / es desatino terrible" (one who cannot be a father is a terrible fate) and dismisses the importance of his "plata" (silver): "si cuando dármela trata, / con el estaño la afrenta / de la vejez que le obliga" (when he tries to give it to me, his decrepitude turns it to tin) (*MP* II.vii). Ridiculing the courtship efforts of the aged, she complains, "me dice amores con tos" (he rasps sweet nothings) (*MP* II.vii). She points to the likely disparity between words and deeds in such a suitor: "en la ejecución fallido / y fecundo de palabra" (fecund with words, but incapable of execution) (*MP* II.vii). Jusepa highlights the antithetical nature of the proposed marriage, declaring that "no es adorno / del mayo el caduco enero" (May is not the right companion for decrepit January) and rejecting the prospect of becoming "monja del matrimonio" (a wedded nun) (*MP* II.vii). The paradoxical description of marriage to an old man emphasizes the way in which the *indiano senex* violates a patriarchal norm in seeking to wed a young woman when he may not be able to produce heirs to whom he would bequeath his financial and social capital.

After Jusepa encounters the Portuguese *galán*, Duarte, her contempt for her aged fiancé increases. Her servant encourages rebellion: "despidamos nuestro viejo / que en tu abril quiere nevar" (let's get rid of this old man who wants to snow on your springtime) (*MP* II.xiii). Duarte's best friend, who engages Bernarda in conversation both to woo her and to speak on behalf of his friend, argues that "prolijos años amenazan hielos" (old age threatens ice) (*MP* II.xvii). Bernarda does come to understand their reasoning, admitting that "setenta años nevados" (seventy frozen years) and "la senectud sin calor" (old age without warmth) are not alluring (*MP* III.iii). The money the captain will give her if the marriage goes through, however, is necessary to Bernarda's hopes for her own remarriage, because her first husband was poor and left her no dowry. Thus, she reassures herself that the groom will die soon and leave her sister a wealthy widow: "pues se queda con la plata" (she will end up with the money) (*MP* III.iii).

The captain's lack of energy and virility is highlighted when he finally arrives in Madrid near the end of the third act. A servant reports that the groom will not visit until the next day, because the trip from Seville has worn him out and made him ill, and he has gone to bed to recuperate (*MP* III.xx). In fact, the old *perulero* never does appear on stage or speak in this play. His attributes and defects are elaborated by his detractors and by his sole champion, Bernarda. This *indiano senex* is the most truly marginalized, the most clearly silenced and subaltern figure of all the *indianos* studied in this chapter, for he is given absolutely no voice or presence with which to define himself—*and* he loses his bride to a young *madrileño*.

In the final scenes, the play shifts focus away from deprecations against the *senex* groom and toward the efforts to persuade Bernarda to permit the marriage of her younger sister and the young suitor, Duarte. Her acquiescence is obtained through a dual strategy. First, Jusepa uses a disguise to escape from her house and visit Duarte, where a private marriage ceremony takes place with the requisite servants as witnesses. Next, Duarte persuades Bernarda that his friend Fernando's financial resources, which she will have access to upon her marriage, are adequate compensation for the money that she loses by not helping the *perulero*. Of course, as Jean Hindson has noted, the issue of private marriage was a thorny issue in the period following the final Council of Trent, which outlawed such secret ceremonies.[24] The manner in which the marriages of Jusepa and Bernarda are arranged in the concluding scenes raise nearly as many problems as they solve, then, for the spectator must accept that a parental figure will accept both an unlawful marriage and much smaller dowries for herself and her ward in exchange for domestic bliss. The second issue is particularly doubtful in light of the prevailing financial concerns Bernarda expresses throughout the play.

The most compelling evidence of Bernarda's priorities is the soliloquy in Act II, where the young widow announces that "La codicia y la afición / pelean dentro en mi pecho" (greed and affection are at war in my heart) (*MP* II.ii) and then decides to continue to encourage an alliance between her sister and the *indiano*. Other indications include the conversation in which she instructs her servant to make inquiries about a young man (Fernando) who has shown interest in her, though she is less interested in his name or title than in his "renta" (annual income) (*MP* II.iii). In another scene, she pressures her sister not to break her engagement, promising that the old man's fortune "le hará mancebo" (will restore his youth) (*MP* III.iii). Bernarda even jeopardizes her future chances with Fernando by asking him to stop trying to help his friend Duarte win Jusepa (*MP* III.v). Finally, just before Duarte arrives, Bernarda informs her sister, "harás lo que yo quisiere / o quitaréte la vida" (you will do as I say, or I will kill you) (*MP* III.xx). In this context, Bernarda's sudden capitulation is indeed problematic. If we are to examine these plays as possible guides for the many financially strapped court families who contemplate marriages to wealthy Others, the resolution provided here is insufficient. The author himself points to this issue in the closing disclaimer: "Tirso escribe mas no afirma" (Tirso writes but does not preach) (*MP* III.xxi).

In *Marta la piadosa,* Tirso addresses the issue of marriage to an *indiano senex* from a different angle, introducing more complex characters. In the opening scene, the protagonist, Marta, like Jusepa, is represented as the typical sympathetic victim of the forced marriage *comedia* plot, describing her current situation as "el que tiene el cuchillo a la garganta" (a knife at my throat) and declaring that "solo el infierno causa pena tanta" (only hell could cause as much pain).[25] Jane Albrecht, however, has observed

---

24. Jean Hindson, "The Fernando-Dorotea-Cardenio-Luscinda Story: Cervantes' Deconstruction of Marriage," *Romance Language Annual* 4 (1992): 484.
25. Laura Dolfi, *Studio sulla commedia di Tirso de Molina* Por el sótano y el torno (Messina-Firenze: D'Anna, 1973), 5.

that as the plot develops, Marta becomes less attractive to the audience as she schemes to compete with her own sister in order to marry the young *peninsular* she prefers—a man who has just murdered her brother.[26] A primary indication of Marta's lack of scruples is her pleasure in easily deceiving her sister, Lucía (*MP* I.i, I.iv), and Captain Urbina (*MP* III.i), her father's old friend who has recently returned to Spain after many years in the Indies. This is particularly notable in the scenes where Marta convinces Lucía that all of her pretenses are part of her plan to arrange for her sister to marry the *galán*, Felipe—and then gloats over the "linda traza" (lovely trick) (*MP* III.xv–xvi). Marta's ultimate success in avoiding marriage to the *indiano senex* does not provide the sense of comic closure and justice served that is typical of many comedias featuring the "forced marriage" plot (Dolfi, *Studio sulla commedia*, 6).

Felipe is also a more complex character than the typical *galán*. Although the audience learns in the first scene that he has just killed Marta's brother, the circumstances surrounding this act are never clarified, so there is no basis on which to determine his guilt or innocence and thus his suitability as a husband. It is also clear from the lamentations of Lucía and Marta in the opening scene that Felipe has previously courted both sisters, and his willingness to pledge devotion to both women in order to dissuade them from revealing his true identity lends ambiguity to another aspect of his character (*MP* III.vi–viii, III.xii). The truth about Felipe's affections is further obscured when the lieutenant reveals that in the past, he had refrained from courting Lucía because of his friend's love for her (*MP* III.xi).

In this play, Don Gómez is represented as the ultimate greedy parent. He freely admits that his daughter Marta's marriage to his old friend, Urbina, is a purely financial arrangement. Unlike Bernarda, however, he offers no compelling reason for his female charge to marry a wealthy man. He calculates that

> con más de cien mil ducados,
> años que están tan dorados
> reverenciarlos conviene.
> Daréle Marta la mano,
> que no es viejo el interés . . .
>
> (*MP* I.ii)

---

26. Jane White Albrecht, "The Satiric Irony of *Marta la Piadosa*," *Bulletin of the Comediantes* 39, no. 1 (1987): 39.

> (He has more than one hundred thousand ducats; it is appropriate to revere such gilded years. I will marry Marta off to him, for greed never ages.)

and subsequently expresses no concern that the "cano . . . compra esta marta / para remediar su frío" (graybeard is buying this ermine to warm him up) (*MP* I.ii). (Note the pun in "Marta" and "marta," or "ermine.") Indeed, the attraction of this dowry is such that it can assuage even the greatest suffering:

> estas nuevas solamente
> poner límite han podido
> al llanto y pena presente,
> por el hijo que he perdido.
>
> (*MP* I.ii)
>
> (Only this news has been able to alleviate the pain and suffering from the loss of my son.)

The esteem for money over every other consideration becomes even clearer in the final scene, when the news that his son's murderer has just inherited a fortune as large as the captain's induces Don Gómez to accept Felipe as his son-in-law.

A multiplicity of voices expresses contempt for the romantic pretenses of the aged suitor in this play, including those of the intended bride and the rival nephew. In addition to the passage cited previously, the lieutenant claims that his uncle is still alive only because "la sangre del interés / anima su cuerpo frío" (avarice animates his cold body), and he describes the forthcoming marriage of Urbina and Marta as the union of "lirio" and "rosa" (lily and rose), the flowers associated with funerals and weddings, respectively (*MP* I.xi). When Urbina declares his intentions to Marta, she asserts, "parece sueño / esa esperanza, que entre verdes años / viene llena de amor como de engaños" (his hope is a mere fantasy, for he is among youths, full of love and self-deception) (*MP* I.xvi). In an aside, Marta repeats a conventional seasonal metaphor used in the condemnation of mixed marriages: Felipe is described as "abril" (April), while Urbina is "este caduco enero" (this decrepit January) (*MP* I.xvi). And Felipe's servant describes the physical "attractions" of an elderly groom as "barba betunada, / tos, catarro, orina, hijada / y mucho diente postizo" (grizzled beard, coughing, sickly, incontinent, effeminate, and with false teeth) (*MP* I.xii). Felipe curses his rival: "maldiga vejez tan seca y verde" (damn this dried-up old man) (*MP* I.xvi).

Urbina, however, is a more complex figure than the nameless captain of *Por el sótano y el torno*. The entire play offers a more dialogical examination of marriage between the young peninsular woman and the *indiano senex*. Although Urbina is ultimately rejected as a husband, he is generous; when Marta feigns a decision to devote herself to chastity and charitable works in order to avoid marriage to Urbina, her suitor offers part of her dowry to help build a hospital, because "el amor que os tengo es tal, / ya no humano mas divino, / daros luego determino . . . ocho mil ducados" (my love for you is so great, divine rather than human; thus, I have decided to give you eight thousand ducats) (*MP* III.i). He also gives his nephew a very generous "dowry" to facilitate the marriage to Lucía, Marta's sister (*MP* III.i). The *indiano* is not jealous or vengeful, either. When Marta's machinations to marry the young man she loves are revealed in the final scene, it is the spurned fiancé who restrains Marta's father from administering corporal punishment to his daughter. Urbina advises temperance: "refrenad . . . el enojo con las canas" (let your years restrain your temper). He adds, "no es de nobles la venganza" (vengeance is not noble) (*MP* III.xxi). Here, the captain enacts an unusual combination of the inappropriate sexual/marital desires of the comic *senex* and the wisdom and temperance of the epic or tragic *senex*. As a final indication of nobility, Urbina allows Marta to keep the money he had contributed to her spurious charity as a wedding gift. In this figure who is marginal due to *indiano* status and age, who is both deeply flawed in terms of his efforts to transgress the decorum of his station in life yet also magnanimous and capable of exercising good judgment, Tirso offers a compelling representation of a liminal type who inhabits the aesthetic and ontological borderlands of early modern Spanish society and culture.

## *INDIANOS* AND MONEY

While it is not uncommon for characters in comic dramas to investigate the family background and economic status of prospective love interests, references to these issues are usually fairly general, using adjectives such as "principal" or "noble" (notable, noble). It is thus particularly striking that in all of these dramas with *indiana/o* brides or grooms, there are repeated references to the specific amounts of "dotes," "rentas," and "haciendas" (dowry, income, and estates). This attention to economic detail is not limited to *indianos* and their prospective mates; competitors also offer concrete numbers. One factor related to this obsession with *indiano* wealth may be found in Mariscal's observation that many *indianos* were also *conversos*. In the writings of the early modern period, even those *indianos* who were *cristianos viejos* were represented with the attributes and epithets associated with *conversos* ("Cultural Studies," 69–71). The strong emphasis on wealth obtained through commercial activities can thus be seen as a constituent element of the discourses that marginalized *conversos, indianos,* and other groups whose ascension to elite status was not based on aristocratic genealogy or military activity.

In *La celosa de sí misma,* the fortune of Magdalena and her brother is specified twice (*CSM* I.ii.189–92, I.vii.914), as is that of Sebastián and his sister (*CSM* II.vii.629, II.x.960–64). The precise amounts of the dowries granted to servants in the mass marriages of the concluding scene are specified, and the amount of spending money that Melchor has brought with him from León is also quantified (*CSM* I.v). In *El premio del bien hablar,* Angela's servant informs her that their *indiana* hostess, Leonarda, has a dowry of one hundred thousand *ducados,* and Leonarda's father details the inheritances of both of his children to the prospective groom (*PBH* I.viii, II.vii). In *La noche de San Juan,* when Leonor broaches the topic of marrying Don Juan, she specifies his income in the very first sentence of her speech to her brother (*NSJ* I.iv). The power that money grants is highlighted when Juan bribes the officials who arrested him for participating in a street brawl and is thus released from jail. In addition to the Quevedoesque references to gold as "caballero" (gentleman), Juan adds, "toda aquella arrogancia / templaron veinte escudos" (twenty coins assuaged all that arrogance) (*NSJ* III.i).

References to sums of money are most frequent in *La villana de Vallecas.* Don Pedro, meeting two total strangers on the road, informs them of the exact amount of his worth (*VV* I.x). The role that money plays in screening a *cortesano* versus an *indiano* mate is obvious in Pedro's description of the betrothal process, during which he made inquiries to Spain concerning his intended bride's honor and virtue, while her father "informóse del estado [de mi padre] . . . de su hacienda, que es copiosa" (made inquiries concerning my father's estate and fortune, which are enormous) (*VV* I.iv). The servant who helps Gabriel steal Pedro's bag refers to the colonies as the sites "que oro derraman" (that flood over with gold) (*VV* II.i). While "copiosa" and "derrama" are less specific references than a cipher, they are also more graphic than the typical descriptives used in *comedias*. Explaining why she believes the first person who claimed the name Don Pedro was telling the truth, Serafina asserts that the "más de treinta mil pesos" (more than thirty thousand pesos) that he possesses are "testigos fieles" (reliable witnesses) (*VV* II.ix).

Likewise, when the *indiano* Don Félix of *El sembrar en buena tierra* inquires about the identity of an attractive woman he has seen, Florencio offers just two pieces of information: her name and the amount of her dowry (*SBT* I.iii). This impressive quantity is specified on many other occasions throughout the course of the play. Monetary sums are also mentioned frequently in reference to Prudencia; the jewelry that she selects costs five hundred *escudos*, and Félix has spent twelve thousand *ducados* on her by Act II (*SBT* II.iv). The play also specifies the exact quantity that Félix receives from his father so that he can prolong his sojourn in Madrid, the asking price of the small diamond that is the last of Félix's pawnable possessions (and the much larger fee that Celia actually pays for the gem), the amount of the unpaid debt for which Félix is nearly incarcerated, and the size of the estate inherited by Félix and his sister after their father dies (*SBT* I.xi, II.v, II.ix, III.viii).

In *Por el sótano y el torno*, we learn the size of the fortune of the elderly *indiano* as well as of the dowries he will bestow on his bride and her widowed sister in the very first speech that refers to the captain (*ST* I.iii). When a young man seeks to court the sister of the *indiana* bride, he specifies his own *renta* in his very first love letter to her (*ST* II.xii). And in the final lines of the play, the exact financial worth of each character is reiterated.

In *Marta la piadosa*, Captain Urbina sends a letter to Marta's father suggesting that their long-standing friendship be converted to familial ties, and he specifies in the second line the amount of the fortune he has earned overseas and can bestow on his bride (*MP* I.ii). In the same scene, Don Gómez, describing the groom's fortune to Marta, reports that the captain "sacó el alma al Potosí" (extracted the core of Potosí), and that this windfall "pone en olvido cuidados" (lays all my cares to rest). The captain's nephew also names the exact amount of *ducados* in complaining to Felipe about his rival (*MP* I.xi). Two additional sums of money are detailed in the *dénouement*: the dowry that Urbina settles on his nephew and Lucía, and the inheritance that allows Felipe to gain Don Gómez's acceptance.

Enumerated sums of money serve more than one purpose in these dramas. In the situations noted above, the numbers emphasize the great wealth of *indianos,* but they are also used to highlight the precarious financial status of many who live at or travel to the court. For example, in *La celosa de sí misma,* Melchor gives the veiled woman a purse that contains two hundred *ducados*—all of the money he has—and his valet notes that Melchor must hurry to meet and wed his wealthy bride or they will have nothing to eat (*CSM* I.v.722). In *El premio del bien hablar,* the information about Leonarda's dowry only deepens Angela's anxiety about her own penurious state: "[l]a fortuna, mi madrastra, / ha guardado para mí / cien mil penas y desgracias" (Fortune, my stepmother, has reserved one hundred thousand pains and disgraces for me) (*PBH* I.viii). The most extreme examples of the fragile relationship between liquid wealth and social status are those of two *indiano* characters. In *La villana de Vallecas,* Don Pedro's very identity is lost when he loses the suitcase that contains all of his wealth. For Don Félix in *El sembrar en buena tierra,* whose love object loses interest after he spends (on her) all the money he brought with him to court, his status is further jeopardized when his father dies, because his inheritance is not a well-defined peninsular estate (*SBT* II.x). Félix expounds upon the condition of the penniless *hidalgo:* "Dura necesidad, madre afrentosa / de la vergüenza . . . para derribar el honor vales" (Harsh poverty, cruel mother of shame, who destroys honor) (*SBT* II.ii). His valet emphasizes the material consequences of Félix's generosity toward Prudencia: "hoy apenas has comido / y cien escudos arrojas / al mar de tus desvaríos" (you have barely eaten today, yet you throw away one hundred *escudos* for the sake of your misguided passion) (*SBT* II.vi). The instability of the *indiano* identity is thus linked with the precariousness of the fortunes gained overseas, consisting of liquid assets rather than a peninsular estate and a title. This issue also appears in *La celosa de sí misma,* where the valet notes that if Melchor's prospective *indiano* father-in-law were to die, "te echase en hora mala" (you would be in dire straits) (*CSM* I.v.730). Don Pedro, in *La villana de Vallecas,* points to yet another factor that makes American wealth undependable: the danger of shipwrecks (*VV* I.x).

## Pretender *Indianos*

Proving the identity of an *indiano* character is particularly difficult, because those who confer identity and those who can confirm it are separated by an ocean. The assumption of such an identity offers a convenient device for *comedias de capa y espada* that depend upon mistaken identity for plot complications.[27] The role of the *indiano* in Spanish society may be fruitfully explored, then, through an analysis of plays in which the stock character *el fingido*, the pretender, chooses to assert an American background.

In *La villana de Vallecas*, it is the loss of his luggage, with the gold and jewelry that constitute one sort of proof of identity, that causes the prospective *indiano* groom, Pedro, to despair, "Con qué despachos entraré en la corte? / Cómo creerá Don Juan que soy Don Pedro?" (What documents can I use to be accepted at court? How will Don Juan believe that I am really Don Pedro?) (*VV* I.x). This automatic equation of *indiano* identity with visible wealth allows Gabriel, who stole the luggage, to usurp Pedro's role as Serafina's fiancé temporarily and thus to perform a variation on *el fingido*. Gabriel's deception is successful mainly because he is able to give the appropriate gifts—he possesses the stolen signifiers of *indianidad*. Pedro emphasizes the uncertainty of the welcome an *indiano* can expect in Spain in his response to his prospective father-in-law's disappointingly cool reception: "Creí que amoroso y tierno, / mi nombre apenas dijera, / cuando os hallara colgado / de mi cuello" (I expected that as soon as I pronounced my name, you would embrace me, affectionately and tenderly) (*VV* II.ix).

Pedro's plight in *La villana de Vallecas* is similar to that of Magdalena's in *La celosa de sí misma;* in both plays, unstable identity serves as a metaphor for the uncertain status of the subaltern *indiano*. Like Pedro, who is rejected if he cannot display enormous wealth at all times, Magdalena has no stable identity. Melchor loves her as the veiled woman in the church, yet he has no interest in her as the *indiana* chosen for him by his family (*CSM* II.ix.770–800). And in *La villana de Vallecas*, when the real Pedro arrives after the usurper, Serafina rejects him, claiming that she believes the man who arrived first, because "autorizan su nobleza / las joyas que con largeza / me acaba de dar" (the jewels that he so generously gave me are proof of his nobility) (*VV* II.ix). The forms of proof that Pedro's valet attempts to provide—familiarity with the food and fauna of the Indies that the false Pedro could not demonstrate—are not accepted, because no one in Serafina's *madrileño* family has the requisite knowledge to validate that form of evidence. The precarious position of the *indiano* at court is further emphasized when Pedro is imprisoned for the crimes committed by the man who borrows his name (*VV* II.xviii) and when he must accept the name "Don Gabriel" in order to end his incarceration (*VV* III.xv).

27. Villarino, *"El indiano,"* 228–29.

Violante, the woman whom Gabriel previously seduced and abandoned, profits from watching her beloved's machinations as a *fingido* to create a temporary obstacle to Serafina's marriage to the false Pedro. She rents a luxurious home in Madrid, appropriating the identity of a wealthy *mejicana*, and she then informs Serafina's brother that she and Pedro were formally betrothed in Mexico (VVIII.ii, III.iii). In this unique instance, the ability to pretend to be an *indiana* simply by virtue of ostentatious display serves the interest of justice within the play.

Another notable example of an *indiano fingido* is Don García in *La verdad sospechosa*. Catherine Larson asserts that all of García's lies are due to his desire to be "famoso, el medio qual fuere sea" (famous, by any means).[28] Claiming to be a *perulero* is indeed one way to stand apart from the crowd of *madrileños*. Alan Paterson notes that family name is one form of "instant signifier of worth"—and the name *perulero* is also an instant signifier, but of another type of worth![29] Harold Veeser points out that García is already an outsider, arriving in Madrid "partly unassimilated" from the exile of the "second son," sent away to a university to prepare for a career. It is thus not surprising that when García chooses a new identity in order to impress the object of his desire, another type of outsider comes to mind. Veeser notes that in many ways, García does resemble the stereotypical *indiano*, "a suddenly fortunate upstart arriving in Madrid with fancy clothes but no manners."[30] García demonstrates his subaltern status—not as *indiano* but as an outsider at court—in his conflation of the compliments and courtesies of courtship with a crass offer to buy jewelry for a woman he has just met (Paterson, "Reversal," 366). Larson's examination of the disagreement between García and his father over the definition of a *caballero* confirms Stoll's observations concerning the period's reexamination of this status (Larson, "Labels and Lies," 97; Stoll, "Dual Levels," 73, 74). The two qualifications debated here, however—birth versus good deeds—constitute a denial of monetary wealth as a basis of nobility not only for the *indiano* but also for many other early modern groups who were enlarging the ranks of the gentry. Although García is not an *indiano*, his character shares many

---

28. Catherine Larson, "Labels and Lies: Names and Don García's World in *La verdad sospechosa*," *Revista de Estudios Hispánicos* 20, no. 2 (1986): 97.

29. Alan K. G. Paterson, "Reversal and Multiple Role-Playing in Alarcón's *La verdad sospechosa*," *Bulletin of Hispanic Studies* 61, no. 1 (1984): 366.

30. Harold A. Veeser, "'That Dangerous Supplement': *La verdad sospechosa* and the Literary Speech Situation," in *Things Done with Words: Speech Acts in Hispanic Drama*, ed. Elias L. Rivers (Newark, Del.: Juan de la Cuesta, 1986), 51, 61.

of the marginalized qualities of that figure and again exemplifies the way in which *indiano* identity functions in conflation with other stock *comedia* "outsider" characters.

Lope de Vega used the false assumption of an *indiano* identity as a plot device in his *entremés, El indiano*, as well as in *El amante agradecido* (Villarino, "*El indiano*, un entremés," 228–29; Urtiaga, *El indiano*, 46). In *El indiano*, a *pícaro* type pretends to be the *indiano* nephew of a wealthy old man, and uses the *Poema del Cid* scheme of offering a chest full of worthless items as collateral for a loan. The twist in this plot is that the old man knows he has no *indiano* nephew, but he goes along with the ruse in the hopes of obtaining some benefit. In the end, both *fingidos* suffer the reversals typical of the farcical *entremés;* the old man loses some of the money he loaned as collateral, and the youth is beaten up by the old man's servants. Here, the manner in which both characters adopt the role of *fingido* points to the corruption nurtured by the prospect of unearned wealth. In all of these plays, the stability of social hierarchies is threatened (though never actually destroyed) because of the mistaken identities and the deceptive behavior whose source is greed for American gold and silver.

The anxiety about deceptive identities found in *indiano* plays and also in many other *comedias* offers significant insights into the early modern Spanish court's psychodynamics as the *madrileño* elite engaged in an unsettling process of redefining itself. This questioning of the categories of elite and commoner must also be viewed in light of the changes in the nature of aristocratic involvement in warfare and the creation of a corps of professional but plebian soldiers. The threatening but liminal *indiano* in this evolving society is positioned within a larger context of other marginalized groups, including professional soldiers, religious converts, and *campesinos*, who gained economic advantage from the gentry's migration to the court and from the demands placed upon Spanish military resources by imperial activity. The wealth of these groups, like that of the *indiano*, sometimes permitted access to the privileges of nobility and demonstrated the permeable boundaries between those who were dominant and those who were dominated (Mariscal, "Figure," 58). As studies of the representation of other marginal groups have indicated, however, the acquisition of titles and noble spouses neither eradicated those groups' ideological alterity and discursive marginalization nor offered a true escape from liminality.

It is important to emphasize that the discursive marginalization endured by the *indiano/a* figure does not constitute a monologic representation. Rather, the conflation of stock figures placing the *indiano/a* in a subaltern position is also one source of dialogic or polylogic interpretation for the early modern (and the postmodern) consumer. The representation of both the *indiano* and the *villano* is dialogic: they are simultaneously outsiders and voices for reformist movements at the court that attracted significant support at various moments in the seventeenth century, particularly during the early phases of the regime of Philip IV and Olivares (Elliott, *Imperial Spain*, 397). In this context, the conflationary move that silences *indianos* on one level grants them an oppositional voice at another level. Lascasian critiques of the treatment of indigenous peoples by greedy Spaniards provide an additional relevant discourse for "epochal" analysis, for the oppression of native workers is an integral component of the system that created spectacular *rentas* and *dotes* for *indianos/as* (Williams, *Marxism and Literature*, 122). Like the other forms of counter-epic writing to be examined in the following chapters, these *indiano* plays offer valuable insights into the myriad competing discourses concerning imperialism's effects both at home and abroad during Spain's "Golden Age."

## 4

## THE EARLY MODERN HISTORY PLAY AS COUNTER-EPIC MODE

Cervantes's *La destrucción de Numancia* and Lope de Vega's *Arauco domado*

Cervantes's *La destrucción de Numancia (The Destruction of Numancia)* and Lope de Vega's *Arauco domado (Arauco Conquered)*, which dramatize imperial battles fought at Numancia in the second century A.D. and in sixteenth-century Chile, are the best-known and most widely studied examples of counter-epic Spanish literature examined in this book. This chapter will analyze the polygeneric, ideologically complex representation of Spanish and Roman imperial practice in the two plays by demonstrating the connections between the counter-epic and contemporary notions (as conceived by Phyllis Rackin and John Loftis) of the nature and function of the early modern history play.

In highlighting the polyphonic nature of these texts, I follow Raymond Williams's practice of "epochal" analysis, a process that recognizes "the complex interactions between movements and tendencies both within and beyond a specific and effective dominance" (*Marxism and Literature*, 120). Williams faults conventional notions of history for their failure to take into account the plurality of discourses in an era and their privileging of the dominant ideological viewpoint (121–22). He identifies residual and emergent elements as the two formations that are most often overlooked. Studies of the counter-epic history plays under consideration here, for example, have not adequately examined the importance of the anti-martial discourses discussed in Chapter 2, resulting in a failure to recognize that the traditional epic is, in Williams's terminology, a residual discourse—one that can no longer adequately express the lived experiences of the culture producing it—rather than the product of a securely dominant formation. Much excellent scholarship has documented the oppositional elements of Ercilla's monumental anti-imperialist poem, *La Araucana*.[1] These insights, however, are just beginning to be used by those reexamining dramatic representations of imperial themes.

The Numancia and Arauco plays analyzed in this chapter were written at pivotal moments of the sixteenth and seventeenth centuries in which military policy was contested not only in the Americas but also in Europe. The Cervantine staging of the siege of Numancia in 1580, for example, coincides with one of the most intense phases of the Spanish struggle to pacify the Netherlands, during which siege warfare was central to Alexander Farnese's strategy (Lynch, *Spain Under the Habsburgs*, 1:288–307). There is no consensus about the date of composition for Lope's play, but all of the dates proposed are years marked by significant military events or debates concerning imperial tactics and strategies. The staging of two moments in Spanish history—the Roman defeat of Numancia and the temporary pacification of the Araucanians by García Hurtado de Mendoza—can be seen as examinations of seventeenth-century Spanish policy toward Flanders, Italy, and France as well as America. And the changing nature of warfare in early modern Europe, described by Michael Murrin, is also relevant to the critique of the ways in which Spanish military goals were achieved.

## THE EARLY MODERN EUROPEAN HISTORY PLAY

The plays under consideration in this chapter share the generic instability of nondramatic works of the period that were assigned the label "historical," such as Burton's *Anatomy of Melancholy* and Sir Walter Raleigh's *History of the World*, as well as theatrical works including Shakespeare's *Henriad*.

1. Among recent articles, see Mejías López, "Testimonio jurídico"; Ralph Bauer, "Colonial Discourse and Early American Literary History: Ercilla, the Inca Garcilaso, and Joel Barlow's Conception of a New World Epic," *Early American Literature* 30, no. 3 (1995): 203–32; Rosa Perelmuter-Pérez, "El paisaje idealizado en *La Araucana*," *Hispanic Review* 54, no. 2 (1986): 129–46; and Roberto Castillo Sandoval, "'Una misma cosa con la vuestra'? Ercilla, Pedro de Oña y la apropiación post-colonial de la patria araucana," *Revista Iberoamericana* 61 (January–June 1995): 231–47.

Phyllis Rackin's *Stages of History* explores the Tudor history play and offers valuable insights for analyzing early modern Spanish dramatizations of its recent and distant past.[2] Rackin notes that the Tudor plays, like the Numancia and Arauco dramas, explore national connections with the Roman Empire in order to create a heroic foundational myth (4); as shown below, Don García is repeatedly compared to Caesar and Alexander the Great. The patronage system that supported dramatizations of the American conquest by Tirso, Mira de Amescua, Lope, and others as a means to glorify the military achievements of the Pizarro and García de Mendoza families can thus be seen as a related form of mythification. Anthony Cascardi describes this process as the "reshap[ing] of the past as an object of desire" (*Ideologies*, 39).

Rackin attributes the history play's rise in popularity to the radical revisioning of the discipline of historiography in the early modern period and to a proliferation of highly popular histories of the British Empire. This interest in historiography is equally keen in early modern Spain, where the recording of the national past entails not only the reconsideration of Roman and medieval events, as documented by such historians as Ambrosio de Morales, Juan de Mariana, Pedro de Mexía, and others, but also the letters and chronicles of the conquistadors, with their competing claims of glory, and the memoirs of professional soldiers (de Armas, *Cervantes*, 8–10; Puddu, *Soldado gentilhombre*, 140–80). In addition to the many links established between Spain and imperial Rome in *La destrucción de Numancia*, Cervantes affirms another mythical variant of early modern Spanish ethnic historiography in the prophecy that links Goths, Numantians, and imperial Spaniards (I.477).[3]

Rackin also points out the importance of the printing press for historiography. Its invention led to a drastic increase in access to classical and medieval historical texts and to the creation of new chronicles, which in turn gave rise to the discovery of multiple versions of historical events and a new skepticism toward the possibility of determining historical truth (*Stages*, 13). In this context, as Herbert Lindenberger correctly asserts, the suspense concerning the outcome of a history play is centered not upon *what* will happen, because the audience already knows the central aspects of the historical event, but upon "a kind of intellectual suspense" about

---

2. I am deeply grateful to Christopher Weimer, who not only suggested that I consult Rackin's study but even went so far as to bestow *Stages of History* as a gift.
3. References to Cervantes's *Numancia* include act and line numbers.

how the play will explain, justify, critique, or celebrate key events and figures in the national past (cited in Rackin, *Stages*, 46). Thus, these representations of the conquests of Numancia and Arauco evoked audience interest in part because the playgoers were aware of multiple viewpoints concerning siege warfare, imperial aggression, and the relative merits of various *conquistador* leaders.

The relationship between generic structure and ideological polyphony in the history play is also relevant to this study. Rackin characterizes Shakespeare's history play as an "experimental genre" that "incorporates a variety of structures that elude traditional generic classification" (27) and as a "hybrid genre . . . [that] transgressed the emergent boundaries between historical fact and fictional artifact" (32). Similarly, Stephen Watt describes the history play as a genre that is always in a "dialogical relationship with one or more antecedent kinds."[4] For John Cox, the ambiguity of the history play stems from its origin in open-ended historiographic inscription rather than the more enclosed nature of literary writing. The history play is thus significantly different from other forms of drama in that it is not "a dramatic mimesis of time's consummation—the definitive end," because "history is defined by the continuum of time."[5] Rackin asserts that ambivalent dramatization offers the theater audience an opportunity for active intellectual engagement with competing political ideologies (29). The representations of the sieges of Numancia and Arauco are even more complex than the Tudor plays, for as Chapter 2 demonstrates, early modern Spain produced several (rather than just two) ideological currents concerning the validity of imperialist activity. This polyvalence can also be seen at the generic level in the Spanish plays. Where Rackin depicts the British history play as the borderland where theatrical and historical writings meet (104), the Spanish history plays juxtapose a plethora of literary forms, including epic, tragedy, amorous intrigue, allegory, and farce as well as chronicle.

Linking generic and ideological complexity, Rackin observes that in *King John,* Shakespeare uses a "diffuse, episodic structure to depict a world

---

4. Stephen Watt, "Shaw's *St. Joan* and the Modern History Play," *Comparative Drama* 19, no. 1 (1985): 59.

5. John D. Cox, "*3 Henry VI:* Dramatic Convention and the Shakespearean History Play," *Comparative Drama* 12 (1978): 56. David Scott Kastan also characterizes the history play as an "open-ended structure" in which form and ideology are problematic because of the difficulty in dramatizing "a mere episode carved from the continuum of human time." See Kastan, "The Shape of Time: Form and Value in the Shakespearean History Play," *Comparative Drama* 7 (1973–74): 268, 272.

where no principle of historic causation can be discovered" (28). She also identifies conservative and oppositional political ideologies coexisting in the *Henriad*. This series of plays attempts to provide a coherent historical explanation of the War of the Roses, giving voice to both traditional, Providential notions of historical causation that celebrate the outcome of the wars (thus validating the Tudor ascension to the throne) as well as Machiavellian interpretations of historical events that could be seen as a challenge to the legitimacy of the Tudor reign (29, 51). Similar notions of the relationship between history and Providence appear in the Cervantine drama. When the character España laments her nation's history of dominance by foreigners, one possible explanation she offers is that "mi maldad lo ha merecido" (from my own sins I could not save me).[6] As Elliott has noted, early modern Spanish historiographers tended to attribute national misfortunes to divine punishment for collective sins (*Spain and Its World*, 246). In *Arauco domado*, Caupolicán evokes Providence in defending his capture by the Spaniards, telling his Amazonian wife, "esto no ha consistido / en mi valor, ni en mis fuerzas, / sino en las de mis fortunas" (this is not an indictment of my valor or strength, but of my fate) (*AD* III, 235–36).[7] He similarly describes his defeat to García as a predetermined event: "así baja y alza el vuelo / la fortuna de la guerra" (thus do the fortunes of war raise up and then bring down men) (*AD* III, 233). This speech may have been intended to convey a sense of Providence concerning Spanish dominance in Chile. In subsequent battles, however, the "sail of fortune" often favored the Araucanians, a situation known only too well by the original peninsular audience.

The early modern history play, like other dramatic subgenres of the Golden Age, often features moments of self-reflexivity in which characters meditate upon the norms and processes of representation. In the history plays, these moments frequently foreground the function of historiography, rather than the theater, as a form of inscription (Rackin, *Stages*, 29). Self-conscious reflection about the process of historical inscription prevails in Cervantes's text. Two allegorical figures, the River Duero and Fame,

---

6. *DN* I.368; the translation of *The Siege of Numantia* is by Roy Campbell, vol. 3 of *The Classic Theater: Six Spanish Plays*, ed. Eric Bentley (Garden City, N.Y.: Doubleday, 1959), 110. Nearly all the translations of *La Numancia* are from Campbell's *Siege of Numantia*, and subsequent references to that work will be abbreviated as SN. In rare instances where the translator has omitted a term or phrase, I provide it in internal brackets (without quotation marks) and refer to the *SN* page number.

7. References to *Arauco domado* (abbreviated as *AD*) include act and page numbers; no standard edition with scene and line numbers exists for this work.

provide reassurances in the opening and closing sections of the play that Numancia's resistance will earn the town a place in the historical record. The Duero predicts, "no podrán las sombras del olvido / obscurecer el sol de sus hazañas, / en toda edad tenidas por extrañas" (the splendid / Exploits of the Numantines will not fade / Or wither in oblivion's dusky shade) (*DN* I.462–64; *SN*, 112), and Fame itself echoes this promise:

> tendré cuidado, . . .
> . . . . . . . .
> a publicar con lengua verdadera
> . . . . . . . .
> el valor de Numancia
>
> (*DN* IV.2426–31)
>
> (I shall take great care . . .
> To publish round the world Numantia's worth
> And peerless valour with truthful tongue)
>
> (*SN*, 159)

Characters who voice concern about their own inscription in the historical record are common in metahistorical dramas. When the Numantian ambassador, Caravino, implies that the Roman siege tactics are cowardly, Escipión communicates not only awareness of his place in history but also the belief that he will be judged for the results of the battle rather than for the means of obtaining victory: "el viento lleve ahora esta vergüenza, / y vuélvale la fama cuando venza" (all that will be whisked off by the wind / When this great victory restores my fame!") (*DN* III.1199–1200; *SN*, 130). This statement offers a rather Machiavellian response to the ethical questions raised by just war theories and Lascasian discourses—and expresses the belief that historical inscription rewards winners and erases troubling details about how victory is achieved.

The Numantians dedicate themselves to disproving Escipión's theory of historical memory. Seeking to ensure that their defeat will be inscribed on their own terms, they at first decide on a glorious death charge, but later choose collective self-destruction. In this scenario, the proto-Spaniards seek to escape the fate of being the objects of inscription, to prevent the victorious Romans from controlling the commemoration of this event—in short, to rewrite the norms of historiography. As Teógenes explains, one purpose of the collective suicide is to reduce the Romans to the status of mere "testigo / que apruebe y eternice nuestra historia" (Rather must our foes / Be witness to blazon forth *our* glory) (*DN* III.1420–21; *SN*, 135, emphasis in original). This reference to manipulating the historical record may be seen as a response to the emergence of the Black Legend (in which imperial Spanish victories were inscribed within Protestant cultures as acts of savagery rather than valor) and to the letters written by *conquistadores* in an effort to influence not only the immediate reception of their accomplishments but also the subsequent inscriptions of the conquest.

Cervantes deploys historical drama as the medium for marginalizing military activity by foregrounding the importance of historical writing. Later counter-epic historical dramatists would develop this mode by incorporating other dramatic genres in addition to metahistorical commentary. Teógenes predicts that "mil siglos durará nuestra memoria" (A hundred thousand years will seem a day / To our immortal fame) (*DN* III.1423; *SN*, 135). His assertion is correct only because, the play reminds us, Cervantes is the latest link in a chain that stretches across more than ten centuries— a chain of scribes who continually revive the memories of ancient deeds. Teógenes thus joins the historiographer with the warrior as the twin pillars of glory. Likewise, the closing lines of the drama foreground historical commemoration as much as the heroic events themselves.

> Hallo solo en Numancia todo cuanto
> debe con justo título cantarse,
> y lo que puede dar materia al canto
> para poder mil siglos ocuparse:
> la fuerza no vencida, el valor tanto,
> digno de en prosa y verso celebrarse.
> Mas, pues de esto se encarga la memoria,
> demos feliz remate a nuestra historia.
>
> (*DN* IV.2441–49)

> (In [Numancia] alone I find
> All that can kindle the poetic mind.
> To fill long ages with sad lamentations,
> Praising the bravest of unconquered nations.
> And now, remembering her matchless glory,
> We give a happy end to our sad story.)
>
> (*SN*, 159–60)

In this stanza, the three passive-voice verbs emphasize that these deeds will be recounted and revered, while the final couplet links memory and written inscription as the dual components of transmission. Here, Cervantes represents the staging of the past as an event nearly as significant as the deeds he dramatizes. This conception of artistic historiography's importance is validated by the subsequent commissioning of historical dramas as vehicles for enhancing *conquistador* family names and fortunes. And, as John Loftis has shown, Olivares confirmed the importance of proper artistic inscription. The minister employed a variety of dramatists during the 1620s, including Calderón and Lope, to write "journalistic" plays celebrating Spanish imperial victories immediately after they occurred. Loftis also notes that most of these plays used the Cervantine history play as their template.[8]

Meditations upon historical inscription are similarly found in *Arauco domado*. Like *Los españoles en Chile*, Lope's American play focuses on the reputation and representation of the achievements of Don García Hurtado de Mendoza. When Don García announces that his first military act as the new governor of Chile will be to lead an expedition to pacify the city of Concepción, a soldier predicts success by vowing, "La fame tu nombre cante" (May fame sing your name) (*AD* I, 114). The power and influence wielded over dramaturgy within commissioned works can be seen as Lope's García envisions his own commemoration within the larger inscription of his family's deeds: "[verá] todo el mundo / aquel valor profundo del que ha dado / la sangre y nombre de Hurtado de Mendoza" (Everyone will know of the great valor that accompanies the name and bloodlines of the Hurtado de Mendoza family) (*AD* I, 129). A loyal soldier predicts that history will acclaim both individual and familial merit as he replies, "este día / Alejandro sería justa cosa / que la fama ambiciosa te llamase, / que aunque el Hurtado pase al mayor hombre, / no será hurtado sino propio nombre" (On this day, it would be right that fame names you another Alexander, for although the title will be passed on, your name will never be forgotten) (*AD* I, 130). Another comparison to classical heroes accompanies the description of Don García's crossing of the Biobío into hostile Araucanian territory—

> allí intentó la más noble
> y más prodigiosa hazaña

8. John Loftis, *Renaissance Drama in England and Spain: Topical Allusion and History Plays* (Princeton: Princeton University Press, 1987), 224, 54–55.

que de general *se cuenta*
(César perdone en su barca)

(*AD* II, 153; emphasis added)

(the most noble and amazing military deed *ever told* about a general occurred there; not even excepting Caesar and his ships)

—and the soldier Alarcón specifically evokes historical commemoration in claiming that this feat is more incredible than any other *recounted* about a military leader, thus dismissing the achievements recorded not only by Roman and Macedonian historians but also in the competing epic poems, chronicles, and letters of early modern *conquistadores*. Lope's *obra de encargo* also stages a scene that appears to be a deliberate attempt to correct the historical record offered in Ercilla's poem. General Avendaño, who led the battle at Purén, rejects the laurel offered to him by García to celebrate this victory: "si algo hice, pues lo hurté / a ti, como dueño suyo, / lo vuelvo y lo restituyo" (if I achieved anything, it was stolen from you, the rightful owner of this victory, and so I restore it to you) (*AD* III, 232). Of course, sponsoring theatrical works does not always have the desired impact. This play is just one of several that the Mendoza family commissioned in its effort to control the commemoration of Don García. The descendants seemed to feel that his deeds required repeated stagings in order to ensure his place at the forefront of the Spanish *imaginaire* concerning America. In addition, the context of all these metahistorical reflections presented within a historical drama reminds members of the audience that they are witnessing a deliberate attempt to manipulate the historical record.

The nostalgia for the imagined simplicity and heroism of the medieval era expressed in the early modern history play described by Rackin can also be found in *Arauco domado,* which evokes Spain's reconquest of its own territory during the Middle Ages. Don García and Avendaño rally their troops to defend the fort at Penco and to prevent the escape of indigenous warriors at Purén with the legendary cry, "Cierra España" (Defend Spain!) (*AD* I, 139; III, 228). The other half of this battle cry is also heard at Purén, where the battle begins when Avendaño calls out, "¡Santiago, Santiago!" (Saint James, Saint James!) (*AD* III, 227). In the context of Arauco's (and Europe's) continued resistance to Spanish domination—and of debate over the validity of imperial practice—these evocations of irreversible victory and unified sentiment serve to highlight the gap between medieval *Reconquista* and early modern *Conquista*.

The ghost of Lautaro describes an additional form of historical commemoration in his efforts to persuade Caupolicán to continue to resist the Spaniards. When his successor is nearly ready to capitulate in the final scene of Act II, Lautaro predicts that a victorious Don García will inscribe his successes upon the land itself by founding cities named Cañete and Mendoza on Araucanian soil (*AD* II, 198–99). Caupolicán rejects this form of inscription as a "deshonor horrible" (horrible dishonor) and calls for a return to battle in order to avoid the shame of Spaniards writing their names within and upon Chilean history and soil. Felipe uses similar diction in the next scene as he predicts the immortal fame that will accompany Don García's feats: "que de inmorales memorias / dejas para siempre al suelo / de tu nombre y de tus glorias!" (Your memorable victories will be commemorated by leaving your name and glory upon this soil!) (*AD* III, 200). Rengo also alludes to Spanish-named cities in support of the decision to continue fighting in Act III; he reports that García has headed for Ancud, "donde la ciudad de Osorno / quiere decir que ha fundado / por un abuelo que tiene" (where his forefather had founded the city, Osorno) (*AD* III, 218–19). Audiences aware of the many occasions upon which the Araucanians succeeded in destroying newly built Spanish cities during the sixteenth and early seventeenth centuries would recall that neither cities nor chronicles—nor plays—guarantee long-lasting fame. García himself is given lines alluding to the vagaries both of city building and of his own fame. He tells Caupolicán that the Araucanian must pay with his life because, among other crimes, "echaste muchas ciudades por tierra" (you razed many cities to the ground), and he worries that the historical record may not give him the recognition he deserves: "pues Felipe, en fin, sabrá / que le doy nueve ciudades / ... aunque envidias atrevidas / oscurezcan mis verdades" (Philip knows that I built nine cities for him, even though envy may obscure my accomplishments) (*AD* III, 232).

Through the scrutiny of written and geographical inscription—and reinscription—these two plays remind audiences that historical theater offers just one mode of presentation among a series of competing interpretations and commemorations of individual and national *fama*. The metahistorical dimensions of the early modern history play highlight key epistemological issues concerning imperial practice, including the elusive and illusory nature of historical truth.

## NUMANCIA, ARAUCO, AND *COMEDIA* CRITICISM

Critical approaches to Cervantes's *La Numancia* over the last quarter-century indicate that this play can be seen as a microcosm of the history of studies of genre and ideology among *comedia* scholars. Many critics have sought to place *La Numancia* within the boundaries of a single genre—tragedy—by demonstrating similarities to classical Athenian theater or to sixteenth-century pre-Lopean drama rather than to the *comedia nueva*. It is important to note that the generic status of the play is seldom the focus of this criticism; it is generally mentioned in passing as part of the process of situating the play in its literary-historical context.[9] For these critics, the generic label and the orthodox tone of the Cervantine work is never in doubt. They seek instead to identify which of the available tragic models Cervantes utilized. (This endeavor was often undertaken to improve the reputation of a play that was revered by the German Romantics but had subsequently been judged deficient.[10]) Although tragic themes, aesthetic structures, and support of the status quo are certainly important elements of *La Numancia* and *Arauco domado*, a fuller reading of these texts requires analysis of the ways in which the tragic elements are juxtaposed with those of epic poetry and comic drama. It is precisely this juxtaposition of multiple genres—in conjunction with a polyphonic view of dominant institutions—that is the hallmark of the early modern European history play. In arguing for a different generic history for these plays, then, I am simultaneously advocating the consideration of a more complex representation of imperialist ideologies. Where an earlier generation of critics sought to carve out a space for *La Numancia* in the canon by pointing to its tragic elements, I seek to use a Cultural Studies approach in order to situate the play within a new canon of anticolonial early modern texts.

---

9. Jean Canavaggio, for example, identifies the speeches by the Río Duero and España as the voices of destiny, like the Greek chorus, thus linking the play to Athenian drama by evoking the concept of unavoidable fate; see Canavaggio, *Cervantes dramaturge: Un théâtre à naître* (Paris: Presses Universitaires de France, 1977), 46. Juan Luis Alborg categorizes the play as tragic because of its affinities with classical theater, despite the nationalist rather than Greco-Roman setting. See Alborg's *Historia de la literatura española*, vol. 1 (Madrid: Gredos, 1966).

10. Joaquín Casalduero, *Sentido y forma del teatro de Cervantes* (Madrid: Gredos, 1966), 259; Edward H. Friedman, *The Unifying Concept: Approaches to the Structure of Cervantes' Comedias* (York, S.C.: Spanish Publications, 1981), 2–3.

One issue that must be explored here is critics' reluctance to use the concept of generic mixture as a way to illuminate difficult texts. Nancy Klein Maguire offers one possible explanation, suggesting that works that mix genres "escape" the binary compulsion that dominates Western approaches to knowledge.[11] To privilege the indeterminacy of the history play, an even more radical form of generic experimentation, is to deconstruct a particular example of binary thought in order to allow this generic phenomenon to escape from its marginal position in seventeenth-century drama study. Another relevant factor is that the two most influential classic authorities—Aristotle and Horace—discouraged the mixing of genres. In the period this study addresses, the two ancients are often mentioned by those who would condemn a text incorporating more than one genre as a "mongrel" (Sidney), a "minotaur" (Lope de Vega), or a "bastard" in need of "legitimization."[12] This peculiar vocabulary highlights the fact that violating (or worse, eliminating) generic boundaries is perceived as an act whose consequences have implications outside the realm of literature: it is a transgression related to inappropriate reproductive behavior, one that therefore poses a threat to social hierarchies. As we have seen, modern criticism often follows the lead of these classical and early modern theoreticians. An important exception is Frederick de Armas's recent reconsideration of his earlier article on *La Numancia*, which focused on Escipión as a tragic hero. In *Cervantes, Raphael, and the Classics,* de Armas demonstrates the ubiquity of *contaminatio,* or generic juxtaposition, in *La Numancia.* His important study documents that Cervantes's reinscription incorporates elements not only of the *Pharsalia* and the *Aeneid* but also of variants on the subgenre of tragedies of defeated empires by Seneca, Euripides, and Aeschylus (14, 90, 138, 166).

Several critics astutely emphasize the epic component in this play. Carroll Johnson and Jean Canavaggio have pointed out the parallels to Virgil's *Aeneid,* because both works narrate the phoenix-like birth of a new civilization out of the ashes of a ruined city. Francisco Ruiz Ramón classifies the play "la tragedia de los sitiados" (a siege tragedy), but, of course, that is only one-half of the plot; he also acknowledges that Cervantes has dramatized an

---

11. Nancy Klein Maguire, ed., *Renaissance Tragicomedy* (New York: AMS Press, 1987), 6.
12. Lope de Vega, *El arte nuevo de escribir comedias,* in *Antología del teatro del siglo de oro* (Madrid: Orígenes, 1989), L. 176; Philip Sidney, *A Defence of Poetry,* ed. and intro. J. A. Van Dorsten (London: Oxford, 1971). Both are cited in James J. Yoch, "The Renaissance Dramatization of Temperance: The Italian Revival of Tragicomedy," in *Renaissance Tragicomedy,* ed. Maguire, 115.

epic theme. Similarly, while Angel Valbuena Prat compares the Cervantine play to Lobo Lasso's *La destrucción de Constantinopla* in order to classify it as a Renaissance tragedy, he concedes that the work of Lobo Lasso is often "novelesca," or novelistic. (The novel—the least determinate of literary genres—is also the genre most like the history play as conceived here, particularly in its late baroque phase, as I will demonstrate in the analysis of González de Bustos and Rojas Zorrilla dramas in the next chapter.) Emilie Bergmann writes that the "timeless" nature of the Cervantine work, which combines projections of the future and reflections on the past through the use of allegorical figures and prophecies, is more suited to a narrative genre like the epic than to drama.[13] All of these critics discuss the play's epic dimension as an element of its affirmation of the status quo, because they have in mind what David Quint calls "the epic of the winners" rather than a more problematic epic text like the *Pharsalia*. It is de Armas's choice of this unconventional epic as a point of comparison that enables him to identify the oppositional elements of *La Numancia;* likewise, my emphasis on generic instability provides the foundation for my arguments concerning ideological tensions.

Other useful observations concerning the generic structure of this play include Edward Friedman's comparison of Cervantes's "superposition of art on history" to the chronicle (*Unifying Concept,* 35). Matthew Stroud emphasizes the similarity of the allegorical characters in the play to those of medieval mystery drama; his paradoxical label of "auto secular" (secular sacramental play) confirms Rackin's assertion that the early modern history play's heritage incorporates a wide range of contradictory elements, "at once learned and popular, literary and theatrical, sacred and profane, authoritarian and subversive."[14] In *La Numancia,* as in *Arauco domado,* the combination of several genres results in the highly complex form of generic indeterminacy that marks the early modern history play. This claim of indeterminacy is similar to that asserted by post-structuralist criticism for textual meaning as a whole, an indeterminacy that validates the *significance* of the lack of closure. In these plays—and particularly in their final

---

13. See Carroll B. Johnson, "*La Numancia* y la estructura de la ambigüedad cervantina," in *Cervantes: Su obra y su mundo,* edited by Manuel Criado de Val (Madrid: Edi-6, 1981), 311; Canavaggio, *Cervantes dramaturge,* 43; Francisco Ruiz Ramón, *Historia del teatro español* (Madrid: Cátedra, 1988), 130–31; Angel Valbuena Prat, *Historia del teatro español* (Barcelona: Noguer, 1956), 53; Emilie Bergmann, "The Epic Vision of Cervantes' *Numancia,*" *Theater Journal* 36 (1982): 88.

14. See Matthew D. Stroud, "*La Numancia* como auto secular," in *Cervantes,* ed. Criado de Val, 303–7; Rackin, *Stages,* 109.

scenes—ideological fault lines are revealed through the deployment of conflicting generic terms. The generic tension remains unresolved, and the lack of a generic dominant is, in fact, central to the polyphonic scrutiny of imperialist ideology.

Carroll Johnson, Willard King, Francisco Ruiz Ramón, Robert Shannon, and Frederick de Armas are among the Hispanists who have begun, in the last twenty years, to recover the oppositional possibilities in plays by Lope and Cervantes that had long been viewed as enthusiastic affirmations of imperial ambition.[15] These studies are only a beginning, their potential impact often muted by the contexts in which subversion is placed. King writes that *La Numancia* is not a "simple exaltation" of empire. Instead, she argues, "in the compassion, understanding and respect with which it views both colony and empire . . . this early play already shows the unmistakable stamp of the Cervantine mind."[16] Here, King contains a powerful questioning of imperial policy in two different fashions. She first joins subversion and affirmation as an essential, inseparable pair, and later, she places this already weakened form of subversion in the controlling context of authorial intention. The result is a glorification of a Romantic vision of genius and creativity, one in which the power of the oppressed voice is reduced to paying homage to the "mind" that conceived it.

Carroll Johnson also emphasizes the "ambiguity" in Cervantes's representation. Johnson repeats King's containing movement in his assertion that, because of this ambiguity, "Una lectura 'correcta,' en el sentido de establecer definitivamente la superioridad de una interpretación sobre la otra, queda así imposibilitada. Precisamente, creo yo, como quiso Cervantes" (A "correct" reading, in the sense of definitively establishing the

---

15. See, for example, Ruiz Ramón, *Historia*, 129; Angela Belli, "Cervantes' *El cerco de Numancia* and Euripides' *The Trojan Women*," *Kentucky Romance Quarterly* 24 (1978): 128; Gustavo Correa, "El concepto de la fama en el teatro de Cervantes," *Hispanic Review* 27 (1959): 283; George Shivers, "La historicidad de *El cerco de Numancia*," *Hispanófila* 39 (1970): 14. Casalduero has even criticized nineteenth- and twentieth-century theatrical revivals that "deformed" the original by using it in the explicitly political context of the Napoleonic siege and the Civil War (*Sentido y forma*, 86). The critical tendency to find affirmation of the status quo in *comedias* is not limited to *La Numancia*. In "Calderón's Late Roman Plays and the Imperial Myth," in *Critical Perspectives on Calderón de la Barca*, ed. Frederick de Armas et al. (Lincoln, Neb.: Society of Spanish and Spanish-American Studies, 1981), David Lanoue writes about the hegemonic representation of imperial mythology in Calderón's Roman plays (92). See also José Antonio Maravall's overview of theater and society in the Golden Age, *Teatro y literatura en la sociedad barroca* (Madrid: Seminarios y Ediciones, 1972).

16. Willard King, "Cervantes' *Numancia* and Imperial Spain," *Modern Language Notes* 94 (1979): 217.

superiority of one interpretation over another, is thus impossible. I believe that this is precisely what Cervantes intended).[17] Similarly, Bruce Wardropper remarks that Cervantes "scrupulously presents both sides of any question."[18] Alfredo Hermenegildo's observations concerning the apparent political criticism in *La Numancia* cannot be used to examine the polyphonic potentials of the text, because these insights are reduced to manifestations of Cervantes's psychological makeup. Hermenegildo links the author to the *moriscos* and "todos aquellos que no forman parte del nucleo sagrado constitutivo" (all of those who are excluded from the sacred homogenous nucleus). Cervantes is "otro Numantino" (another Numantian). For Hermenegildo, as for the others cited here, the political elements are ambiguous: "son las claves interpretativas de la intencionalidad del autor" (they are the interpretive keys to the author's intentions).[19] The valuable insights of these critics are thus rendered unusable for progressive historical criticism: their studies privilege closure and unity through the structural device of authorial intention. They do not consider the possibility that these early modern texts might constitute a component of a debate that was carried out in many different discursive fields but treat them instead as isolated cases of social critique from the pen of a uniquely visionary writer.

In his study of *Arauco domado*, Francisco Ruiz Ramón, like Johnson and King, argues against the earlier generation of critics who interpreted the New World plays as crude propaganda for imperialist policies.[20] Unlike the work of King and Johnson, however, his study does not include nonliterary texts; it is purely formalist. He emphasizes the ambiguous representation of empire in a play "donde resonaba el orgullo de la empresa acometida y, al mismo tiempo, una insobornable conciencia de culpa" (where both pride for imperial achievements and an undeniable sense of guilt can be heard) (246). Ruiz Ramón's observation is made in the context of a universalizing view of "el gran oximorón *esencial* al teatro en la sociedad occidental . . . desenmascarar enmascarando y vice versa" (the great, essential oxymoron

---

17. Johnson, "*La Numancia* y la estructura de la ambigüedad cervantina," 316.
18. Bruce Wardropper, "Cervantes's Theory of Drama," *Modern Philology* 52, no. 4 (1955): 218.
19. Alfredo Hermenegildo, La Numancia *de Cervantes* (Madrid: Sociedad General Española de Librería, 1976), 50, 123, 52.
20. Francisco Ruiz Ramón, "El héroe americano en Lope de Vega y Tirso: De la guerra de los hombres a la guerra de los dioses," in *El mundo del teatro español en su siglo de oro: Ensayos dedicados a John E. Varey*, ed. J. M. Ruano de la Haza, Ottawa Hispanic Studies 3 (Ottawa, Canada: Dovehouse Editions, 1989), 230.

of Western theater . . . to reveal by masking and vice versa) (247, emphasis added). In this case, the eternal nature of the theater is the force that tames subversion through its double role, celebrating the dominant ideology and serving "la función catártico-conjuradora" (the cathartic and exorcising function) (246). In a later essay on the same topic, Ruiz Ramón reworks this notion of the theater as a space outside ideological critique as he considers the "dialectic" nature of the *comedia*.[21] Similarly, after pointing out significant contradictions in Lope's representation of both Spaniards and Araucanians, Robert Shannon concludes, "Lope was neither historian nor philosopher. His *personal vision* of the Araucanian wars and the participants in them is difficult to discern because he was a dramatist principally concerned with conveying events in a manner that would instruct and delight. . . . it is clear that he did seriously question the events which occurred across the Atlantic but seemed confused or perturbed by the many conflicting reports."[22] All of the critics cited here take for granted a conception of Art—in the form of the genius author or the unchanging theater—that neutralizes the potentially radical implications of granting meaning to the questioning of the imperial project. It is important to note that the King and Johnson pieces appeared in the late 1970s, just prior to the emergence of the new forms of historical study that problematized conventional approaches to literature and history. Ruiz Ramón's essays, written ten years later, must exclude history entirely in order to read subversion without entering into the territory where New Historicists and materialists were exploring the relative power of subversion and containment. Shannon's 1989 book does address the debate over applications of just war theories to the conquest of the Americas, but his conclusion emphasizes the individual vision of Lope rather than the larger discursive theater in which this debate occurred. The depiction of Cervantes and Lope as lone visionaries precludes the contextualization of their work within the debates of their era, an omission that this book strives to remedy.

Frederick de Armas's thought-provoking analysis of imperialist discourses in Cervantes does not seek to neutralize the oppositional discourses he identifies. Instead, de Armas asserts that Cervantes "goes beyond any fixed ideology" in order to reveal "the subversive nature of [artistic] beauty—it

21. Francisco Ruiz Ramón, "La voz de los vencidos en el teatro de los vencedores," in *Relaciones literarias entre España y América en los siglos XVI y XVII*, ed. Ysla Campbell (Ciudad Juárez: Universidad Autónoma de Ciudad Juárez, 1992), 8.
22. Robert Shannon, *Visions of the New World in the Drama of Lope de Vega* (New York: Peter Lang, 1989), 157 (emphasis added).

can destabilize even the most carefully thought-out ideology" (*Cervantes*, 15). And in *Renaissance Drama*, which examines seventeenth-century Spanish and English "journalistic" dramatizations of the very recent past, John Loftis cites Cervantes's *La Numancia* as a "source" for such works as Lope's *Los españoles en Flandes* (*The Spaniards in Flanders*) and *El asalto de Manrique* (*The Assault of Manrique*) as well as Calderón's *El sitio de Bredá* (*The Siege of Breda*) (224). According to Loftis, in Cervantes's rendition, "Spain's foreign wars on both sides of the Atlantic are horrible and unnecessary" (58). Loftis does not explain why he sees the Cervantes play as univocally critical of the imperial project, nor does he explain why the other plays he chose to study should be viewed as less oppositional, offering instead a "double vision of war, of victory bought at an absurdly high price" (56–57). Still, Loftis's study of dramatic inscriptions of Spain's battle to dominate the Dutch provides many useful insights into the nature of theatrical scrutiny of military discourse. His elaboration of Cervantes's *La Numancia* as the main *hypotexte* providing counter-epic motifs and structures for the "Flanders plays" is also relevant to this study of the connections among Numancia and Arauco plays.

*Arauco domado* has received less critical attention than *La Numancia*, despite the recent surge of interest in Ercilla's representation of the same event. Some critics assert that *Arauco domado* and other texts written about the Araucanians are inherently conservative, due to their origin as *obras de encargo* designed to flatter the Hurtado de Mendoza family.[23] Melchora Romanos offers a common perspective on the orthodoxy of the Arauco texts. She uses Marc Vitse's notions of the *comedia* as a stage for archetypal Oedipal conflict to analyze character development in Caupolicán and the other native leaders as a transition from the rebellious adolescent "espacio de la libertad" (space of freedom) to the mature and submissive "espacio de la autoridad" (space of authority).[24]

In his study of *Arauco domado*, Glen Dille notes that Lope's play does offer many passages that seem to question Spanish motives and advocate Amerindian liberty ("America Tamed," 117). Dille posits the ubiquity of

23. Romanos, "La construcción del personaje de Caupolicán," 194; Jack Weiner, "La guerra y la paz espirituales en tres comedias de Lope de Vega," *Revista de Estudios Hispánicos* 17, no. 1 (1983): 70; Juan M. Corominas, "Las fuentes literarias del *Arauco domado*, de Lope de Vega," in *Lope de Vega y los orígenes del teatro español: Actas del I Congreso internacional sobre Lope de Vega*, ed. Manuel Criado de Val (Madrid: Edi-6, 1981), 162–63.

24. Romanos, "La construcción del personaje de Caupolicán," 193; Fausta Antonucci, "El indio americano y la conquista de América en las comedias impresas de tema araucano (1616–1665)," in *Relaciones literarias*, ed. Campbell, 29.

the yoking metaphor, however, as the "fundamental sign" of support for the imperialist project and repeatedly refers to the notion of textual unity to emphasize the *yugo* (yoke) and dismiss the importance of other ideas expressed. He attributes critical attention to this topic to a "wish to dissociate [Lope] from his nation's perceived colonial sins" (118). Dille dismisses the relevance of nonliterary writings during the period that questioned the compatibility of Christianity and imperialism, stating that although "many influential Spanish intellectuals lamented the horrifying mortality among the Amerindians, there were few Spaniards who questioned the benefits, indeed the duty of their presence in the New World" (122). It is not necessary for a populace to reject the dominant ideology unanimously in order for alternate belief systems to have an impact on a society, however. Once again I refer to Williams: the representations of "opposition and struggle are important not only in themselves, but as indicative of what the hegemonic process has in practice to work to control."[25] The examination in Chapter 2 of the "intellectuals" Dille dismisses is a fundamental component of a materialist reading of these texts, one that is central to identifying their counter-epic thrust.

Critical awareness of the heterodox dimensions of *Arauco domado*'s polyphonic nature can be found in many recent articles, although the significance granted to the oppositional elements varies greatly. Romanos, for example, does concede that the play reveals "ambivalencias and contradicciones, emergentes de la ideología dominante" (ambivalence and contradictions stemming from the dominant ideology) ("La construcción del personaje de Caupolicán," 194). Her study of dramatic representations of Caupolicán, however, emphasizes the indigenous leader's final conversion as an exemplary submission to European rule (193). Fausta Antonucci recognizes that Lope gives voice to Lascasian discourse by allowing the indigenous peoples to express justifications for their uprisings against the Spaniards, but she asserts that Lope advocated "la necesidad de [la] inclusión pacífica o forzosa en el orbe español" (the need for voluntary or forced inclusion in the Spanish orb) for the Amerindians ("El indio americano y la conquista," 32). Jack Weiner asserts that Lope's *Arauco* voices the same limited support for imperialism found in Las Casas: affirmation of Spain's right to conquer the indigenous peoples through conversion and assimilation rather than through armed combat ("La guerra y la paz espirituales," 71).

25. Williams cited in Jonathan Dollimore, *Radical Tragedy: Religion, Ideology, and Power in the Drama of Shakespeare and His Contemporaries*, 2d ed. (London: Harvester Wheatsheaf, 1989), 14.

Viviana Díaz Balsera offers a compelling study of the ideological dimensions of *Arauco domado,* arguing that this play expresses a fundamental but unspoken concern of imperialist debate—the "anxiety that there might be something unconquerable about the Other's desire that will forever return to split the Spanish colonizer's valued fantasy of spiritual domination."[26] She adds that even texts intended "to serve the colonizer's interests" may unintentionally raise problematic issues and contradictions concerning imperial practice ("Araucanian Alterity," 36). Teresa Kirschner also makes a valuable contribution toward identifying pro-American discourse through her analysis of the play's nonverbal elements, which would have had greater impact on early modern viewers than on postmodern readers. She notes that indigenous characters greatly outnumber Spaniards, that the most fully developed character is Caupolicán rather than Don García Hurtado de Mendoza, and that many of the most visually interesting scenes take place in the Araucanian camp.[27] In this chapter and the next, I will build upon these explorations of contestatory ideology and generic polyphony in the Numancia and Arauco dramas in order to examine the ways in which the plays of Cervantes, Lope de Vega, Rojas Zorrilla, and González de Bustos utilize complex aesthetic tactics to dramatize the equally complex issue of ideological inscription within the counter-epic history play.

## A Distant Mirror: Numancia and Chile

In *Empire and Emancipation,* Jan Nederveen Pieterse points out that an examination of the parallels between "nation building (the Reconquista) and empire building (the Conquest)" is relevant to the study of Spanish imperialism (132). The New World *encomienda* system of labor "recruitment" conforms to the pattern set during the peninsular *Reconquista,* where land grants to military leaders included rights over the inhabitants of the land (133). In both campaigns, military victory was followed by the devel-

---

26. Viviana Díaz Balsera, "Araucanian Alterity in Alonso de Ercilla and Lope de Vega," in *Looking at the "Comedia" in the Year of the Quincentennial,* ed. Barbara Mujica, Sharon D. Voros, and Matthew D. Stroud (Lanham, Md.: University Press of America, 1993), 36.

27. Teresa J. Kirschner, "Encounter and Assimilation of the Other in *Arauco domado* and *La Araucana* by Lope de Vega," in *Christian Encounters with the Other,* ed. John C. Hawley and Erik D. Langer (New York: New York University Press, 1998), 34, 35–36.

opment of an explanation for subsequent power relations. Pieterse cites Stanley and Barbara Stein and Julio Caro Baroja to assert that the Renaissance preoccupation with "purity of blood"—the absence of Islamic or Jewish ancestors—and a focus on Spain's Gothic origins, as seen in *La Numancia,* were the ideological precursors to the discourses concerning European superiority over Amerindians represented in *Arauco domado* and *Los españoles en Chile.* These developments are, according to Pieterse, a carryover from the civilization/barbarism binary that dates back to antiquity (240–43). And in all of these cases, we can see that this binary *produces* race, which is "essentially a social category, an expression of social relations ... namely, *unequal* social relations" (227). These discourses are part of the process through which "a temporary advantage has been obtained by virtue of *uneven development,* whether of a military nature or a combination of political and economic circumstances, and these differentials of development are masked and mystified as differences of *descent*" (252). Pieterse concludes that the determining factor in the production of racial or ethnic categories is struggle (228). It is significant that Cervantes contributes to the mythification of the status quo through an elegiac representation of the heroic Goths or Spaniards but also problematizes the arrogance of the Roman imperialists. It is also relevant that *Arauco domado* represents a native civilization that had *not* yet been fully "domado" (tamed) and was still a site of struggle at the moment of the play's production (Dille, "America Tamed," 118; Díaz Balsera, "Araucanian Alterity," 36).

The questioning of imperial practice in the two plays is achieved through critical scrutiny of Spanish military goals and methodologies combined with a contradictory representation of the vanquished groups. The "natives" are portrayed not only as freedom-loving warriors who display idealized chivalric traits and deploy Western literary discourses in their treatment of their mates (and their enemies) but also as barbaric Others who practice necromancy, cannibalism, or suicide (de Armas, *Cervantes,* 103; Díaz Balsera, "Araucanian Alterity," 32–33). In addition, Lope and Cervantes incorporate innovative aesthetic strategies—e.g., the juxtaposition of epic and many other genres and the open-ended concluding scenes—in their construction of polyvalent history plays. Although many of the counter-epic elements listed above have been previously noted on an individual basis in connection with a single play and in comparisons of the Numancia works and the Arauco corpus, critical studies of the *comedia* have not explored the connections among these aesthetic and ideological dimensions within the two groups of plays.

## CRITIQUE OF CONQUEST

As indicated in Chapter 2, politicians, jurists, soldiers, and theologians engaged in intense debate over the validity of Spain's imperial policies. The Numancia and Arauco plays dramatize the tensions among competing visions of Spain's foreign policy in the late sixteenth and early seventeenth centuries and contribute to that debate as well. The theatrical representation of military activity as unjust, barbaric, and unchristian—and heroic and glorious—constitutes both participation in sociopolitical debates and a counter-epic literary discourse. These plays question the ethical and moral dimensions of empire through a strategy that reveals the degraded aspects of the Spanish enterprise, what Díaz Balsera calls "the gap between that lofty fantasy [of a truly Christian conquest] and the reality of its implementation," and the "indomitable spirit and independence" of the Araucanian nation, which is "fully equal to the European in [its] iron-willed determination to defend territorial sovereignty" and in its refusal "to accept in the name of freedom a Spanish domination represented as saintly, superior and irreproachable" ("Araucanian Alterity," 25, 26, 36). (Although Díaz Balsera refers only to Ercilla's and Lope's texts, her observations concerning the questioning of Spanish imperialism as it was actually conducted and the fierce struggle for autonomy of the besieged groups are also relevant to the Cervantine play. And as John Loftis has shown, these two factors are also relevant to the polyphonic representations of Spain's attempts to subdue the Netherlands.)

The legitimacy of wars of imperialism is a central theme in *La destrucción de Numancia*. Some passages in the play express support for imperial adventures; for example, in the beginning of Act I, Escipión condemns the Roman soldiers for their laxity and compares their pampered hands and complexions to those of people born in England or Flanders—the primary enemies in the European theater of Spain's imperialist expansion (*DN* I.72–73). In addition, the monarch whose vision drives this venture is referred to by an allegorical figure, the River Duero, as "el segundo Felipo sin segundo" (Philip the Second who has no peer [my translation]), and the leader of the king's bellicose faction is praised as "el grande Albano" (the great Alban) (*DN* I.512, 493; *SN*, 112). The River also refers to the sack of Rome as one of the future accomplishments of the heir to the Roman Empire (one of the more questionable deeds of this Christian empire, as Frederick de Armas has noted [*Cervantes*, 57]). And in Act IV, the allegorical figure War calls the imperializing policies of Ferdinand, Charles, and Philip "la dulce ocasión" (the happy reigns) (*DN* IV.1999, *SN* 148).

In Cervantes's play, the drive to conquer new territories can be linked both to epic glory—the successes of Philip II and Alba—and to the tragedy of the many Spaniards and others who continued to die in this pursuit. In constructing a critique of empire, Rome's appetite for new lands is decried as an inappropriate arrogance that prevents Escipión from agreeing to negotiate a settlement with the proto-Spaniards of the town of Numancia (*DN* I.279). Like the Spaniards in *Arauco domado*, the Romans use the imagery of taming beasts to describe their goals. In the opening scene of Act III, Escipión chooses the verb "to tame" to describe his plans for the town (*DN* III.1115). Later, he rejects the challenge to resolve the conflict through a Homeric contest of individual heroes by describing the besieged Numantians as animals:

> La fiera que en la jaula está cerrada
> por su selvatiquez . . .
>
> . . . . . . . . . .
>
> Bestias sois, y por tales encerradas
> os tengo donde habéis de ser domados
>
> (*DN* III.1185–92)

> (Beasts you are, I say,
> And caged as beasts: to learn, the only way
> That beasts can learn, their masters to obey)
>
> (*SN*, 130)

In his very first speech, however, Escipión also emphasizes the tremendous cost of war even for the imperial victors as he expresses reluctance to pursue again "guerra y curso tan extraña y larga / y que tantos romanos ha costado" (Such a long and monstrous war / That cost so many Roman lives) (*DN* I.5–6; *SN*, 101). Both Cervantes and Lope dramatize an imperial general who stands out above his military peers, who enjoys unparalleled success. The primary difference between the Roman leader of the Numancia play and the Spaniard of the Arauco play is that the former relies upon siege warfare to achieve victory, while the latter enjoys a technological superiority based upon firearms and cavalry. Even in Cervantes's day, this hagiographic description of a perfect general was not totally matched by reality. By the time of the later play, written while Spain was losing important battles or being forced by financial problems to accept unfavorable treaties, the gap between the effectiveness of the staged generals and the ineffectiveness of actual imperial efforts was glaringly obvious. Thus, evocation of grand military skill and leadership itself may be seen as an indirect critique of contemporary military reality, especially for the seventeenth-century author. For example, Jugarta praises Escipión lavishly: "quien tiene la ventura, / el valor, nunca visto, que en ti encierras, / pues con ella y con él está segura / la vitoria y el triunfo destas guerras" (For you contain / Both luck and peerless valour in your person, / and both will make your victory secure" (*DN* I.9–12; *SN*, 101). But this tribute may also serve as a reminder that at the present moment, Spain cannot boast of even one invincible commander. Likewise, Jugarta assures Escipión that all of the troops will gather together eagerly to hear his speech, because "no hay soldado / que no te teme juntamente y ame" (there's no soldier here / Who does not love you or does not fear / You, too" (*DN* I.33–34; *SN*, 102). This assertion of devotion may also indirectly criticize the lack of respect felt toward aristocratic but incapable officers who held their rank because of Philip II's habit of using such positions as reward for courtly rather than military virtues, as indicated in the memoirs of professional soldiers of the time (Lynch, *Spain Under the Habsburgs*, 1:33–35).[28]

Escipión, however, offers another perspective on the Roman struggle—one that is more in line with the hierarchical values of Cervantes's age. He locates vice and disorder in the ranks rather than among the leaders in his *allocutio* to the Roman troops:

> el vicio sólo puede hacernos guerra
> más que los enemigos de esta tierra . . .
>
> . . . . . . . . . . . .
>
> El general descuido vuestro, amigos,
> el no mirar por lo que tanto os toca,
> levanta los caídos enemigos,
> que vuestro esfuerzo y opinión apoca.
>
> (DN I.46–77)

> (First, we need to bridle and to quiet
> The vice that seems amongst them to run riot
>
> . . . . . . . . . . . .
>
> . . . your joint negligence in not
> Heeding what most concerns your good

---

28. See also Puddu's account in Chapter 2 of this volume.

> Revives a fallen enemy to seek your lives,
> Despising both your prowess and your fame)
>
> (*SN*, 102–3)

In the Cervantine rendition, the troops accept this blame. Cayo Mario speaks for the entire assembly, reporting that

> ... el temor y la vergüenza a una
> nos aflige, molesta e importune:
> vergüenza, de mirar ser reducidos
> a término tan bajo por su culpa,
> que viendo ser por ti reprendidos,
> no saben a esta falta hacer disculpa;
> temor, de tantos yerros cometidos,
> y la torpe pereza que los culpa
> los tiene de tal modo, que se holgaran
> antes morir que en esto se hallaran.
>
> (*DN* I.175–84)

> (the shame and fear that now afflicts
> And punishes us all—shame to behold
> To what a level they have been reduced
> By their own guilt, and that, when chid by you,
> They could not find the least excuse to offer
> And fear at having made such fatal errors
> And having sunk into such drowsy sloth
> That they would rather die than do their duty)
>
> (*SN*, 105)

Although Cervantes gives voice both to attacks upon the officer corps and the rank-and-file soldiers, the distribution of speeches could be seen to indicate more sympathy for the leaders than for the troops. (This partisanship is quite the reverse of that expressed by the Rojas Zorrilla diptych fifty years later, as the next chapter shows.)

Escipión's praise of military wile in a conversation with his ally, Jugarta, emphasizes the unproductive dimensions of unrestrained military fervor—the very quality lionized in epic literature as glorious *furor*:

> El esfuerzo regido con cordura
> allana al suelo las más altas sierras,
> y la fuerza feroz de loca mano
> áspero vuelve lo que está más llano.
>
> *(DN* I.13–16)
>
> (Force, when applied with prudent moderation,
> Humbles the steepest mountains to the earth,
> But, when it's fiercely plied with a mad hand,
> Trenches the smoothest plains to rugged wastes)
>
> *(SN,* 101)

Escipión's defense of strategic rather than heroic battle emphasizes that the loss of glory will be compensated by the saving of Roman lives: "no quiero yo que sangre de romanos / colore más el suelo de esta tierra; / basta la que han vertido estos hispanos" (I do not wish the wasted blood / Of any more Romans to discolor / This ground again. Enough blood / Has been shed by these cursed Spaniards" (*DN* I.321–23, *SN,* 108). Escipión continues to defend siege warfare tactics as the third act opens and victory seems imminent: "esta libre nación soberbia domo / sin fuerzas, solamante con cordura" (to be taming this free, stubborn people / By prudence, without wasting strength" (*DN* III.1115–16; *SN,* 128). The general asserts that he has created new definitions of the terms "honor" and "glory."

> ¿Qué gloria puede haber más levantada,
> en las cosas de guerra que aquí digo,
> que, sin quitar de su lugar la espada,
> vencer y sujetar al enemigo?
>
> *(DN* III.1129–32)
>
> (What victory can redound to greater glory,
> Judging it from the point of view of war,
> Than one that's won without a single sword,
> Leaving its sheath, and yet can subjugate
> And conquer a strong enemy completely?)
>
> *(SN,* 128)

The high cost in human suffering that accompanies conventional warfare, even for the conqueror nation, is once again emphasized by Escipión in his defense of siege tactics as a way to limit Roman casualties:

Que cuando la vitoria es granjeada
con la sangre vertida de un amigo,
el gusto mengua que causar pudiera
la que sin sangre tal ganada fuera

(*DN* III.1133–36)

(But when a victory's acquired with loss
Of friendly blood, it spoils the joy of it
To win with blood what might be won without)

(*SN*, 128)

The Numantians characterize Roman reliance upon strategy rather than force as humiliating and antithetical, labeling the imperial troops as "liebres en pieles fieras disfrazadas" (Rabbits! who go disguised in lion's hide) (*DN* III.1229; *SN*, 130). A related metaphorical condemnation of Roman imperialism, employing typically Lascasian critiques of the Spanish treatment of indigenous peoples, can be found in Lira's description of the Romans as "hambrientos y fieros lobos" (The Romans are as wolves ferocious, / Rapacious, bloody and atrocious" (*DN* III.1377; *SN*, 134). This rationale could serve either to bolster imperial aggression or to censure it. As John Loftis notes, some advisors questioned the validity of military victories in Flanders that were extremely costly in terms of blood and money and comparatively insignificant in their strategic value (*Renaissance Drama*, 56–57).

In this context, Escipión's response to the Numantian suggestion of a duel as the proper mode for resolving the conflict emphasizes the fact that heroic combat is completely anachronistic. The suggestion does not merit any serious consideration: "donaire es lo que dices, risa y juego, / y loco el que pensase hacello" (What quips and jests are these? / What mad hilarity would you excite?) (*DN* III.1179–80; *SN*, 1229). The contempt that the Roman leader voices toward the Numantian proposal demonstrates the complete incompatibility of chivalric ideals and early modern military practices. Such ridicule of medieval notions of military heroism in early modern Spanish society anticipates one of the major themes later developed by Cervantes in *Don Quijote*.

The Numantian justification for rebelling against Roman dominion offers the most direct parallel with the situation of the resistant Araucanians. Here, Cervantes clearly links ancient and modern concerns with this evocation of Lascasian and Ercillan discourse. The ambassador who seeks to persuade Escipión to desist in his military ventures explains the legitimacy of the town's uprising,

> ... nunca de la ley y fueros
> del Senado romano se apartara
> si el insufrible mando y desafueros
> de un cónsul y otro no le fatigara.
> Ellos con duros estatutos fieros
> y con su extraña condición avara
> pusieron tan gran yugo a nuestros cuellos,
> que forzados salimos dél y dellos
>
> (*DN* I.241–48)

> (... never from the laws
> And statutes of the Roman Senate will [we]
> Depart as long as we have not to suffer
> Weight of one consul's rule after another.
> They, with their cruel laws and vicious greed,
> Placed such a heavy yoke upon our necks,
> We were compelled to shake it off by force.)
>
> (*SN*, 106–7)

Complaints about the greed and unjust mandates of the imperial governors may refer to the excesses of the *encomienda* system that compel indigenous groups to revolt. The evocation of "fueros" (compacts) and "desafueros" (misrule) links this speech to the ideas of natural human rights asserted by Las Casas and other reformers as well as to the possibly apocryphal but popular early modern notion of a medieval system of peasant rights (Elliott, *Imperial Spain*, 30). The Numantian decision to burn every item of value in the town may hark back to Lascasian discourses that condemn avarice as a primary and shameful motivator in Spanish imperial efforts—and may also advance a critique of imperial troops' frequent sacking of Dutch towns (Loftis, *Renaissance Drama*, 40). Thus, Teógenes urges the destruction of all property in order to assure that the villains will not benefit from their capture of the town, burning "desde la pobre a la más rica cosa" (*DN* III.1429). The purpose of the fire is to assure that "no quede cosa aquí en Numancia / de do el contrario pueda hacer ganancia" (all that those swine desire, / Of trinkets, even from the poorest penny / Of the poor pauper who has hardly any. / ... each priceless jewel / And heirloom too, is sentenced to be fuel) (*DN* III.1424–25; *SN,* 135). Lira concurs with this recommendation, emphasizing imperialist greed: "abrásense en un punto los trofeos / que pudieran hacer ricas las manos, / y aun hartar la codicia de romanos" (Let us pile and burn in one fixed place / Aught that by way of trophy might enrich / The Roman's hands or feed his avarice) (*DN* III.1455–57; *SN,* 136).

On two occasions, Escipión paradoxically praises Numantian valor in order to defend the need for total domination of this group, which will otherwise prove a source of constant resistance. After Quinto Fabio describes the impressive results of Marandro and Leonicio's food-stealing endeavor, in which the two killed six nameless guards plus four men who could be presumed to be officers known to Escipión because they are named, the Roman leader muses,

> Si estando deshambridos y encerrados
> muestran tan demasiado atreviemiento,
> ¿qué hicieran siendo libres y enteredas
> en sus fuerzas primeras y ardimiento?
> ¡Indómitos! ¡Al fin seréis domados,
> porque contra el furor vuestro violento
> se tiene de poner la industria nuestra,
> que de domar soberbios es maestra!
>
> (*DN* IV.1788–95)

> (If having been starved so and circled in,
> They show such huge excess of valor, what
> Would they not do were they in prime fettle
> And free to come and go? O, tameless hearts!
> But in the end you will be tamed at last,
> For your fierce violence is not in the running
> With calculation, industry, and cunning)
>
> (*SN,* 144)

Later, the discovery of the collective self-destruction confirms this diagnosis. Escipión claims that the Numantians' hyper-valor

> me forzó con razón a usar el medio
> de encerrallos cual fieras indomables
> y triunfar dellos con industria y maña,
> pues era con las fuerzas imposible.
>
> (*DN* IV.2252–55)

(Their valour and dexterity in arms,
Force me, with perfect reason, to immure them
As if they were untamable, wild beasts,
And conquer them with assiduity
And wiles—it was impossible by force)

(*SN*, 155)

Here, "industria"—military technology—is associated with civilized society as the only means by which to subordinate a group that is physically indomitable but culturally inferior and lacking in sophisticated weaponry. In this instance, *furor* is redefined as a stigma associated with the vanquished rather than as a mark of pride for the victorious group. This marginalization of physical bravery constitutes one important component of counter-epic questioning of military and imperial activity and of the role of the warrior in a mercantile, proto-capitalist world. Escipión's last lines, after witnessing Bariato's final act of *furor,* emphasize the mixed nature of the victory achieved. In this case, the lack of a single prisoner or trophy will rob Escipión of a true triumph, according to Roman definition. There will be no victory parade, no recognition by the Senate. Further, as Fame indicates in the prediction cited previously, history will commemorate the Numantian resistance rather than the Roman victory. Thus, the victory that Escipión attains by means of technological superiority is hollow, partial, and uncelebrated. Cervantes points to a paradox concerning historical inscriptions of colonialism that connects early modern Spanish counter-epic writers and contemporary postcolonial theorists.

This double-voiced representation of the practice of siege warfare, one of the most effective weapons in Spain's imperial arsenal both in the Americas and in Europe, serves to highlight the negative similarities between Counter-Reformation Spain and imperial Rome. Willard King is one of many critics who have pointed out that the Spain of Cervantes resembles Scipio's Rome just as much as the town of Numancia. She cites the River Duero's prophecy, which depicts "a victorious Spain, feared and envied by a thousand foreign nations, embroiled in constant war—in sum, a Spain which mirrors the militant, aggressive, Rome of Scipio" ("Cervantes' *Numancia*," 215). In this representation, Spain itself is indeterminate, the sign that refers simultaneously to the morally victorious Numantians and to the decadent Roman Empire, its achievements in the early modern period shown to be both epic victories and tragic slaughters. The Cervantine play is able to suggest individual heroic combat as a viable option because of its remote historical setting. In her examination of *La Araucana*, Adrienne Laskier Martín notes that Ercilla can plausibly create such an encounter in a work of *contemporary* history only in the Americas, because the indigenous peoples are the only enemies of Europe who do not possess the weapons and techniques of "guerra a sangre y fuego" (total war).[29] Many dramatists of New World events took advantage of the unique nature of the American encounter to foreground anachronistic chivalric duels.

A wide range of perspectives concerning Spanish imperial ideology and practice can also be seen in *Arauco domado*. Support for notions associated with just war theory can be heard in Rebolledo's joyous announcement in the opening scene that Don García is coming "a domar a Chile y a la gente bárbara que en Arauco se derrama" (to conquer Chile and the barbarians who live there) (*AD* I, 108). (The double meaning of "derrama"—"geographically located" or "spilling blood"—is particularly significant.) García's confirmation that his twin goals are "ensanchar la fe de Dios" (to establish faith in God) and "reducir y sujetar / . . . esta tierra y este mar / para que Filipe tenga / vasallos a mandar" (to conquer and rule . . . this land and this sea so that Philip may have vassals to rule) also follows that line of reasoning (*AD* I, 112). Don García is described by his followers in glowing terms as a young Caesar or Alexander; the religious ceremony in which the newly arrived young governor symbolically prostrates himself before God is termed a "hazaña santa" (saintly act) and a "divino ejemplo" (divine example) (*AD* I, 107, 110–11). These early scenes indicate that the messengers, not the mission, have been flawed. Lope distorts historical chronology in order to allow Don García to punish the (long-dead) Villagrán and Aguirre for their "ambición de poder," or hunger for power—the internal rivalry, also criticized in Rojas Zorrilla's *Numancia cercada*, that made them vulnerable to indigenous rebellion. Unlike his predecessors, Don García is represented as devoted to the crown rather than to his own glory. When he orders that Galvarino's hands be cut off, the purpose is to send a message to all Araucanians "que han de ser / de Carlos de Austria" (that they must be ruled by Charles of Austria) (*AD* III, 202). The news of Charles's abdication and Philip's ascension to the throne renews and energizes García's determination to subjugate Chile for his sovereign: "si allá se muestra España agradecido, / no menos de su imperio satisfecho / se ha de mostrar Arauco" (if faraway Spain is willing, Arauco must show itself no

---

29. Adrienne Laskier Martín, *Cervantes and the Burlesque Sonnet* (Berkeley and Los Angeles: University of California Press, 1991), 101.

less satisfied to be ruled by him) (*AD* III, 220). García incites a chorus of "Viva Felipe!" (Long live Philip!) so that he can reply, "Y por su rey Chile reciba" (And may Chile accept him as its king) (*AD* III, 220). In the final scene of the play, García once again emphasizes service to the crown as he dedicates the victory celebration to an effigy of the new king, whom he addresses respectfully:

> veis aquí nueve banderas
> nueve batallas de Arauco
> que en vuestro nombre he vencido
> pacificando su estado.
> Nueve ciudades también
> os doy, ofrezco y consagro.
>
> (*AD* III, 245)

(Here you see nine flags, signifying the nine battles through which I have conquered Arauco and pacified this land in his name. Nine cities as well I give, offer, and dedicate to you.)

The play succeeds in lionizing Don García as an ideal leader, then, but the representation of his success and loyalty cannot erase the audience's awareness that this period of pacification, like others that followed during the seventeenth century, did not long endure. This staging raises as many problems as it "solves" concerning the historical and philosophical issues involved. Although it does "correct" Ercilla's marginalization of a single figure, it does so in a context that undermines the very basis of Mendoza's (and Spain's) enterprise.

The questioning of the imperial mission is achieved primarily though scenes that dramatize the indigenous peoples, who offer a different interpretation of the conquest. In the war council scene, they are shown to possess a recognizable political organization and thus to be civil enough to exercise their own *dominium* (see Chapter 2). Tucapel condemns Spanish attempts to conquer Chile, using arguments that reflect sixteenth-century discussions of the ethics of ocean-crossing imperial ventures:

> que vengan por mil mares, no es bajeza
> a ponernos los pies en la cabeza?
> Si el soberano Apó juntar quisiera

chilenos y cristianos españoles
no con tan largo mar nos dividiera.

(*AD* II, 168–69)

(Is it not base for them to cross a thousand oceans in order to place our heads beneath their feet? If Holy Apo wanted Christians and Chileans to live together, he would not have divided us with such a vast sea.)

One aspect of imperial practice debated among Romans and early modern Spaniards was the size of the empire. Vázquez de Menchaca cited Roman jurists to argue, like Tucapel, that the sea was a God-given barrier intended to limit empires to those who live in proximity and share customs. Saavedra Fajardo and Thomist thinkers took a contrary approach, viewing the sea as a medium for communication and connection, one that God created to encourage and facilitate exploration (Pagden, *Lords,* 60–61). Tucapel also gives voice to the philosophy of natural sovereignty in claiming that "Dios se ofende / que os sujetéis a un hombre, / y hombre extraño" (God is offended that you let yourself be ruled by any man, especially a foreigner) (*AD* II, 169). The sophisticated philosophical arguments incorporated in this speech may also be read as a critique of Spanish stereotypes of indigenous peoples as primitive and thus as beneficiaries rather than victims of conquest.

Kirschner astutely observes that a key element of dramaturgy—what the audience actually experiences when attending the theater—is overlooked by contemporary critics who work primarily with texts. She notes that Caupolicán's conversion, often posited as the key to a pro-imperial interpretation, is given a scant four lines, while his heroic, Christlike death is staged in the discovery space—the very same space in which the effigy of Philip II appears in the closing lines. Kirschner asserts that "superimposition of [these two] images in the same location of the stage points out and emphasizes that the true perpetrator of savagery is the Spanish crown" ("Encounter and Assimilation," 38). The fact that Lope later wrote an *auto sacramental* in which Caupolicán stands in for the crucified Christ provides support for this analysis (39).

A Lascasian critique of Spanish motivations can be found in Tucapel's description of the Christians as hypocrites who disguise their personal greed as a desire to serve their king's interests: "ladrones, que a hurtar venís / el oro de nuestra tierra, / y disfrazando la guerra, / decís que a Carlos servís" (You come as thieves who seek to steal our gold, and disguise your true motives by saying that you serve your king) (*AD* I, 133). Contempt for Spanish greed is reiterated when the Spaniard Rebolledo admits, "Los que las Indias hallaron / vinieron por oro y plata" (those who found the Indies came for gold and silver). He takes care, however, to distinguish the campaign in which he participates from earlier ventures in Chile: "No viene así Don García, / ni plata intenta buscar" (Don García does not come for this reason; he does not even intend to look for silver) (*AD* I, 149). The Chileans do not concur with this distinction. When Reinoso confronts a Spanish attack, he calls out,

> ¿Adónde venís, ladrones,
> cobardes por vuestra infamia?
> . . . . . . . . . . .
> Venid, que como a Valdivia
> os sacaremos los almas
> donde la codicia viene
> del oro antártico y plata
> 
> (*AD* II, 156)

(Why do you come here, thieves, cowards, criminals? Come on, and as we did with Valdivia, we will pluck out your souls, the root of your greed for Chilean gold and silver.)

This critique is repeated in the war council scene as Tucapel condemns the Christians for coveting both riches and indigenous labor: "que enriquecerse del sudor pretende / de nuestra mina de oro y fértil año" (they seek to enrich themselves by the sweat of our brow and the fruit of our productive mines) (*AD* II, 169). In addition to evocations of avarice, the Spaniards are also depicted as the source of excessive violence. The guns used for the clash at the Biobío River produce "tan sangriente batalla / que al mar de Chile corrían / arroyos de sangre humana" (such bloody battles that streams of human blood run all the way to the sea) (*AD* II, 157). In these scenes, the indigenous peoples are given a voice that echoes the most trenchant Lascasian critiques of the *encomienda* system. (William Mejías López has identified a similar perspective in Pedro de Oña's *Arauco* poem.)

## Imperialist Diplomacy

Many counter-epic history plays stage scenes of diplomacy that are significant on a number of levels. As a pragmatic consideration, the direct verbal confrontations between the two groups allow each side to display the *agon* necessary to maintain interest in a theatricalized representation of warfare where large-scale battles cannot be waged. Most important, these scenes provide dramatic space in which to explore the mechanisms of negotiation as an essential component of imperialism. As Elliott and others have shown, disagreement concerning the proper selection of times to negotiate and times to engage in battle was central to debates about imperial policy throughout the early modern period (see Chapter 2). When Escipión agrees to meet with the two Numantian ambassadors, he underlines the utility of such encounters:

> Oír al enemigo es cosa cierta
> que siempre aprovechó más que dañase,
> y, en cosas de guerra, la experiencia
> muestra que lo que digo es cierta ciencia.
> 
> (*DN* I.221–24)

> (To give an audience to one's enemy
> Has always done more good than harm. Experience
> In things of war has taught me what I say,
> And one acquires sure knowledge in this way)
> 
> (*SN*, 206)

Escipión rejects the offer of a truce, however, employing language similar to that of the Alvista forces who advocated domination rather than negotiation with the Dutch: "a desvergüenza de tan largos años, / es poca recompensa pedir paces" (For the shame / Of these long years, it is small recompense / To sue for peace) (*DN* I.273–74; *SN*, 107). Considering the comparative brevity of the Chilean and Dutch resistance at the date this work was composed, Cervantes's words are a startlingly prescient description of Spain's future as a waning imperial power embroiled in struggles it could not resolve.

In *Arauco domado*, all but one of the scenes of diplomatic maneuvering take place within the American camp, and the indigenous peoples themselves argue the cases for both resistance and capitulation. Over the course of the play, even Tucapel and Caupolicán, the two most feared leaders, come to express doubts about the viability of continued rebellion. Each of these scenes concludes, however, with an evocation of the glory of liberty and the shame of enslavement that puts an end to the prospect of negotiated peace. These scenes serve to emphasize an indigenous honor based on autonomy, as shown below, but they may also be seen as references to Spain's own prioritization of its national honor: throughout the reigns of Philip II and Philip IV, tactical and economic considerations were often marginalized out of an impractical desire to maintain Spain's empire at any cost. The sole, brief diplomatic scene staged in the Spanish camp dramatizes Don García Hurtado de Mendoza's successful effort to persuade Caupolicán to acquiesce to a deathbed conversion.

## THE PERSONAL AND THE POLITICAL

Showing the "human face of war" has been a popular technique in counter-epic films of the post-Vietnam era. It is equally effective for Lope and Cervantes. The history play derives emotional and ideological force from the juxtaposition of epic, comic drama, pastoral eclogue, and tragedy, of battles, courtship, and death—that is to say, of the political and the personal dimensions of imperial policies. In the counter-epic early modern history play, the emphasis upon the personal lives of the vanquished provides a "humanizing" element that is central to the counter-hegemonic ideological dimension of these works (Díaz Balsera, "Araucanian Alterity," 26; Ruiz Ramón, "El héroe," 232).

To scrutinize the effects of war on individuals, *La Numancia* juxtaposes epic and tragedy—in particular, the form of tragedy found in Euripides' *The Trojan Women*, which highlights the suffering of a vanquished group. In Act II we learn that the marriage of Lira and Marandro has been delayed by the war, because "no está nuestra tierra / para fiestas y contento" (our country's now no place for feasts / And happiness) (*DN* II.755–56; *SN*, 118). By the final act, Lira's hunger has driven her fiancé to brave the Roman camp in order to bring back bread, which is stained by the blood he shed to obtain her "triste y amarga comida" (sad and bitter meal [my translation]) (*DN* IV.1847). Marandro's dying words are followed by Lira's soliloquy to the corpse in her arms:

> Que, por excusar mi muerte,
> me habéis quitado la vida . . .
> 
> . . . . . . . . .
> 
> mi esposo feneció por darme vida
>
> (*DN* IV.1878–79, 1966)

> (You made a sortie to prevent my death
> And by it took away my life)
>
> (*SN*, 145–46)

Her declaration that "primero daré a mi pecho / una daga que este pan" (I'd sooner give a knife / To my throat than this bread) (*DN* IV.1928–29; *SN*, 146) reinforces the contradictory imagery of life, bread, and death. The sufferings not only of couples but also of families are represented with extreme pathos. An ironic link between food and death is again foregrounded when a starving mother laments that her infant also suffers because, instead of milk, it suckles blood. This mother, who cannot provide the food her older child requests, replies, "te daré la muerte por comida" (we will throw into the fire / Our pain, our hunger and despair, / And burn them up entire) (*DN* IV.2115; *SN*, 142). One of the companions of War, Hunger, describes the tragic role reversals that result when the townspeople decide to commit mass suicide rather than submit:

> Contra el hijo, el padre, con rabiosa
> clemencia levantado el brazo crudo,
> rompe aquellas entrañas que ha engendrado,
> quedando satisfecho y lastimado.
>
> (*DN* IV.2045–48)

> (Against the son, his father and his sire,
> Whom these contrarious clemencies conspire,
> Lifts his strong arm, and what he did beget
> Is unbegotten—though with fierce regret,
> Yet with deep satisfaction)
>
> (*SN*, 149)

The effects of this war on lovers, parents, and children constitute an unnatural collision of the elements of life and death, conveyed through terms such as "lastimado" (pitiful) that have specific generic—i.e., tragic—connotations.

A militarized culture's effects upon family life can also be seen in the prevalence of voluntary, aggressive military action, even when failure and death are certain. For example, when the Numantians realize that their defeat is inevitable, their initial response is to advocate one last charge of the Roman camp, so that the Numantian men will achieve glory through heroic (epic) death on the battlefield instead of dying from hunger or disease within the walls of the besieged town. A counter-epic viewpoint is presented by their female relations, who point out the terrible consequences the men overlook in devising this plan of action. One of the nameless Numantian women warns the male leaders—and the audience—of the fate that would be suffered by the warriors' widows and orphans, the tragedies of rape or concubinage for virtuous women and enslavement for their offspring (*DN* III.1313). The men agree, in this case, to forfeit their dreams of military glory in favor of the alternate form of fame to be earned as a result of the mass suicide. And indeed, in regard to national military policy, Spain's leaders often pursued a course of action that bears a striking resemblance both to the proposed death charge and to the collective suicide: victories and defeats alike produced great losses of life along with a gradual strangulation of the Castilian economy, especially in rural areas (see Chapter 2).

In *Arauco domado*, the human face of war is represented in connection with two genres: the pastoral eclogue, as Lope explores the ways in which warfare interrupts the flow of human lives, and tragedy, through the play's haunting evocation of the price of conquest. The scene in which Fresia and Caupolicán first appear, attempting to find a stolen hour of pleasure in the midst of the turmoil of Araucanian resistance, is one of the most frequently cited passages of the entire play. Caupolicán's invitation to bathe together—"Deja el arco y las fleshes, / hermosa Fresia mía" (put aside your bow and arrows, Fresia)—emphasizes that only at rare moments may weapons be forgotten (*AD* I, 114). Even during this tender scene, war intrudes, as the warrior instructs his spouse that if she wishes to adorn the beauty he is praising (in Petrarchan terms), she should ask for necklaces decorated with Spanish skulls rather than conventional jewels (*AD* I, 118). Similarly, even Fresia's amorous feelings are determined by military considerations: she is proud to have captured not the man most desired by the women of her group, but "el pecho / a quien se rinde España" (the heart of the one who defeats Spain) (*AD* I, 117).

The evocation of simple domesticity as a means to highlight the disruptions of war is particularly powerful. As the wives of the four Araucanian leaders gather near the Penco fort, they discuss the food they have brought while waiting for their husbands to claim their suppers. Talk of exotic cuisine unknown to the peninsular audience—"maní," "perper," "concaví," and "muday"—soon gives way to concern for the safety of their mates. Guava worries,

> ¿Cuánto me apuestas, Quidora
> que aquel mi amor, temerario,
> como es en el ordinario,
> entra por el fuerte ahora,
> y que sacarlo de allí
> hasta que vida no quede,
> ni Talguén su amigo puede,
> ni el amor que tiene en mí?
>
> (*AD* I, 140–41)

(How much do you want to bet, Quidora, that my love, audacious as always, is going into the fort now, and that he won't come out even if his life depends upon it, not for the sake of his friend Talguen, nor for his love of me?)

Gualeva concurs that the valor they admire in their spouses may also cause their deaths: "mi esposo es un león, / y temo en esta ocasión / que por su furia peligre" (my husband is a lion, and I'm afraid that this time his courage will put him in danger) (*AD* I, 141). The desolation that these indigenous women experience increases as night falls and their husbands do not appear. Fresia declares, "yo muero de soledad" (I am dying of loneliness), and Gualeva replies, "y yo" (and I, as well) (*AD* I, 143). These lamentations, like the medieval romance of Doña Alda (which also describes a victory from the perspective of a woman from the vanquished group), remind the audience of the personal costs associated with military conquest.

Although Rengo is an aristocratic warrior, his support for peace with the Spaniards during the war council scene is grounded in his awareness of the high costs of war: "La guerra, qué puede hacer / sino robos, muertos, daños?" (War, what is it good for, but thefts, deaths, damage?) (*AD* II, 170). Galvarino, on the other hand, employs references to the fate of the women and children of defeated groups similar to those found in the Numancia plays of Cervantes and Rojas Zorrilla, making the opposite argument—that the war should be continued in order to avoid dishonor.

> ¿Será mejor que esos hijos
> vayan de leña cargados,
> y que sus madres les den,
> con vuestra afrenta y agravio,
> siendo amigas de españoles,
> otros mestizos hermanos,
> que los maten y sujeten,
> con afrentas y con palos?
>
> (*AD* III, 216)

(Would it be better that your children serve as beasts of burden, and that their mothers, in affront to your memories, become concubines of the Spaniards and give birth to mixed-race siblings, who will be beaten and subjugated by their half-brothers?)

In addition, the fallen indigenous leader, Caupolicán, last appears on the scene not as a dangerous warrior but as a man who leaves behind a widow and an orphaned son. After viewing her husband's impaled body and listening to his brief conversion speech, Fresia mourns, "Hay ojos que aquesto vean / sin que aneguen llorando?" (Can any eye view this without shedding tears?), and she laments the early death of "mi esposo, / muerto en la flor de sus años" (my husband, cut down in the bloom of his youth) (*AD* III, 243, 244). Engol vows "de no me llamar tu hijo . . . hasta que vengue tu muerte" (not to call myself your son . . . until I avenge your death) (*AD* III, 243). The total absence of references to the Spanish soldiers' personal lives, in conjunction with the dramatization of the indigenous families' tragic suffering, contributes significantly to a critique of Spanish depredations upon American societies.

## Staging the Other: Humanization

One of the key components in the challenging of imperial doctrine is the representation of the conquered Other in a positive manner that emphasizes the common elements of the victorious and the defeated societies. In the Numancia and Arauco plays, the besieged nations express a love of freedom and deploy idealized Western literary genres—particularly the pastoral eclogue and chivalric romance. Both moves establish a common humanity shared by imperialist and "primitive" societies. Díaz Balsera points to a key contradiction in Spain's justification of military conquest as the necessary prerequisite to conversion: she observes that the Spaniard reveals himself as the true barbarian, "because in crushing the desire for freedom, he destroys that part of the Other's humanity the colonial subject clearly recognizes as part of himself" ("Araucanian Alterity," 31). Pieterse notes that "challenging the empire in terms of its own stated ideals play[s] a major part in all anti-imperialist movements." In these plays, the representation of conquered peoples who embrace the empire's ideal of freedom accomplishes this goal (*Empire and Emancipation*, 361). Of course, the practice of grounding the worthiness of the Other in its similarity and assimilability to the European is a patronizing and ultimately hierarchical gesture, one that maintains the dominated culture in a subaltern position. But the granting of a sympathetic voice and a significant presence to the "losers" is nonetheless a key element for the counter-epic dimension of this text, for it allows—forces—the spectator or reader to see and hear, if only in a mediated fashion, the peoples whom imperialist discourses seek to silence and erase. Beatriz Pastor argues that during the early modern period, the humanization of the American Other *requires* an idealization based upon "Spanish ideological and aesthetic models." She adds, "to erase otherness [is] essential if the humanity of the native is to be accepted in a world for which *human* means *European* . . . paradoxically, this humanity can be conveyed to a European audience only by rejecting all problematic aspects of the new reality and by replacing accurate or realistic characterizations by idealized models."[30] This paradox is one of many that contribute to the polyphonic representation of empire in the early modern history play.

In Cervantes's *La Numancia*, as described above, the Numantians voice chivalric ideals in their request to decide the town's fate through a heroic duel. This offer reflects a view of war that is clearly anachronistic in its emphasis on individual heroism but is nonetheless attractive to the original audience (as noted above, Rackin has shown that nostalgia for the medieval period is a fundamental aspect of the early modern history play). Here, the Numantian evocation of "breve y singular batalla" (one-on-one combat) as glorified in the chivalric romance displays a revered component of European sensibility and tradition on the part of this ostensibly barbaric group (*DN* III.1160). According to Rackin, anachronisms play an

---

30. Beatriz Pastor, *The Armature of Conquest: Spanish Accounts of the Discovery of America, 1492–1589*, trans. Lydia Longstreth Hunt (Stanford: Stanford University Press, 1992), 235–36 (emphasis in original).

essential role in the dramatic scrutiny of hegemonic discourse, for they "break the frame of historical representation to mark the difference between historical past and present reconstruction of that past" and also "call attention to . . . the present degeneration that made the recuperation desirable" (*Stages*, 98). Thus, Caravino condemns the Romans as "cobardes" (cowards) and "canalla" (craven) before launching into a tirade of fifteen pejorative adjectives in sequence, claiming that the Romans are "estáis acostumbrados / a vencer con ventajas y mañas" (known rather for base cunning than for bravery") (*DN* III.1206–26; *SN*, 130). By condemning the use of strategy instead of the methods conventionally associated with war and glory, Caravino calls attention to the unbreachable chasm between past and present modes of warfare, to the "degradation" of the military enterprise in an age marked not only by sieges but also by cannons and the proliferation of mercenaries. The association of the "losers" with this privileged discourse closes the distance between civilized imperial cultures and "barbaric" peoples.

In the Cervantine *La Numancia*, the emphasis on the native people's love for liberty, expressed in several scenes, is the cornerstone of their humanity—and thus of the critique of imperialism (Ruiz Ramón, *Historia*, 233). For example, as España complains to the heavens about the Roman siege of Numancia, she refers to the loss of the town's "amada libertad" (beloved liberty) as the most serious consequence of this defeat, as well as of previous occupations where Spain found herself "esclava de naciones extranjeras" (each strange nation in its turn enslave[s] me) (*DN* I.370, 388; *SN*, 110). In the powerful scene where the women and children of the town persuade the men not to launch a doomed final offensive that would result in glorious deaths for the men but shameful captivity for the Numantian civilians, one character defines the life span of the Numantians through evocations of liberty: "os engendraron libres" (begot free), "libres nacistes" (born free), "vuestras madres tristes / también libres os criaron" (your mothers reared you / In freedom) (*DN* III.1346–49; *SN*, 133). In conclusion, she beseeches the walls of the town to affirm freedom as the highest good: "decid / y mil veces repetid, / '¡Numantinos, libertad!'" (Cry out these words, a thousand times repeat them, / Numantines! Free [yourselves]) (*DN* III.1355–57; *SN*, 133). Although no further speeches about freedom occur in the final act, the piteous series of farewell scenes among friends, lovers, and family members demonstrates more clearly than words the Numantian commitment to "live free or die" and thus earn the eternal commemoration promised by Fame in the closing lines of the play. It may be argued that the trait for which this town is commemorated is precisely its courageous commitment to liberty.

The Numantians also utilize Platonic discourses of idealized friendship. When Marandro risks his life to bring food for Lira from the Roman camp, Leonicio proves himself to be the ultimate loyal friend, willing to risk his life to defend Marandro:

> ... no los miedos de la muerte
> de tí me apartarán un solo punto
>
> . . . . . . . .
>
> ¡Contigo tengo de ir; contigo junto
> he de volver, si ya el Cielo no ordena
> que quede en tu defensa allá difunto!
>
> (*DN* III.1601–6)

> (... not fear nor death itself
> Can swerve them from you by a single hair.
> Nothing is stronger than my will to serve you.
> I *will* go with you and with you return
> If Heaven does not bid me to remain,
> Killed in defense of you, upon the plain.)
>
> (*SN*, 139)

Upon discovering that Leonicio has not survived the attack upon the Roman camp, Marandro delivers a neo-Platonic, homosocial farewell speech that indicates a devotion as passionate as his love for Lira, expressed using the same terminology of celebrated loyalty and a disinclination to live on when the beloved has died:

> Tú al fin llevarás la palma
> de más verdadero amigo;
> yo a disculparme contigo
> enviaré presto el alma.
>
> (*DN* III.1816–19)

> (You carry off the palm in the contention
> As to which of us was the better friend.
> Soon, to excuse me, I'll send you my soul)
>
> (*SN*, 144)

The staging of perfect friendship between the two Numantian men serves to humanize the "barbarian" Others by allowing them to display a form of idealized masculine behavior that does not run the risk of excess. Representations of great physical valor on the part of non-European groups, however, may ultimately serve to dehumanize the Other by characterizing battle prowess as mindless carnage.

An emphasis upon the indigenous desire to maintain autonomy is also central to the positive representation of the Araucanians in the Lopean drama. Again, Díaz Balsera notes how the Araucanians' refusal to accept "a Spanish domination represented as saintly, superior and irreproachable maps out a space of difference that promises to clash with the colonizer's loftiest truths and best-meaning efforts" ("Araucanian Alterity," 36). Díaz Balsera lists six different evocations of liberty in Lope's text. To my mind, the most memorable declaration appears in Act III, as the Araucanian leaders meet to decide how to respond to the Spanish victories that are decimating their population. Although Caupolicán and Tucapel urge a negotiated settlement, Galvarino, who has just returned from the Spanish camp with bloody stumps in place of hands, carries the day with his argument:

> ¿Cuánto mejor es morir
> con las armas peleando
> que vivir sirviendo un noble
> como bestia y como esclavo?
>
> (*AD* III, 213)

> (Isn't it better to die in armed resistance than to live serving a nobleman as his beast and slave?)

This is the same argument that leads to the mass suicide closing the Cervantine and Rojas Zorrilla Numancia plays, in which the protagonists are described as the distant ancestors of Cervantes's Spain, thus establishing a link between civilization and the worship of liberty over life itself. Although Romanos, like many other scholars cited above, privileges the orthodox elements of Lope's play, she does concede that the indigenous people's fight for their freedom "inclina la adhesión del espectador/lector a favor de los vencidos" (does induce the spectator/reader to sympathize with the losers) ("La construcción del personaje de Caupolicán," 190). Díaz Balsera goes further, claiming that the play produces an impression of

Spanish barbarity, which "creates anxiety in the colonizing subject because it disrupts his triumphal fantasies, because it rifts the illusion of truth he needs to produce about himself in order to act and to exercise power" ("Araucanian Alterity," 31). In keeping with the materialist reception of poetics outlined in Chapter 1, I would argue that both modes of reception were possibilities for early modern audiences—as well as for contemporary readers.

Certain identification of the dates of composition and initial performance of *Arauco domado* (which has been dated variously as 1599, 1610, and 1625) could provide additional insight into this dramatization of the Araucanian devotion to freedom.[31] Chapter 2 describes in detail the history of the Chilean enterprise during this tumultuous quarter-century in which all of the three suggested dates were marked by frustrated efforts to achieve even a limited victory. If the earliest date of composition put forth is correct, then the eruptions of successful Araucanian rebellion at Valdivia and Concepción and the total collapse of Spanish influence in southern Chile at the turn of the century would have served to emphasize for the Spanish public the indigenous people's tenacious resistance to domination. The middle date posited coincides with the debates in the Council of the Indies concerning defensive versus offensive tactics. The latest date put forth coincides with the onset of the reign of Philip IV and the termination of the defensive tactics approved by his father, tactics that had not produced the desired results: neither pacification nor security had been achieved in the designated safe area. The successful indigenous opposition provoked both admiration and frustration on the part of the would-be conqueror, a point underscored in Lope's dialogic evocation of the resistance.

Pastor points out that the representation of excessive, cruel violence on the part of the Other is an important element of dehumanization. She asserts that in Ercilla's *Araucana,* violence is directly linked to honor, "thus justifying it and making it part of a value system directly associated with the canons of medieval chivalry" (*Armature of Conquest,* 220). This observation is also relevant to the representation of indigenous aggression in Lope's play, for each debate concerning whether to continue the resistance is resolved by evocations of liberty as the primary element of human dignity and honor.

Ruiz Ramón indicates a key scene that humanizes the Amerindians in *Arauco domado* by allowing them to use European discourses. Early in Act I, as the Araucanian ruler and his wife bathe together in a lake, Caupolicán

---

31. See Shannon, *Visions,* 100–107, for a comprehensive consideration of the date controversy.

praises his wife's beauty in Petrarchan terms: "Tú, que a sus vidrios en blancura excedes / Desnuda el cuerpo hermoso, / dando a la luna envidia, / y quejaráse el agua por tenerte" (You are whiter than crystal, your lovely nude body makes the moon envious of the water that touches you) (*AD* I, 113). Ruiz Ramón observes that their amorous dialogue is reminiscent of the poetic space of Garcilaso's eclogues ("El héroe," 232). This scene not only humanizes the enemy forces and problematizes their subjugation, then, but also contributes to the generic polyphony of the text. Díaz Balsera cites the same passage in support of the contention that Lope's polyvalent dramatization of the Araucanians "open[s] up the possibility of [indigenous] amelioration under colonial rule, but also pose[s] a threat to the logic of that rule" ("Araucanian Alterity," 32). As many critics have noted, the epic genre requires two virtuous groups, so that victory can be inscribed as a glorious triumph over a meritorious group. In the process of transformation from single-genre poetic narrative to multi-generic history play, incorporation of this particular form of poetics serves both aesthetic and ideological purposes, for disputes over indigenous capacity to assimilate to Western standards of civilized behavior were central to the Lascasian/Sepulvedan debates, as Díaz Balsera observes (26).

The representation of indigenous female characters as Amazons is multivalent. It may be read as an example of humanizing discourse in the sense that the American woman is rendered more familiar through the evocation of classical Western myth. The choice of this particular mythical figure, however, simultaneously dehumanizes the Araucanian women, for, as Pastor notes in her analysis of Ercilla's indigenous Amazons, "to give a female figure the same attributes as those of the male would mean turning her into an inconceivable monster from the perspective of European culture" (*Armature of Conquest*, 224). When Gualeva berates Rengo for having left her husband, Tucapel, behind when he escaped from the Spanish after the failed Araucanian attempt to capture the fort at Penco, she presents herself as the valiant warrior who will accomplish the task Rengo ought to have completed: "que por no me detener / en buscar mi dueño amado, / no te mato, afeminado" (The only reason I will not kill you, sissy, is because I don't want to delay my search for my love) (*AD* I, 146). If her compatriot has shown himself less than ideally masculine in failing to rescue his fellow captives, then Gualeva will violate gender norms as well in order to compensate. Here, both genders of native peoples are shown as unbalanced. (Fresia's Amazonian and Medea-like qualities have also been well documented by scholars of this work.)

## Staging the Other: Demonization

Lope and Cervantes combine representations of the civilized dimensions of the Other with sensational scenes that reveal the Numantians or Amerindians as idolatrous and savage, according to European social norms. The aberrant behaviors presented include cannibalism, necromancy, and suicide, and they act as a counterbalance to the Westernizing discourses cited above (de Armas, *Cervantes*, 113). This contradictory staging of the victims of conquest is a central element in the polyphonic examinations of the imperial project, and as Díaz Balsera explains, it points to an ideological fault line in early modern Spain: "it suggests that the logic of the Conquest was never totally mastered by the *conquistador*" ("Araucanian Alterity," 36). (Nor, I would add, by the *conquistador* polity.) The critique of cannibalism is also a problematic issue, for as Todorov notes, the punishment for this act—death at the stake—is itself a form of brutality. The act of singling out as barbaric some forms of torture and murder but not others plays a crucial role in the ideological dimension of discursive dehumanization (*Conquest of America*, 179).

In the Cervantine *La Numancia*, the Roman characters make frequent references to the barbarity of the Celtiberians they struggle to dominate. At the end of his famed *harenga*, Escipión, who has been dialoguing about the efforts against the Numantians for more than 150 lines, refers to his opponents as "enemigos bárbaros españoles" (base, barbarian Spaniards) (*DN* I.164; *SN*, 105). In addition, there are several key scenes in which the future Spaniards display unchristian practices and thus appear as "barbarous Others whose excesses make them appear less than human" (de Armas, *Cervantes*, 113). De Armas has shown that the primary tactic through which Cervantes voices support for the imperial enterprise is through the dehumanization of the Numantian population as practitioners of a barbaric, necromantic religion. In the two scenes where illicit prognostication is practiced, Cervantes makes extensive use of stage directions to ensure that these events will be staged in a shocking manner, reducing the audience's empathy with the Celtiberians. Thus, the description of the preparations for the animal sacrifice constitutes nine lines (*DN* II.798–806), five lines of stage directions are dedicated to the depiction of the sorcerer Marquino and his magical potions, and the disruptive figure that puts an end to the sacrifice is specified as a half-demon (*DN* II.884–85). The stage directions also specify the colors of the potions used on two occasions upon the resuscitated corpse (*DN* II.1024–25, 1040–41).

Each of the acts of *La Numancia* presents Numantian otherness in a unique manner. As we have seen, Act I focused upon Roman denigration of the Celtiberians, while Act II staged grotesque religious rituals. The third act makes concrete reference to (though does not stage) cannibalism as an additional barbaric characteristic of the vanquished group. Teógenes, seeking to alleviate the hunger of his compatriots as they destroy their homes and possessions and prepare to destroy themselves, orders that all Roman prisoners be killed and consumed. The Numantian leader's diction inscribes this act in multiple registers. As "nuestra comida celebrada" (our final feast) (*DN* III.1440; *SN*, 135), this meal evokes the Last Supper and the cannibalistic dimension of the Eucharist itself. As an action that is simultaneously cruel and necessary, the blame for this barbarity is partially displaced onto the Romans themselves, who have used military technology that leaves the Numantians with cannibalism and starvation as their only options (*DN* III.1441). Likewise, the graphic descriptions of the collective suicide victims, detailed above, serve to elicit sympathy for the hideous fate of the civilians. These acts, however, also distance the spectator from a group whose mass suicide, although pitiful and tragic, is also anathema to the spiritual values of a Christian society. Ironically, it is a Roman soldier, a member of the culture that early modern Europe viewed as the primary architect of the Stoic doctrine of heroic suicide, who condemns the suicide as an act of "bárbaro furor" (barbarous fury) (*DN* IV.2238; *SN*, 155). The dramatizations and descriptions of necromancy, cannibalism, and self-slaughter, in conjunction with the representation of the humanizing elements described above, combine to present the non-Christian Other as a being who embodies a borderland ontology, disconcertingly familiar yet also incomprehensibly different.

Lope's *Arauco domado* also alludes to cannibalism and devil-worship on the part of the colonized subjects. Several Araucanian characters refer with pride to past experiences that involved eating the flesh and drinking the blood of their European oppressors. Upon capturing Rebolledo, the Araucanians discuss with great pleasure the possibility of cannibalism. Tucapel urges, "Asale entero, que quiero / comérmele todo entero" (Roast him whole, for I want to eat up his entire body), and Gualeva advocates that her fellow Chileans refrain from killing him with bows and arrows because "quiero / que le aséis vivo" (I want you to roast him alive) (*AD* II, 162–63). In the climactic celebration in Act III, the indigenous leaders do indeed drink blood that "está caliente" (is still warm) from Valdivia's skull (*AD* III, 227). As in *La Numancia*, non-Christian religion is staged as necromancy.

Pillán, the spirit the Araucanians worship, is construed in the text as a diabolical figure; as in the Cervantine play, the scene of prophecy emphasizes the strangeness of the ritual and the spirit summoned. When Pillán first appears on the stage, the directions describe him "con un medio rostro dorado y un cerco de rayos, como sol, en la cabeza" (with a golden mask and a crown with rays like the sun upon his head) (*AD* I, 120).

Just as the Romans describe the Numantians as savage Others, García also characterizes the battle song of the Araucanians as "extraña" (strange). Here, though, his denunciation is highly complex, for this epithet is followed by the admission, "si de questa suerte fueran / los indios que vio Colón, / tarde en aquesta región / los españoles se vieran" (if Columbus had encountered natives like this, the Spaniards would have taken a long time to conquer that region) (*AD* I, 134). Rebolledo disputes the relevance of Lascasian accusations concerning Spanish slaughters of innocent Americans to the Chilean situation. He asserts that the Araucanians are quite different from "los indios desarmados / que hallaba en selvas y prados, / como corderos, Colón" (those unarmed natives that Columbus found in forests and meadows, gentle as lambs) (*AD* I, 150). By contrast, the Spaniards in Chile oppose "los hombres más fieros, / más valientes, más extraños / que vio este Polo en mil años" (the fiercest, bravest, and strangest men that have been seen in one thousand years) (*AD* I, 150). This barbaric excess of valor is found even among the female members of the group. Fresia's fierce dedication to freedom becomes inhuman and cruel as she condemns both husband and son for preferring shameful captivity to death. After the failed nighttime assault, she orders her son to find his father in the Spanish fort, "y si vive, dile que por qué es infame, / y en su cara le apercibe / a que mujer no me llame / quien tal afrenta recibe" (and if he is alive, tell him that he is unworthy, and that he may not call me his wife after insulting me so) (*AD* II, 194). Fresia's later decision to kill Caupolicán's infant offspring—out of rage and disgust that Caupolicán let himself be captured rather than dying in battle—is central to all critical analyses of the representation of Amerindian excess in the fierce pursuit of freedom. Thus, the very elements that mark the Chileans as Others are also crucial to the discourse that humanizes them as valiant warriors and lovers of liberty. Díaz Balsera points to the ambiguous characterizations as key components of the Spanish defense of the Conquest, for the fear of "illegitimate usurpation loses much of its anxiety-producing force when enunciated by a subject lying inside and outside the boundaries of the European universal" ("Araucanian Alterity," 33). This theatrical demonization of the non-Christian colonial subject influenced their material circumstances, for, as Díaz Balsera asserts, "Spanish colonial literary texts were shaped with some awareness of the connections between the representation of the truth about American natives and the exercise of power over them" (23). The polyvalent inscriptions of the Other incorporate significant points in both Lascasian and Sepulvedan discourse. Cervantes's and Lope's portrayals of the Numantians and Araucanians, then, offer the opportunity for a specifically ideological investigation of early modern Spanish notions of "humanness." The contradictory elements of these portraits should not be reduced to a baroque or theatrical aesthetic of ambiguity; rather, they should be viewed as a nuanced analysis of the process through which early modern Spaniards sought to define themselves by determining whom to exclude, discursively and materially, from the community of humankind.

## Ideology, Genre, and Closure

In the final scenes of Cervantes's *La Numancia* and Lope's *Arauco domado*, the juxtaposition of epic and tragic modes contributes to the generic indeterminacy that produces ideological instability and marks these works as history plays according to the criteria established above. The early, parallel scenes of prophecy in the two dramas set the stage for later deployments of multiple generic tones. After the elaborate sacrifice to Jupiter and the priest's gloomy interpretation, one Numantian observer advises, "lloremos, pues es fin tan lamentable, / nuestra desdicha" (We'll grieve in such a way for our misfortune / That future ages never will forget) (*DN* II.900–901; *SN*, 122). Leonicio rejects the prediction, declaring that "el ánimo esforzado" (strenuous effort) is more powerful than any "agüero" (omen) (*DN* II.918, 916) and that a good soldier

> esas vanas apariencias
> nunca le turban el tino:
> su brazo es su estrella o sino;
> su valor, sus influencias.
>
> (*DN* II.919–22)

> (... mistrusts the vain
> Appearances of things from the outside
> Which should not make him lose his common sense.

Your arm's your lucky star or else your doom.
Your valour is the talisman in which to trust.)

(*SN*, 123)

In a similar fashion, the Araucanian warrior Tucapel dismisses the prophecy of Pillán, the god summoned by their priest, Pillalonco. He boasts that he will kill his more credulous companion in order to be sent to the underworld dwelling of "ese loco" (this lunatic) so that he can demonstrate the power "del brazo riguroso del soberbio Tucapel" (of proud Tucapel's mighty arm). Asserting his doubt even more strongly, Tucapel concludes, "no hay Pillán; yo basto y sobro / contra el mundo" (There is no God, I alone suffice and exceed against the world) (*AD* I, 243). Thus, the meaning of the future—tragic defeat or epic victory—depends upon the prophet chosen: priest or soldier. In *La Numancia*, however, both Leonicio and his companion agree that the forthcoming necromantic rites of Marquino are more meaningful than the sacrifices of the priests. Leonicio still finds a way to denounce the "tristes signos" (dismal omens), though, this time using the explanation that the practices are "diabólicas invenciones" (of diabolical invention) and "poca ciencia" (irrational), offering the additional rationale that "poco cuidan los muertos / de lo que a los vivos toca" (the dead don't care for living folks' affairs) (*DN* II.1085, 1100–1104; *SN*, 127). In these passages, Retógenes, Leonicio, and Tucapel give voice to the early modern period's growing confidence in the power of the rational individual subject to control its own destiny, rejecting pagan notions of fate. In this light, the tragic dimensions of the endings may be viewed as a confirmation of the power of prophecy, but the actualization of predestined defeat may also affirm the efficacy of Roman (and Spanish) innovations in waging war.

I will now examine more fully the way that the indeterminate juxtaposition of tragedy, comedy, and epic in the final scenes of *La Numancia* and *Arauco domado* constitutes a generic deployment that is a meaningful element of imperial discourse. Paul Lewis Smith takes an important step toward recognizing generic indeterminacy in the play when he observes that *La Numancia* is both a tragedy and a tragicomedy.[32] Smith also argues that Cervantes himself was ambiguous about the appropriate generic designation, pointing out that Fame refers to the play as neither *comedia* nor *tragedia* but rather as *historia*. The *historia* and its close relative, the novel,

---

32. Paul Lewis Smith, "Cervantes' *Numancia* as Tragedy and as Tragicomedy," *Bulletin of Hispanic Studies* 64, no. 1 (1987): 23.

are the two most significant examples of early modern generic innovation. They are also "genres" that embody indeterminacy in their combination of elements from many other forms, including the epic, romance, tragedy, and comedy as well as medieval chronicles and morality plays. In addition, historic and novelistic discourses are often manifested in the dramas, anatomies, and political treatises of the period. I place the word "genre" in quotation marks in this situation precisely because early modern texts that sought to represent national history are both inclusive and variable; they lack either a stable group of features to which formalist criticism can refer or a consistent social function upon which a materialist analysis can focus. Although the early modern term *historia* does not necessarily imply the collision of genres that is so notable in these plays, current critical discussions of the early modern history play posit generic polyphony as a complement to polyvocal ideology. This mingling of generic features is particularly striking in the final scenes of the plays, where the characters' diction specifically and metadramatically evokes differing genres. Cascardi asserts that historical dramas such as *Fuente Ovejuna* "reconstruc[t] historical narrative as a form of literary romance" (*Ideologies,* 3). Such a characterization applies only partially to the dramatizations of the battles for Arauco and Numancia, because romance is only one of several modes present in the concluding scenes.

In the last scenes of the Cervantine drama, the Romans describe their fates in language that resonates generically. Mario declares that the valor of the Numantian deed will earn the town eternal fame, so that "sacado han de su pérdida ganancia" (they have cheated you [the Romans] of all your winnings) (*DN* IV.2267; *SN,* 155). Upon witnessing the suicide of Bariato—and with it the last hope for any sort of meaningful victory—Escipión laments, "tú, con esta caída levantaste / tu fama y mis victorias derribaste" (you, with this fall, have raised your fame on high / And leveled all my victories to the ground!) (*DN* IV.2407–8; *SN,* 159). Escipión's final self-description also juxtaposes tragic and epic fates, victory and defeat: he is "[e]l que, subiendo, queda más caído" (Him who, exalted high, you've now brought low) (*DN* IV.2416; *SN,* 159). The generic fate of the future Spaniards is also equivocal, however, for although the coming generations descend "de tales padres herederos" (From ancestors and fathers of such merit) (*DN* IV.2436; *SN,* 159), referring to the link between Numantians and Castilians, there have been many indications that the House of Austria descends from Escipión as well.

The final scene of Lope's play also combines genres in an ultimately indeterminate manner as it juxtaposes the celebration of the Spanish victory over the Araucanians with the Christlike crucifixion of Caupolicán. It gives a voice to Engol, son of the slain Indian leader, as he vows, "padre, yo te vengaré" (Father, I will avenge you) and also to Caupolicán's wife, Fresia, who echoes that threat. The cries of "¡Viva Felipe!" that close the play in celebration of the young king's coronation were heard by an audience who had seen that Philip II's reign was not nearly as successful as that of his father. The historical record bears witness to the validity of the Araucanian threats of revenge. As noted previously, Araucanian resistance continued successfully throughout the colonial period. During the reign of Philip III, the battle against this group was considered a major drain on the Castilian treasury at a time when peace had been procured throughout the European segments of the empire (Elliott, *Spain and Its World*, 24–25).

In the counter-epic history play, the deployment of multiple genres collapses the boundaries between them; moreover, the ascription of conflicting genres to the events and ideologies represented, without closure, further problematizes the identification of a generic dominant or of a definitive political statement. This conflation of genres, tones, and contradictory ideologies in the dramatic representation of recent and remote episodes from Spanish history demonstrates the oppositional potential of historical drama, for contradictory ramifications outside of the theater are implicit in this open-ended staging of the controversies over imperialism that engaged the period. In their refusal to ascribe a fixed genre, a fixed "signified" to national policy and history, and in their deployment of counter-epic discourses, history plays such as *La destrucción de Numancia* and *Arauco domado* participated in and helped produce and refine the conflicting discourses concerning militant imperialism that circulated in the sixteenth and seventeenth centuries. A materialist poetics of genre that examines the wider field of discourses in which the *comedia* was deployed makes it possible to acknowledge the role played by such innovative genre constructions in the questioning of the dominant martial ideologies of early modern Spain.

# 5

## THE NOVELISTIC HISTORY PLAY
Rojas Zorrilla's *Numancia* Diptych and González de Bustos's *Los españoles en Chile*

The dramatization of Spain's Roman period as presented in Rojas Zorrilla's diptych, *Numancia cercada (Numancia Under Siege)* and *Numancia destruida (Numancia Destroyed)*, constitutes not only a counter-epic history play as described in Chapter 4 but also a reinscription of the Cervantine drama upon the same topic written more than a half-century earlier. Similarly, *Los españoles en Chile (Spaniards in Chile)* offers a meditation on Spanish attempts to pacify the indigenous peoples of Chile and on the series of epic poems and dramas that inscribed that effort.[1] This chapter will continue to explore the counter-epic history play's aesthetic and ideological dimensions and will also analyze its evolution over the course of the eighty years that passed between the composition of the Cervantine play and *Los españoles en Chile*. This process of transformation is marked by a shift in counter-epic strategies: questioning of imperial military activity and ideology gives way to a marginalization of military activity and the dramatization of the combatants' private lives. Dramatizing the personal concerns of historical figures, rather than their military achievements, constitutes an innovative counter-epic

---

1. The text of *Los españoles en Chile* that I will cite is James T. Abraham's digitized critical edition, available online at http://www.coh.arizona.edu/chile (May 2001). I am also heavily indebted to Abraham's critical introduction, which provided many important bibliographic leads.

strategy—a novelization of the history play. This counter-epic tactic is also found in the Arauco romances of the period, which feature "el desplazamiento del espíritu épico histórico hacia lo novelesco" (a replacement of the epic, historical spirit with a novelistic tone).[2] An analysis of the novelistic and counter-epic dimensions of the Rojas Zorrilla and González de Bustos plays can help trace one particular form of the early modern Spanish history play's development and demonstrate the linked ideological and aesthetic dimensions of these two counter-epic works.

The juxtaposition of military and amorous discourses and foundational mythology found in these two plays has a precursor in the most popular sixteenth-century romance epic, *Orlando Furioso*.[3] Peter Marinelli points out that Ruggiero's most important battle takes place in a city that was conquered by the Turks just before Ariosto wrote this work, and he asserts that the poet "creat[ed] fictional situations for his characters that mirror, with alterations, the circumstances and personages of later times" (*Ariosto and Boiardo*, 91). Just as Spanish dramatists used a similar template for staging the battles at Numancia and Arauco, Ariosto represents the eighth-century Moorish invasions as a distant mirror for the Turkish conquests of his own moment. In particular, Marinelli suggests, Ariosto sought to discourage the internecine warfare among the Catholic nations in order to focus Christian energies on the battle against Islam (93). Although this work does not condemn imperial ideology in the same terms as the Numancia and Arauco plays, it does present similar just war arguments in its attempts to distinguish moral warfare from that motivated by greed (94).

The ideological significance of the later Numancia and Arauco plays can be more fully appreciated by taking into consideration the military history of their periods. The Rojas Zorrilla diptych, written at the end of the 1620s, coincides with Spain's failed attempt to win control over the Duchy of Mantua and with Breda's repudiation of the Spanish yoke—just two short years after its much-celebrated conquest.[4] *Los españoles en Chile* was written about 1665, as Philip IV stubbornly pursued dreams of an Iberian empire, signing treaties with the Dutch and bringing an end to the Thirty Years' War only to turn his attention to futile attempts to recapture Portugal. At

---

2. Aurelio González, "Los Romances de la Conquista: Enfoques y perspectivas," in *Relaciones literarias*, ed. Campbell, 223.

3. Peter V. Marinelli, *Ariosto and Boiardo: The Origins of* Orlando Furioso (Columbia: University of Missouri Press, 1987), 84, 91.

4. Frederick de Armas, "Numancia as Ganymede: Conquest and Continence in Giulio Romano, Cervantes, and Rojas Zorrilla," in *Echoes and Inscriptions*, ed. Simerka and Weimer, 254.

this same time, Spanish troops in Chile were compelled to realize, after a century of failed attempts at pacification and forced labor, that the colonization of Arauco would never follow the model set forth by Cortés and Pizarro (Lynch, *Spain Under the Habsburgs*, 2:133).

## CRITICAL RECEPTION OF LATE BAROQUE DRAMA

The critical reputation of Rojas Zorrilla has not been a favorable one. Key arbiters of Golden Age drama, including Schack, Cotarelo, Mesonero Romanos, and Menéndez y Pelayo, criticized his works as excessively bizarre, monstrous, extravagant, and lacking in verisimilitude. In short, his work contains all of the components of late baroque drama that aroused critical contempt during the initial period of canon formation.[5] Raymond MacCurdy, the primary modern scholar of Rojas Zorrilla's dramaturgy, interprets Rojas Zorrilla's reinscription of the Cervantine drama according to the notions of tragedy set forth by A. A. Parker. He thus labels the diptych a personal tragedy, in place of Cervantes's collective tragedy, and attributes the emphasis upon the personal lives of the characters to the aesthetic requirements of this alternate tragic mode.[6] Such a modification of dramatic form leads to an inversion in the relative importance of war and human relations, so that in the two Rojas Zorrilla plays, the war is a mere "pretext" for the examination of personal conflicts: "dominan los seres humanos, que borran muy a menudo el fondo de la guerra" (human beings dominate the action, often relegating warfare to the backdrop).[7] This explanation validates the later author's revision of the Cervantine drama by positioning the work within an acceptable alternate tragic framework. MacCurdy employs this particular critical strategy in order to improve the reputation of these unappreciated plays. His important efforts to reinterpret Rojas Zorrilla provide the basis on which other forms of analysis may launch their interpretations (*Numancia*, ix). Harriet Powers also makes an important contribution to the study of these plays with her praise for Rojas Zorrilla's "intentional

---

5. Dietrich Briesemeister, "El horror y su función en algunas tragedias de Francisco de Rojas Zorrilla," *Criticón* 23 (1983): 160; Harriet B. Powers, "The Grotesque Vision of Rojas Zorrilla," *Bulletin of the Comediantes* 23 (1971): 6.

6. Raymond R. MacCurdy, *Francisco de Rojas Zorrilla* (New York: Twayne, 1968), 65.

7. Ibid., 61; MacCurdy, critical introduction to Francisco de Rojas Zorrilla, *Numancia cercada y Numancia destruida*, ed. and intro. by Raymond R. MacCurdy (Madrid: Ediciones José Porrua Turanzas, 1977), xxiii.

cultivation of the grotesque" as an effective aesthetic strategy ("Grotesque Vision," 1). This aesthetic makes a statement about both literary and military matters, as Powers observes, for the outrageous reinterpretations of well-known stories serve to ridicule "prevailing dramatic conventions and public taste" and offer "deliberate satirization or subversion of cherished public notions," including "the necessity for social order" (4–5). The following chapter seeks to build upon these important studies by exploring in detail the symbiosis of generic and ideological complexity in the two plays. Using materialist and cultural studies models of textual study to delineate the ideological dimensions of late baroque aesthetic practices, this chapter will argue that these two plays merit consideration within the new canon of postcolonial literatures.

Ada M. Coe describes what might be the earliest critical evaluation of *Los españoles en Chile*, citing a review of a 1789 performance in the *Memoria Literaria:*

> Son tantos los episodios que se gastan en enredos amorosos, que más parece hecha para conquistas de Cupido, que de Marte; por lo que la acción queda muy desnuda de interés y de trama.[8]

> (So many episodes focus on amorous interludes, that it appears to be about the conquests of Cupid rather than Mars; for this reason the plot is dull.)

This rejection of late baroque stylistic techniques—and the subsequent marginalization of the dramas of González de Bustos, Rojas Zorrilla, and their contemporaries in the Golden Age dramatic canon—is not limited to critics of earlier eras, however. Abraham asserts that scholars generally view *Los españoles en Chile* as the "weakest" of the Arauco plays, a denigration that is based in part on its lack of unity.[9] Melchora Romanos disparages the text because "el drama histórico se desdibuja a una absurda comedia de enredos" (the historical action is erased for an absurd comedy of misunderstandings) and "está totalmente alejada del principio de verosimilitud" (it totally

---

8. Ada M. Coe, *Catálogo bibliográfico y crítico de las comedias anunciadas en los periódicos de Madrid desde 1661 hasta 1819* (Baltimore: The Johns Hopkins University Press, 1935), cited in Abraham's introduction to *Los españoles en Chile*, available online at http://www.coh.arizona.edu/chile/introtext.htm#gonzalez (May 2001).

9. See Abraham's introduction to *Los españoles en Chile*.

violates the principles of verisimilitude) ("La construcción del personaje de Caupolicán," 198). Because of the many courtship episodes, Fausta Antonucci also describes this play as a "comedia de enredos" that totally lacks the "didactic" dimensions of earlier versions ("El indio americano y la conquista," 40). Although Antonucci notes the change in the representation of the Marquis, who in this version orders the torture of indigenous captives (other plays had attributed the command to lesser figures), she denies that any Arauco play highlighting amorous intrigue could also contain ideological commentary about imperialism (41–44). But in a seeming contradiction to this assertion, she also asserts that all the Arauco plays demonstrate an awareness of the potential for abuse within the imperial system, "y quizás por eso, *cada vez* que llevaba a la escena conquistas y reconquistas, tenía que justificarlas con intentos religiosos y políticos, y con cualidades negativas de los conquistados" (and perhaps for this reason, *every time* that conquest and reconquest were dramatized, they had to be justified with political and religious motivations and by the negative representation of the colonized peoples) (46, emphasis added). Although her attempt to draw a clear boundary between serious and comic works detracts from this study, Antonucci's useful overview of the entire corpus of Arauco plays provides an important contribution, especially as she underscores the role played by national historical dramas "que sirven de 'pretexto' para evocar preocupaciones más cercanas y concretas" (that serve as pretexts for exploring more contemporary and pressing issues) (45). A. Robert Lauer characterizes the typical depiction of imperialism in Chilean *comedias* as a

> doble visión . . . lo que no se logra ver en estos dramas es una visión clara y única, sino, al contrario, dos posturas opuestas en las cuales las acusaciones de crueldad, tiranía y rebelión se pueden aplicar tanto a un grupo como el otro.[10]
>
> (double vision . . . what is never achieved in these dramas is a clear and unified vision, but rather, two contradictory viewpoints, through which the accusations of cruelty, tyranny, and rebellion are equally applicable to both sides).

---

10. A. Robert Lauer, "La conquista de Chile en el teatro español del Siglo de Oro," in *El escritor y la escena II: Actas del II Congreso de la Asociación Internacional de Teatro Español y Novohispano de los Siglos de Oro, 17–20 de marzo de 1993*, ed. Ysla Campbell (Ciudad Juárez: Universidad Autónoma de Ciudad Juárez, 1994), 103.

Analyzing the development of this double vision in the context of the late baroque techniques employed by both Rojas Zorrilla and González de Bustos will help illuminate the aesthetic and ideological evolution of the counter-epic history play and may serve as a stimulus for reconsidering the marginalized status of these dramatists.

## Controlling the Historical Record

The hallmarks of the Elizabethan and Jacobean history play, according to Phyllis Rackin, John Loftis, and others, include the tracing of national connections with the Roman Empire in order to create a heroic foundational myth, self-conscious exploration of historical inscription, generic polyphony, and ideological complexity. Both plays of Rojas Zorrilla's diptych assert that the control of historical inscription constitutes a significant element of victory or defeat. In *Numancia cercada*, Cipión describes for his enemy Retógenes the form in which history will record the fall of Numancia:

> . . . ansí en los siglos futuros
> las reliquias y antiguillas
> de esas insignes murallas
> dirán en mármoles duros:
> "Aquí verás, caminante,
> en gloria postrada y viva,
> que murió Numancia altiva
> y venció Cipión constante"
>
> (*NC* II.1574–81)[11]

(In future times, commemorative marble plaques will be placed upon these famous walls, proclaiming, "Passerby, here you see the glorious site where arrogant Numancia fell and constant Scipio triumphed.)

And in the opening scene of *Numancia destruida*, Retógenes concludes his speech about national glory with a reference to his place in history:

---

11. References to *Numancia cercada*, *Numancia destruida*, and *Los españoles en Chile* (abbreviated *NC*, *ND*, and *EC*, respectively) include act and line numbers; there are no standard editions with scene numbers for these works.

> . . . Proseguid el triunfo;
> que no han de ser indecisas
> las glorias que me atribuyo.
> ¡Ea, cantad mis hazañas!
>
> (*ND* I.462–65)

(Let us move forward to total victory, for the glories attributed to me must not be fainthearted. Let my accomplishments be sung!)

In the long hymn to the town of Numancia near the end of the second act, Retógenes compares the Numantian legacy to that of other empires, claiming superiority to all those previously celebrated in the annals of history.

> Bien pueden los anales
> del griego, el medo y tracio
> contar en largo espacio
> hazañas inmortales,
> pero son, si a las tuyas las reduces,
> átamos breves de tus santas luces.
>
> (*ND* II.1425–30)

(Let the records of the Greeks, Medes, and Thracians relate their immortal deeds at length; they are brief paragraphs compared to the volumes of your accomplishments.)

Cipión also links battle strategies to his place in history when he decides to lay siege to Numancia rather than suffer further defeats in combat: "no es razón que yo pierda / la reputación ganada / tan sin seso" (there is no reason for me to squander so senselessly the fame I have won) (*ND* I.912–14).

In the dream sequence in which the two nations and El Olvido appear, personified, announcing to Retógenes the tragic but glorious and historically memorable destiny of his town, both sides express a desire not only to triumph and be commemorated but also, in doing so, to erase the other's memory from the historical record. Thus the figure Numancia declares, "moriré contenta / cuando del mundo tu memoria borre" (I can die happily when the memory of you is erased from the world) (*ND* II.1485–86). Numancia adds, "el valor de mis hijos me alienta / cuya fama de polo a polo corre" (my sons' valor, whose fame travels from one pole to the other, sustains me) (*ND* II.1489–90) and will earn not only present recognition but will also constitute "materia altiva a célebres historias" (material worthy of notable histories) (*ND* II.1492). Rome replies, "tu nombre he de entregar al viejo Olvido" (I must consign your name to Oblivion) (*ND* II.1510). Upon learning that the town is doomed, Numancia inscribes the collective suicide as an evasion of enslavement and as a means to obtain a symbolic triumph, so that "con eterna gloria / cante yo de mí misma la victoria" (with eternal glory will I sing of myself and my victory) (*ND* II.1523–24). Numancia's final words in the dream sequence are addressed to Olvido, rather than to Rome, as the ultimate enemy over which she will triumph.

> Olvido, cuando muero dando espanto
> al mundo, he de vencerte. Del Leteo
> parte a habitar las lóbregas cavernas;
> que mi memoria y mi fama son eternas.
>
> (*ND* II.1529–32)

(Oblivion, with my heroic death, I will overcome you. Return to the gloomy caverns of Lethe, for my glory and fame are eternal.)

The Rojas Zorrilla diptych, like the Cervantine drama, alludes to the role that desire for historical immortality plays in early modern Spain's policy formation and military planning.

In the final scenes of *Numancia destruida*, references to the town's inscribed immortality abound. Florinda suggests collective death as the key to future commemoration: "vive siempre el valor contra el olvido" (courage always triumphs over oblivion) (*ND* III.2210). Retógenes concurs, proposing the self-slaughter of all the inhabitants and the destruction of their belongings: "hagamos / un hecho ilustre, una invencible hazaña, / inmortal honra de la madre España" (Let us commit an illustrious act, an invincible deed, for the eternal honor of our motherland) (*ND* III.2222–24). Cipión himself predicts that Retógenes's valor will be remembered: "¡Oh, ejemplo / de valentía, la fama / te inmortalice!" (Oh, model of valor, you will be immortalized!) (*ND* III.2623–25). Because he has captured no trophy that could allow him to portray this action as a triumph in Rome, Cipión's last speech is a command to destroy the city, "porque no quede memoria / de una ciudad, que, cercada / de mi gente, me ha vencido" (so that no memory will remain of the city, besieged by my troops, that defeated me)

(*ND* III.2651–53). The fact that this hope is expressed within a play that resuscitates his defeat more than a millennium later—a play that is itself a *refundición* (rewriting) of a drama written in a prior generation—demonstrates to the audience that, despite the preoccupation of great nations and leaders with the way in which history will inscribe them and despite their efforts to control the historical record, individuals and societies alike cannot dictate the terms under which they will be remembered, "re-membered," or forgotten. Indeed, the play's references to the variability of historical commemoration may allude to the emergence of the Black Legend and western European condemnations of Spanish colonial practice. This metahistorical commentary also underlines the ultimate futility of the conquistadors' attempts to shape the record with their letters or of their descendants' desires to enhance their ancestors' reputations by commissioning literary testimonials.

In *Los españoles en Chile*, it is the commemoration of individual leaders, rather than the Spanish nation, that is foregrounded. According to Antonucci, concern with personal *fama* dictated the form of inscription in these works, which were commissioned by the conquistadors' families. Thus, in the González de Bustos composition, the Araucanian warrior Fresia tells Tucapel that her hatred for Don Diego is grounded in the fact that the Spaniard's military victories threaten Tucapel's place in the historical record:

> . . . me corro de ver
> que sus hazañas altivas
> borren las que de vosotros
> hoy tiene la fama escritas
>
> (*EC* II.1326–29)

(It infuriates me to see that their accomplishments erase what Fame has written of your deeds.)

Of course, such metahistorical speeches also remind the audience that the entertainment they are viewing itself constitutes a form of historical inscription—and that the proliferation of commemorations by court historians, chroniclers, epic poets, painters, and balladeers as well as dramatists has produced conflicting versions of past events, particularly in the case of the brief history of Spanish imperial activity in Chile.

## LATE BAROQUE AESTHETICS

Rojas Zorrilla and González de Bustos deploy similar artistic and ideological strategies in their novelistic reinscriptions of the counter-epic history play. Their insertion into historical dramas of the conventions of the Renaissance epic and the *comedia*—with its focus on the personal lives of military heroes, including episodes of jealousy, rivalry, and mistaken identity, women who dress as men in order to recapture their honor, and farcical scenes involving plebian characters—has been interpreted on a purely stylistic basis. These texts are often viewed as inferior to those produced by the Lopean and Calderonian circles and are seen as manifestations of a late baroque practice that goes to extremes in its inclusion of multiple genres, styles, tones, and subplots.[12] The three plays under consideration here have suffered from critical neglect and contempt for this reason, as well as from assertions that the later, personalized epic dramas lack an ideological dimension (Antonucci, "El indio americano y la conquista," 40–41), providing a diverting but ultimately trivial and inferior nonideological theatrical experience. I would argue, to the contrary, that the generic juxtaposition and other forms of polyphony found in these (and other) late baroque history plays offer a framework for a common vision in which hegemonic ideologies are scrutinized and questioned through a dramatic structure that marginalizes military and overtly political considerations. Generic juxtaposition thus serves to ridicule or minimize the aristocratic and bellic elements of the epic tales reworked in these plays. This form of counter-epic drama, which trivializes rather than overtly criticizes imperial practice (and which, like *indiano* drama, emphasizes personal rather than public activity), constitutes an important development in the history of theater. Dramatists of the early modern period experimented with new genres, tones, and themes in order to stage and engage with the changes in hierarchy that accompanied the waning of the feudal social and economic order and the emergence of mercantile and proto-capitalist societies.

One major aspect of the representation of warfare within these plays is the competition between Mars and Venus—the conflict experienced when the exigencies of wartime threaten to block the fulfillment of personal desires. The marginalization of epic material occurs because, unlike the

---

12. Raymond R. MacCurdy, "The Numantian Plays of Cervantes and Rojas Zorrilla: The Shift from the Collective to Personal Tragedy," *Symposium* 14 (1960): 102–5; de Armas, "Numancia as Ganymede," 250.

characters staged in *La Numancia* and *Arauco domado*, the protagonists of the later plays often opt for personal gratification rather than communal benefit.[13] This inclination to prioritize individual goals is related to the critique of Spanish imperial officers explored in Chapter 4; here, however, I will emphasize those moments in which the conflict marginalizes emplotment of military matters and battles. In his diptych, Zorrilla displaces battle activity through a series of amorous encounters between the avatars of empire and enemy women as well as through reinscriptions of the conventions of farce. González de Bustos's *Los españoles en Chile* also reduces military issues to background matter, dramatizing a series of conflicts between passion and duty as well as providing a series of interwoven cross-ethnic courtship subplots, a *gracioso gloriosus*, chivalric encounters, a baptism scene that evokes medieval drama, and even a potential *drama de honor*.

In *Numancia cercada*, the conflict between personal and national goals first erupts when Cayo Mario and King Jugarta's rivalry over Florinda leads to a clash of swords. The Numantian Amazon observes that this duel, which divides her enemies, helps her own cause: "eso sí, verted vosotros / vuestra sangre" (this is great, yes, spill each other's blood) (*NC* II.1338–39). Then, even though Cayo Mario and Jugarta admit that their actions have caused the Romans to lose this battle, they continue to interrupt their dialogues with Cipión by interspersing asides directed to Florinda. Megara's betrayal of Numancia is another example of the conflict between personal and national interest. He admits, "quiero por el sol que adoro / intentar una traición" (because of the sun I adore, I will commit treason) (*NC* II.1660–61). Megara highlights the similarity of military and passionate diction as he redefines glory as the possession of Florinda rather than the conquest of her city (*NC* II.1668).

In the second play of the diptych, the arrival of Jugarta's African fiancée, Artemisa, provides additional opportunities to explore the ways in which personal lives are disrupted by war, although in this case Venus gives way to Mars. Artemisa tells Cipión that Jugarta left her side in order to gain fame. She quotes his farewell speech:

¿Qué me importa que herede
el reino, el oro y las joyas
del valiente Masinisa,

---

13. In Lacanian terms, they fail to display the homage to the Law of the Father that marks appropriate social interpellation. For an excellent study of the Lacanian dimension of early modern Spanish plays that dramatize conflicts between passion and duty, see Henry Sullivan,

> si no le imita en las obras?
> Deja que a España me parta,
> donde en la escuela famosa
> de Cipión, estudiar pueda
> lo que a mi valor importa
>
> (*ND* I.179–86)

(What do I care about inheriting a kingdom and all its riches, if I do not equal brave Masinisa in my deeds? Let me depart for Spain, where I can learn what I need at Scipio's famous school.)

This scene demonstrates that in a militarized culture, where leadership and merit are equated with battle success, even those monarchs whose kingdoms are not involved in disputes will seek out military action to acquire the renown attached to imperial ventures, heedless of the effects upon their loved ones. Here, Jugarta resembles the Numantian soldiers who wished to die in a blaze of glory that would have left their wives and children defenseless at the hands of the Roman conquerors. Jugarta's assertion to Artemisa that he cannot pay attention to her because of his military responsibilities—"no se mezcla el amor con la arrogancia" (love and ambition do not mix)—could be seen as an indication that Rojas Zorrilla will foreground Mars rather than Venus in the sequel to *Numancia cercada*. It soon becomes evident, however, that the Numidian wishes to be free of Artemisa in order to pursue Florinda, not armed combat. Later, when Jugarta repents this error, he must enter the enemy camp for a personal errand—rescuing Artemisa, who has been captured by Florinda (*ND* II.989).

The competition between Mars and Venus in the Numancia diptych centers upon battlefield encounters among imperial soldiers and female warriors from the "barbaric" opposing group. The first battlefield encounter between Florinda and the Roman heroes of the Rojas Zorrilla *Numancia* is noteworthy for the rapid transition from military action to amorous dialogue. This unheroic response to an enemy marks the imperial leaders as less masculine (according to the gender norms of the period) than the leading female soldier on the opposing side, and it sets the stage for a form of dramatic emplotment seen in both the Rojas Zorrilla and González de Bustos plays: the actual crossing of swords is nearly always avoided in favor

---

"Lacan and Calderón: Spanish Classical Drama in the Light of Psychoanalytic Theory," *Gestos* 5, no. 10 (1990): 39–55.

of staging the personal lives of the heroes. Throughout the two parts of the diptych and in *Los españoles en Chile,* battle scenes are generally framed by—or even displaced by—scenes of courtship intrigue more common to comic drama. In that first encounter, Florinda's response to Cayo Mario and Jugarta's employment of standard courtly love military metaphors in their attempts to woo her (rather than accepting her challenge to cross swords) emphasizes their degradation of the military ideal. Florinda reinscribes the Roman and Numidian using the same adjective normally applied to her own people: these two are barbarians because of their desire "de gastar locas palabras" (to waste their time with silly speeches) (*NC* II.1311). Rojas Zorrilla presents here one of the many counter-epic moments in which the supposed superiority of the civilized nation over the savage enemy is rendered suspect.

In the third act of *NC,* it is Jugarta who seeks to meld military and amatory adventures. In order to cheer Cipión after the devastatingly successful Numantian attack on the Roman camp, Jugarta tells him about Cayo Mario's captive beauty:

> para que olvides, señor,
> este disgusto presente,
> a un gusto y gloria excelente,
> hoy te convida el amor
>
> (*NC* III.2129–32)

(to distract you from the current disgrace, sir, today love invites you to enjoy this glorious beauty)

Of course, Cipión is the one Roman who does not permit his attention to stray from Mars to Venus. He advises his assistant to follow his example: "toma la luciente espada; / deja la delectación" (take up the shining sword, leave behind pleasure) (*NC* III.2171–72). The structure of the diptych, however, requires that Cayo's amorous interest continue into the second play. The first play of the diptych closes in a scene that moves from an inconclusive duel between the two opposing leaders to an exchange of chivalric courtesies, and then to a speech in which Retógenes confirms the inextricability of Venus and Mars in this play, telling Florinda that Numantian success depends upon his love for her and her fighting ability, expressed through the synecdoche "tus ojos y tu acero" (your eyes and your steel) (*NC* III.2915).

The second play continues to represent love and war as inseparable components of human experience, adding a new character, Artemisa (the jilted fiancée of Jugarta), who hopes to reconquer her lover as he seeks to put an end to Numantian resistance. Even though Cipión is the strongest advocate of the separation of personal and military issues, he cannot resist the validity of her request—or the appeal of her tearful beauty: "¿A quién no obliga una hermosura rara?" (Who can resist such rare beauty?) (*ND* I.262). Because he has expelled all the women from the Roman camp, however, Cipión instructs Artemisa to dress as a man in order to pursue her goals, thus providing a new twist to the popular *comedia* convention of cross-dressed heroines in pursuit of their honor. In following the letter (if not the spirit) of his edict, Cipión emphasizes that no one must find out about the invasion of Venus into the territory of Mars:

> al punto
> que por el campo llegue a murmurare,
> . . . . . . . . . .
> veréis montes de nieve en vuestro fuego
> 
> (*ND* I.251–54)

> (if any word of this gets out in the camp, you will find mountains of ice upon your fire)

In a notable departure from the Cervantine drama, Rojas Zorrilla inscribes the Roman leader as susceptible to—although not in thrall to—the passions that afflict his troops. This portrait is simultaneously more humanizing and more heroic, for the figure who experiences temptation but can resist exists on a different plane from the being who is totally immune to Venus's influences.

Because Jugarta's newfound zeal for the battlefield over the boudoir is really just a pretext for his desire to continue to court Florinda, it is easily extinguished. Although he initially chastises Cayo Mario for raving about "una Circe, una Medea / que de sus ojos divinos / mata con flechas" (a Circe, a Medea whose divine eyes kill with their arrows), reminding his companion that "es vergüenza / que se aviven los deseos / y se aniquilen las fuerza" (it is shameful that desire nullifies force), a glimpse of the Numantian women suffices to change his attitude. He concedes that Florinda's charm "mi valor afemina" (feminizes my valor) (*ND* I.633–35, 641–43, 656). Jugarta reconciles with Cayo Mario—"ya disculpo tu flaqueza" (I now pardon your weakness) (*ND* I.661)—although jealous rivalry remains a potential source of future conflict. Both Florinda and Cipión harshly remonstrate the two lovesick swains for their misplaced priorities. She wonders, "¿Hay infamia como aquesta?" (Has there ever been such infamy?), and he condemns "vuestra infame bajeza" (your infamous baseness) (*ND* I.663, 701).

The very first scene of *Los españoles en Chile* emphasizes the potential conflict between personal and military issues, as the priest Colocolo advises, "Vuelve en tí, Caupolicán, / ardid en más nobles incendios / que en los del amor tu orgullo" (Control yourself, Caupolicán, let your passions burn for a more noble fire than love) (*EC* I.164–66). Caupolicán vehemently rejects this advice and gives priority to love for Fresia, which sets the stage for the marginalization of warfare in this play. Similarly, when Fresia learns that Mosquete is servant to Don Diego, the Spaniard for whom she has formed an attraction, she frees her captive with the condition that upon his return to his master, Mosquete must bring him to meet her. Likewise, not wishing to bring sadness to her "lover," Gualeva also sets her captive, Juan/a, free. In a scene that vividly contrasts personal and national interest (inscribed, as in the Numancia plays, as the competition between Venus and Mars), Caupolicán becomes infuriated at Colocolo's efforts to remove him from Fresia's sphere, claiming that she is the source of support for all of his martial accomplishments:

> ¿No sabes que mis hazañas
> y mis gloriosos trofeos,
> . . . . . . .
> vienen de Fresia . . .
>
> (*EC* I.221–25)

(Don't you know that my glorious deeds and triumphs are inspired by Fresia?)

The following scene also juxtaposes amorous and bellic interests, as the arrival of Tucapel and Rengo is marked by exchanges of battle news interspersed with asides concerning the other two Araucanian captains' frustrated desires for Fresia and Gualeva, which cause them to come to blows in front of Caupolicán. This scene comes to an end as Caupolicán agrees to ignore the insults to his pride caused by the fight and by Tucapel's assertion that "en lances de pundonor, / no guarda humanos respetos / a nadie" (when honor is at stake, men respect no one) (*EC* I.299–301). Here, Colocolo does convince the leader to put aside personal pride for the benefit of the group: "es bien que te persüades / al perdón, que estas espadas /

defensa de Arauco son" (it is best that you forgive each other, for these swords must be used to defend Arauco) (*EC* I.331–33).

The Spaniards staged in *Los españoles in Chile* also face conflicting personal and military dilemmas, and like the Araucanians, they often give highest priority to individual goals. Diego, like the Roman warriors Cayo Mario and Jugarta, views a beautiful female warrior from the enemy group through the lens of poetic conventions that conflate love and war: "ya me has muerto / con los rayos de tus ojos" (the darts from your eyes have killed me) (*EC* I.991–92). Diego returns Fresia's sword to her, restores her freedom—even though she is an enemy soldier—and gives her a horse so that she can return safely home (*EC* I.999). Fresia reciprocates, brandishing her weapon in his defense when the Araucanians attack, although she defends her action as chivalric obligation rather than personal passion.

## Epic and Comedia

Within these two plays, the subplots typical of the *comedia* contribute to the Mars versus Venus theme and constitute an important component of generic polyphony. In *Numancia destruida*, when Retógenes misinterprets snippets of a conversation and a hug between Florinda and her captive, Artemisa, who is still dressed in masculine garb, the jealous intrigue typical of comic drama erupts among the Numantians and the siege retreats to the background. As Retógenes ponders the proper course of action, obligation and personal honor once again conflict. If he kills her, "a Numancia quito / en Florinda la mayor / defensa" (I destroy Florinda, who is Numancia's greatest warrior) (*ND* II.1143–45). He cannot ignore her infidelity, however, because "mi honor / da voces contra el delito" (my honor shouts out against this crime) (*ND* II.1145–46). Seeing Retógenes confront the disguised captive, Florinda experiences pangs of jealousy as she overhears him describe "el fuego que hay en mi pecho" (the fire that burns in my breast), unaware that this flame is of jealousy rather than amorous passion (*ND* II.1199). Both characters utilize the apparent deceptions to spew a litany of stereotypical defamations of the opposite sex. Retógenes condemns the natural laws of procreation and wishes that "para conservación / del linaje humano fuera / mejor que las plantas diera" (it would be better if the preservation of the human species were bestowed upon plants), and Florinda likewise questions God's order: "nunca el cielo criara / al hombre" (if only heaven had not created men) (*ND* II.1127–29, 1229–30).

Jugarta's arrival in Numancia, as he seeks to reclaim his captured "page," gives rise to an equally bitter speech from Artemisa, who believes that the exchange in which Florinda and Jugarta discuss her true identity is a continuation of Jugarta's prior pursuit of the Numantian beauty. Such a web of confusion could give rise to an entire comic drama in which to unravel these misunderstandings. Here, this action is a mere subplot; a speedy *desengaño* and reconciliation for all characters involved occurs within the space of two short scenes, and the amorous intrigue of comic drama gives way to romance conventions when Rojas Zorrilla shifts gears to stage exaggerated chivalric exchanges between the two male characters.

The competition among military concerns, courtship issues, and the farcical commentary of a *gracioso* is a structural component of *Los españoles en Chile* as well as a thematic concern. In the second scene of Act I, two Araucanian soldiers present their Christian captives to Caupolicán. The identities of the two Spanish "warriors," however, undermine the epic nature of such an event: one is the cowardly *gracioso*, Mosquete, whose first speech consists of an accusation that the indigenous soldiers are drunk, while the other is a jilted *dama* who has dressed as a man to pursue her erstwhile lover, Don Diego. *Comedia* conventions are brought to the foreground and an additional level of nonmilitary intrigue presents itself as one of the noble Araucanian women, Gualeva, expresses sexual interest in the captive she receives: "no tiene mala presencia, / prima, aquel mozo español" (Cousin, that young Spaniard is quite attractive) (*EC* I.371–72). She also appears possessive when Fresia praises Juan/a: "¡Santos cielos, / no es bueno que tenga celos / de que me prima le alabe!" (Heavens, it is not right that I should be jealous when my cousin praises him!) (*EC* I.384–86). Of course, because Gualeva has taken charge of the disguised Juan/a, this desire is prohibited for its transgression of gender as well as ethnic/religious barriers.

The revelation of Fresia's interest in Don Diego further enmeshes the Spanish and indigenous intrigues. The Araucanians who love Fresia (Caupolicán and Tucapel) and Gualeva (Rengo) complicate the intrigue with their jealousy. Diego's interest in the battle-garbed captive, Fresia, adds to the tangled web of desires (*EC* I.986–87). Taking into account the two Araucanian men, the rivalries form four triangles whose innermost angles involve the two Spaniards, Diego and Juan/a. These subplots give prominence to the captive *gracioso*, the jilted Spanish *dama*, and the sexual intrigue and jealousy among the Araucanians, and they greatly overshadow the representation of battles and epic encounters among the warriors.

Indeed, this play marginalizes warfare to an even greater extent than the Rojas Zorrilla diptych. (Although Lope de Vega also addresses the possibility of cross-ethnic attraction, Gualeva's encounters with Rebolledo and Felipe in Act II take up fewer than one hundred lines and do not have a significant impact on the plot.) Lia Schwartz Lerner has noted in her study of Ercilla's *Araucana* that the indigenous women in the poem "become involved in adventures that are purely literary in tone and in no way reflect historical reality."[14] Similarly, in the González de Bustos play, the many amorous subplots draw upon standard romance and dramatic *topoi*. As these subplots are developed, his dramatic technique—often criticized as an excess akin to "throwing in the kitchen sink"—may be seen as a dazzling display of the entire range of comic dramatic conventions within a miniature *comedia de capa y espada,* or as a form of metadramaturgy in which the very profusion of baroque comic devices serves to "lay bare" the function of such standard motifs and stylistic elements as the elaborate, extended metaphor; gender and ethnic cross-dressing; deceiving by telling the truth; parallel construction between main plot and subplot; and final reconciliation.[15]

The main comic subplot within this history play focuses upon the fiancée abandoned by Don Diego, one of the three military heroes of the Spanish camp. The highlighting of the personal concerns of the two lesser Spaniards, Diego and Pedro (Juan/a's brother), and the silence about the nonmilitary activity of the marquis of Cañete may be interpreted as González de Bustos's show of respect for the family who commissioned this work. (Rojas Zorrilla's reinscription of a far more ancient battle provided the latitude necessary to explore the desires that preyed upon *all* the main military figures in his works.)

In her first soliloquy, Juan/a gives voice to the familiar *comedia* plot of the woman who leaves her family in order to avenge her own honor. Juan/a's speech incorporates metadramatic references to other victimized *comedia* characters. Her "Cielos, piedad, que me abraso" (Have pity on me,

14. Lia Schwartz Lerner, "Tradición literaria y heroinas indias en *La Araucana*." *Revista Iberoamericana* 38 (1972): 615–25, cited in Pastor, *Armature of Conquest,* 229.
15. This self-reflexivity may be seen as an example of Alastair Fowler's concept of the tertiary phase of generic development, which is characterized by the use of an established genre's conventions "as material for symbolic developments," and which is, in Schiller's terms, "sentimental" or reflexive rather than "naïve." See Fowler, *Kinds of Literature* (Cambridge: Harvard University Press, 1982), 160, 62. For an exploration of the function of metadrama in Golden Age Spanish drama, see my "Generic Dimension of Self-Referentiality: Calderón's *El médico de su honra* as *metadrama de honor,*" *Bulletin of the Comediantes* 46, no. 1 (1994): 103–17.

heavens, I'm burning up) (*EC* I.619) recalls Tisbea's despairing monologue in *El burlador de Sevilla* (I.995–1000), while her "¿Mi pecho no aborta un Etna?" (an Aetna burns within my breast) (*EC* I.616) provides a complex allusion to *La vida es sueño (Life Is a Dream)*. Here, Juan/a borrows a metaphor spoken by Segismundo in reference to his suffering in the tower (I.ii.164), even though it is another character, Rosaura, whose situation parallels Juan/a's. This quandary also resembles the plight of Leonor/Leonardo in *Valor, agravio, y mujer,* who courts Estela so that Estela will not marry Leonor's lover. Juan/a makes fun of her ability to inspire love in the wrong place—"buena estoy / para enamorar de veras" (I'm really good at making people fall in love with me)—even as she decides to feign a reciprocal attachment to Gualeva in order to pursue her own goals (*EC* I.665–66).

Imbricated desires, rather than battles, close the first act of this history play, as Juan/a communicates in asides her pain at the flirtation now developing between Diego and Fresia, then hides her face and maintains her pose as an Araucanian soldier who has granted Diego his freedom at Fresia's request. The final scene of Act I emphasizes that the intrigue upon which the audience will focus in the remaining two acts will alternate between amorous and military concerns. Diego acknowledges the chivalric obligation he owes to the "man" who freed him, and Juan/a replies, "mas me debéis que pensáis" (you owe me more than you can imagine) (*EC* I.1055). Her last words emphasize that the original obligation is the more important one: "yo haré que pagues mi amor" (I will make you return my love) (*EC* I.1073).

Amatory interests remain at the forefront as Juan/a opens the second act with a long soliloquy that recapitulates her dilemma and as Tucapel learns of Fresia's love for Diego. González de Bustos's mastery of comic emplotment shines forth as Fresia convinces the Spanish soldier Juan/a to take a message from her to Diego; here, a cross-dressed woman must act as the go-between for her rival and the lover who abandoned her. Juan/a acquiesces with the paradoxical assurance that "es uno mismo / tu cuidado y mi cuidado" (your concerns and mine are as one) (*EC* II.1255–56). Her foray into the Spanish camp provides *admiratio,* for this crossed-dressed figure now carries a gun (*EC* II.1642). Juan/a's meditation upon her liminal state, "no soy mujer, soy soldado" (I am not a woman but a soldier), parodies the use of military metaphors in love poetry (*EC* II.1661). After describing her difficult situation as "la guerra en mi pecho" (a war in my breast), she lays bare this conceit through exaggeration:

mi amor es el general,
capitanes mis deseos,
artilleros mis cuidados,
y aun centinelas mis celos

(*EC* II.1661–64)

(my love is the general; my desires, captains; my worries, gunners; and my jealousy, sentries)

Juan/a makes use of her masculine attire to enact the part of Fresia's outraged lover, sending a message via Mosquete that Diego must cease his pursuit of "esa dama [que] tiene dueño" (this woman who is already claimed) (*EC* II.1738). Where Ana Caro's Leonor/Leonardo disrupted her lover's pursuit of another woman by wooing that woman, thus demonstrating the ability to engage in active amorous pursuit, Juan/a violates a different component of the gender code by presenting herself as a source of physical violence.

Like Act II, the final act opens with a soliloquy in which Juan/a laments her personal situation, continues with an encounter in which an indigenous male character overhears his beloved speaking of her passion for a Spaniard, and moves forward with a scene in which Fresia asks Juan/a to carry a message to Diego—but it is Rengo rather than Tucapel who eavesdrops, and it is Gualeva's rather than Fresia's declaration that is heard. Just as Tucapel reminds Fresia that her people drink from the skulls of defeated Spanish enemies, Rengo condemns Gualeva's action as "infamia" (infamous) (*EC* III.1285) and describes her interest in a Christian as shameful: "¿A tan bajo pensamiento / te abates?" (How can you lower yourself like this?) (*EC* III.2196–97). Here, the parallel construction ends briefly, for, unlike Fresia, Gualeva does succeed in her attempt to deceive the indigenous suitor and calm his fury. (González de Bustos improves upon the traditional baroque motif of deception via truth-telling: Gualeva is unaware of the truth in her assertion that Rengo need not be jealous, because Juan is a woman in disguise!)

The parallel construction between the second and third act resumes when, once again, Fresia asks Juan/a to carry a message that goes against her true interests. In this message, the Araucanian woman offers Diego two choices: to marry her or to be killed by Caupolicán as revenge for the Spanish mistreatment of indigenous prisoners. Juan/a's ironic promise to fulfill this mission "como si a mí me importara" (as if it mattered greatly to me) points once again to González de Bustos's skilled handling of the baroque technique of deceptive honesty that is central both to the emplotment and to the atmosphere of *desengaño* found in the most successful canonical comic dramas (*EC* III.2363). Fresia's ironically self-confident assertion, "Cierto, que anduve discreta / en fiarle mi cuidado" (I knew I was right to entrust my cares to you) (*EC* III.2367–68), also emphasizes the baroque character of the comic portions of this drama: in plays ranging from *La verdad sospechosa* to *Don Gil de las calzas verdes,* characters are never more deceived than in the situations where they use the term "cierto" (certain). This series of scenes is central to the metadramatic component of the play, as González de Bustos combines exaggerated stagings of parallel scenes and highly familiar forms of baroque dramatic irony to provoke reflection upon the function of these comic clichés.

Another memorable example of a polyvalent deployment of generic norms involves the manner in which Rojas Zorrilla's and González de Bustos's protagonists are inscribed as heroes of chivalric romance. When Retógenes and Cipión first meet on the battlefield, the Numantian matches the Roman leader in producing formulaic expressions of mutual admiration and in adherence to the codes of chivalric warfare. Cipión urges Retógenes to flee in the face of an onslaught of Roman troops, so that the two might meet in a future battle: "que no te quiero vencer, / español, con tal ventaja" (I don't want to kill you, Spaniard, in such an unequal contest) (*NC* II.1500–1501). Later, when Cipión demonstrates his generosity by returning the kidnapped Florinda to Retógenes (and returns the ransom so that it can serve as part of her dowry), Retógenes labels the Roman a new Alexander (*NC* III.2365). As the first play in the diptych closes, Retógenes fulfills his obligation to Cipión by returning the favor the Roman had extended earlier, letting the general flee in order to avoid capture by enemy troops: "la vida me diste un día, / aquí la vida te vuelvo" (you once granted life to me; here, I give your life back to you) (*NC* III.2884–85). In these encounters, the dignity, valor, and morality of the two leaders reinforce the ideals of military chivalry. (Rackin argues, however, that in historical drama, the evocation of an outdated literary genre linked to an era perceived as gilded but irretrievable also emphasizes the shortcomings of the contemporary moment.)

In *Los españoles en Chile,* one complex episode provides further generic polyphony yet illustrates the problematic role of a literary discourse's role in early modern society. The scenes in which characters display archaic chivalric ideals highlight the conflict between individual honor, as prescribed by chivalric codes, and public honor, which requires the sacrifice of personal goals in order to serve the king's needs. Tucapel's challenge to Diego over Fresia brings this issue to the fore. Although the Marquis orders Diego to ignore the challenge and to save his sword for the defense of the plaza, Mendoza rather paradoxically decides to fight the duel in Diego's name: "yo tomaré a mi cargo / su despique" (I will take up your affront) (*EC* II.1616–17). It is difficult to see the logic in this decision, for surely the life and health of Mendoza is as important as Diego's to the conquest of Chile. Here, the Marquis's participation in the duel on Diego's behalf puts him in the very position he advised Diego to avoid. By valuing personal honor rather than duty to the king, this scene undermines the idealized portrait of a model colonial leader established earlier. The Marquis himself gives voice to the legitimate criticism that this act could provoke: "diránme que no es cordura / el que yo salga" (it could be said that it is not rational for me to do this) (*EC* II.1865–66). González de Bustos fully exploits the dramatic possibilities of this situation, for the Marquis and Diego both arrive at the duel site claiming to be the man Tucapel challenged. In the end, Tucapel designates which of the two he believes to be Diego (*EC* II.1984). Because Tucapel chooses correctly, the Marquis must leave the field, vowing revenge for Diego's violation of the command he issued and for prizing personal honor above loyalty to his general: "me ha de pagar, ¡Vive Dios! / haber quebrantado el bando, / y no haber guardado el orden" (By God, he will pay for having disobeyed and not followed the order) (*EC* II.2019–21).

When a real battle actually erupts, Tucapel and Diego do give priority to national interests, agreeing to suspend the duel "hasta mejor ocasión" (for a more appropriate time) (*EC* II.2057). Tucapel later informs the imprisoned Diego that the Spaniard will be killed that day as Caupolicán's vengeance for Spanish mistreatment of indigenous prisoners, but Diego expects the Araucanian to address the personal debt owed to Diego rather than loyalty to his people:

> ¿Y es
> de pechos agradecidos
> cuando estáis de mí obligado,
> ser quien me traigas tu mismo
> la sentencia de mi muerte?
>
> (*EC* III.2593–97)

(What kind of gratitude is this, that the one who owes me a debt of honor brings me my death sentence?)

Tucapel is indeed sensitive to the dilemma and seeks diligently to identify a mode of action that will allow him to fulfill both of his obligations. He resolves to free Diego, in order to show proper gratitude, but then to kill him in a fair duel, so that the Spaniard will not endanger Arauco: "aunque a Arauco le quito / esta venganza, ¿qué importa, / si le he de dar yo mismo?" (Although I take this vengeance from Arauco, what does it matter, since I take vengeance myself?) (*EC* III.2636–38).

Tucapel's ultimate failure to defeat Diego and to reconcile personal and national goals plays a role in the downfall of the Araucanians. This episode may thus be viewed as a condemnation of the conflicts between military priorities and aristocratic privileges that were perceived as undermining imperial endeavors (Puddu, *Soldado gentilhombre*, 148, 162). Here, as in *Don Quijote*, the incorporation of chivalric situations emphasizes the negative effects of this archaic genre for early modern life and audiences. The intertextuality presents an additional level of "meta-art," as González de Bustos, like Cervantes, constructs an "anatomy"—examining within the space of a single three-act play the artistry and ideology of a wide variety of ancient and post-classical genres.[16]

Both of the late baroque writers utilize farce as still another weapon in their counter-epic arsenal. Juxtaposing plebian characters and heroic concerns violates both aesthetic notions of decorum and ideological ideals of heroism. The representation of the Numantian plebian couple, Tronco and Olalla, is highly complex and produces ideological polyphony by mixing farcical slapstick conventions with aristocratic social motifs. In their first appearance near the end of Act I of *Numancia cercada,* Tronco and Olalla immediately launch into a metafictive parody of courtly love conventions. When Tronco invokes his right to dominate and punish his wife, Olalla grants this privilege to "los maridos cortesanos / y discretos" (honorable courtier husbands) but not to "hombres ingeridos / en asnos como sois vos" (beastly men like you) (*NC* I.636–37, 646–47). The dispute over which member of the couple has the right to address the noblemen with whom they wish to share the discovery of the inscribed tablet continues unabated after the entrance of Megara and Aluro. Olalla ignores three direct commands from Aluro to be silent and let her husband speak (*NC* I.688, 703, 721). This farcical representation of Olalla's rejection of class and gender power dynamics can be seen as a critique of the hierarchical and patriarchal value system that grounds military enterprise.

---

16. James A. Parr, *Don Quixote: An Anatomy of Subversive Discourse* (Newark, Del.: Juan de la Cuesta, 1988), xv.

Tronco's next appearance undermines epic discourse in a different fashion. Here, Rojas Zorrilla reinscribes the stock figure of the lower-class servant who questions heroism through the redefinition of physical cowardice as prudent self-preservation. Tronco enters, dressed in armor, announcing that he is ready to go off "a matar hombres / de estos romanillos viles" (to kill those vile little Roman men) (*NC* II.1205–6). Tronco's willingness to serve may reflect the ever-growing corps of professional but nonaristocratic soldiers and affirm their contributions, which do not register in the conventional epic scale of accomplishments (Puddu, *Soldado gentilhombre*, 11).

When Tronco returns to the Numantian camp, he plans to disguise himself and to present news of his own death in order to test Olalla's fidelity. The *examen* (test) of an actual or potential spouse—a literary commonplace normally deployed in conjunction with aristocratic characters—serves here as yet another potential rupture of the social order, like Tronco's decision to fight the Romans. The possibilities of generic and ideological discord, however, are not carried through. Instead, this scene evolves in a standard way: Olalla, who recognizes her disguised husband, feigns willingness to marry the messenger who brought news of her husband's death and thus provokes a typical farcical argument.

In the final act of *Numancia cercada*, Tronco openly questions social hierarchies, deciding that he will invade the Roman camp alone and try to kill Cipión, "porque se diga / que en España aun los villanos / tienen valor, tienen manos, / y que el honor les obliga (so that it can be said that in Spain, even the commoners have courage, have hands, and live up to their honor) (*NC* III.2460–63). His aspiration to a higher level of existence is further demonstrated as Tronco explains, "quiero morir / con fama" (I want to die with glory) (*NC* III.2477–78). Although Tronco chooses the wrong tent and kills the Roman prefect rather than Cipión, his success in entering the camp, killing a prominent leader, and escaping detection and capture mark him as both brave and clever, blurring the boundary that separates him from the Numantian leaders.

The first five acts of the Rojas Zorrilla diptych, while incorporating the essential plot elements of the Cervantine *Numancia*, deviate significantly from that model by marginalizing combat activity and concerns and exploring the effects of war upon the private lives of military leaders and ordinary citizens alike in a multi-generic fashion. These acts question militaristic and hierarchical ideologies as they stage a peasant who is both ridiculously henpecked yet also valiant and effective in combat and as they reduce warfare to a source of *agon* for comic representations of the obstacles to aristocratic courtship and marriage.

The majority of the diptych's final act returns to the Cervantine model of counter-epic dramatic inscription of historical events analyzed in Chapter 4. The one truly innovative moment of the last act of *Numancia destruida* reinscribes, as farce, the tragic Cervantine scene in which Marandro sacrifices his life raiding the Roman camp in order to bring back food for the starving Lira. Here it is the *gracioso*, Tronco, who has taken bread from a Roman soldier, although he is not mortally wounded. When he returns, Olalla asks him to share his bounty, pleading for just a mouthful "que estoy preñada y aquí / malpariré" (because I'm pregnant and fear a miscarriage) (*ND* III.2030–31). The addition of pregnancy to the pathos of the Cervantine characters' suffering is completely at odds with Tronco's refusal to share his food, which he grounds in a parody of neo-Platonic and mystic conventions concerning the idea of living through the beloved. He urges her, "pues tenís mi vida allá, / no os dé pena, muérase" (because you hold my life, don't worry, go ahead and die) (*ND* III.2101–2; MacCurdy, *Numancia*, xxiii). Here, Rojas Zorrilla interrupts the flow of tragic action in the third act to rewrite one of the most touching moments of the Cervantine tragedy—one that highlighted the ultimate nobility of human love and altruism—as a shockingly brutal demonstration of the dehumanizing effects of war's deprivations. Tronco's degeneration, which repeats and magnifies stereotypical *gracioso* greed and gluttony, is particularly unexpected because, in the previous five acts, this plebian character nullified many negative traits conventionally associated with lower-class characters. Here, the play reveals that the survival instinct, brought to the forefront in wartime, overwhelms the restraints of civilization.

Farcical episodes are deployed in *Los españoles en Chile* both to displace true battle narrative and to question epic values. Mosquete combines the comic braggadocio of the *miles gloriosus* with an underlying critique (similar to Ercilla's) of Spain's use of superior military technology as he informs his two captors, "hoy he muerto por mis manos / veinte carros de araucanos" (Today I have killed twenty carts of Araucanians with my own hands) (*EC* I.404–5). After the first battle, Mosquete fabricates for Diego a tale of intense participation in the bloody skirmish: "nos vimos / bebiendo la muerte a tragos" (we were gulping down blood) (*EC* II.1369–70). Elaborating upon the imaginary mistreatment of one victim, he adds, "de un bigote / en un arbol le colgué" (I hung him from a tree by his moustache) (*EC* II.1381–82). Even though these particular events occur only in

Mosquete's imagination, they serve as evocations of actual battle excesses and thus as reminders of the horrors of war. Mosquete again emphasizes imperial cruelty in the farcical prison scene that contrasts Diego's heroic, stoic suffering with Mosquete's worries about his empty belly and imminent death. The servant's comic admission of military impotence simultaneously presents a serious scrutiny of imperialism, for he argues that it should be easier for his master to accept his fate, because Diego has earned indigenous enmity, while he has not:

> que te empalaran a tí,
> vaya que derecho o tuerto,
> mil araucanos has muerto;
> mas que me impalen a mí . . .
> . . . . . . . . . .
> que no haya muerto de horquilla
>
> (*EC* III.2503–19)

(Let them impale you, for you have killed a thousand Araucanians, in every way possible, but don't let them kill me, for I have not strung up anyone.)

This passage highlights the fact that Mosquete's chief characteristic, like that of many *graciosos,* is his sensible self-preservation in dangerous situations, a trait that is depicted as cowardice in standard epic contexts. The Infantes of Carrión portrayed in Quevedo's burlesque rendition of the Cid's encounter with a lion defend their flight from the beast as practical rather than fearful (see Chapter 6); similarly, Mosquete claims that his retreat was "escrupuloso" (prudent) (*EC* I.944). These scenes also establish parallels with Sancho Panza, whose preference for saving his skin rather than seeking glory is an important element of *Don Quijote*'s questioning of chivalric ideals.

Mosquete's humorous dialogues also interrogate hegemonic notions of social hierarchy. He combines amusing self-deprecation with an ideological reversal of the discourse that questions the humanity of indigenous peoples, describing himself through bestial vocabulary as he declares, "soy la peor bestia" (I am the lowest beast), and "tengo hambre canina" (I'm as hungry as a wolf) (*EC* I.447, 451). The servant attributes these less-than-human attributes to his social order: "huelo de ochenta leguas / a hombre bajo" (from a mile away, I smell like a plebian) (*EC* I.454–55). Nonetheless, the delineation of likenesses among native peoples and European commoners reveals to the audience the similarities among the forms of discursive oppression operating in a hierarchical society and questions the harsh treatment of Amerindian workers. In addition, by placing stock dramatic clichés criticizing the gluttony and greed of lower-class characters into the mouth of Mosquete himself rather than that of his master, González de Bustos provides yet another moment of self-conscious dramaturgy. When the *gracioso* accedes to Juan/a's demand that Mosquete convey a threat from "him" to Diego rather than carrying amorous messages between Diego and Fresia, he explains his humiliation as "esto y mucho más merezco / por alcahuete" (I deserve this and more for acting as a go-between) (*EC* II.1748–49). By naming himself a pimp in the tradition of the lower-class characters in *La Celestina,* Mosquete once again confirms his own lack of status. This terminology, however, also reduces the status of his master, who had inscribed himself as an idealized lover through the deployment of more elevated poetic genres. This meta-artistic reinscription on Mosquete's part recalls the deflation of noble characters found in burlesque counter-epic texts, where idealized poetic discourses are revealed to be mere "window dressing" used to fulfill sexual desire.

When Tucapel comes to the prison to liberate Diego, who has already been freed by Juan/a, Mosquete pretends to be his master in order to escape confinement. Here, Mosquete, like Clarín in *La vida es sueño*, assumes an identity that is difficult to maintain. He attempts to avoid resuming the interrupted duel by employing chivalric discourse appropriate to his master's station: he tells Tucapel, "no he de reñir con quien / me ha dado la vida" (I must not fight the one who has given me life) (*EC* III.3026–27). As Tucapel presses the issue, however, Mosquete's excuse becomes vulgar: "no tengo ganas" (I don't feel like it) (*EC* III.3029). Upon hearing that Tucapel wishes to carry Diego's head to Fresia as a trophy, Mosquete completely abandons any pretense of aristocratic discourse: "usted llevará una alhaja / muy vacia, porque son / mis cascos de calabaza" (you would carry an empty noggin, for I have a pumpkin for a skull) (III. 3039–41). Unlike Clarín, Mosquete does not pay for this transgressive usurpation of a false identity with his life, for Tucapel is once more called away from personal pursuits by the ensuing battle.

In *Los españoles en Chile,* the laying bare of the tricks of dramatic convention is so prevalent that it merits sustained attention. In the third act, this aesthetic element is particularly central to a materialist analysis. The proliferating scenes of disguised identity are an important metadramaturgical component of the play, as they foreground through excess the ubiquity of this convention as a cornerstone of comic emplotment.[17] Both men and women disguise their true identity for a variety of purposes. In addition to the Marquis's and Mosquete's impersonations of Diego, Caupolicán presents himself as an ordinary indigenous soldier in order to see the new Spanish leader for himself. Juan/a's alternate identities include not only a Spanish soldier, as she pursues Diego, and a Spanish woman pretending to be a soldier to alleviate Rengo's jealousy (a costume that, ironically, presents her true self), but also a guard who cannot remember the password of the day (so that her brother will not come close enough to recognize her) and finally, a *mestiza* woman garbed in native fashion in order to carry a message from Fresia to Diego. This final disguise is accompanied by an ironic stage direction that Juan/a appears "lo más disfrazada que pueda" (as heavily disguised as possible), perhaps as a mockery of the dramatic conventions requiring that characters do not recognize intimate acquaintances when disguised and are not aware of physical discrepancies during instances of gender cross-dressing. The subsequent dialogue confirms the metadramatic and parodic intent: Juan/a insists that Diego's fear of death must be the source of "este engaño" (this deception), while Diego wonders, "¿yo engañarme puedo, / si las señas que averiguo / me afirman *todos* que es ella?" (can I be mistaken, when *every* attribute tells me that this is she?) (*EC* III.2729–31, emphasis added). Diego's acceptance of the disguise is based on the most flimsy, superficial aspect of physical appearance, her attire: "el mayor testigo / de que no es ella, es mirarla / en un traje tan indigno" (the best indicator that this is not she is to see her dressed in such lowly garb) (*EC* III.2743–45). His confident declaration, "estoy corrido / de imaginar que ella fuese" (I was wrong to think it could have been she) (*EC* III.2758–59), in conjunction with all the other examples of disguised identity in this drama, serves to rupture the "willing suspension of disbelief" essential to the conventional enjoyment of theatrical performance, providing instead an alternate aesthetic experience in which pleasure is derived from sharing the "insider" perspective of the work's creator. The widespread manifestations of meta-artistry in all forms of seventeenth-century Spanish literature can be seen as a testament to its popularity and as an affirmation of that particular form of aesthetic *jouissance*.

The repetition of plot elements in the first three scenes of the final two acts, staged with the subtle yet significant variations described above, is an

---

17. See Abraham's introduction to *Los españoles en Chile*.

additional metadramatic technique that reveals through exaggeration the effects produced by parallel construction. Here, the military dimensions of the drama nearly disappear as the play leads the spectator to meditate upon the conventions of comic dramaturgy. At the same time, though, the technique can draw the audience back into the world of epic and tragic dramatic conventions, for another form of parallel construction—alternating scenes at the camps of the imperial forces and their victims—is a constant in stagings of Numancia and Arauco materials. The spectator who has noticed other thematic references to the earlier plays might also take note of this stylistic similarity. These scenes, finally, lay bare the primary aesthetic basis of all dramatic *refundición*, a form of parallel construction in which a play engages in dialogue with earlier treatments of the same subject. By highlighting the practice of dramatic reinscription, the play invites the audience to compare its treatment of imperialist material with previous renditions of the topic. *Los españoles en Chile* expands significantly upon the historical awareness demonstrated by the characters in the other four plays, and González de Bustos moves to a deeper level of metahistoriography through his scrutiny of the process of inscription and reinscription. Consideration of historiography thus replaces the evaluation of actual military affairs—a situation that may mirror the events of the time when this work was written. By 1665, all of the major European initiatives had ended in failure and Arauco remained unconquered. With little hope for significant military action under Carlos II, all that remained for imperial discourses was discussion of past events, mediated through the multiple inscriptions of the battles of the previous century.

The final five hundred lines of the play shift attention to a self-conscious staging of the conventions of dramatic closure, in which *anagnorisis*, heroic military victory, Christian conversion, honor tragedy, mass marriage, and farce vie for attention. Diego's reawakened love for Juan/a occurs as he examines his conscience in preparation for death, and it is presented as a tardy and therefore tragic recognition of an error: "¡Ay doña Juana, qué tarde / se acuerda de ti mi olvido!" (Oh, Juana, how tardily I remember my love for you) (*EC* III.2687–88). Soon after, Caupolicán meets defeat with his own moment of *anagnorisis* and lamented hubris over his mistreatment of the priest, Colocolo: "todas estas desdichas / por no creerte me asaltan" (I have brought all these miseries upon myself by not believing you) (*EC* III.3073–74). In a brief victory scene, the Marquis rejoices, "al cielo le doy gracias / de tan feliz victoria. / Gran día le ha dado España" (I thank heaven for this wonderful victory. God has honored Spain greatly today)

(*EC* III.3108–10). Then, as Tucapel and the indigenous survivors request conversion, the European Christian fantasy of benevolent conquest is briefly fulfilled. Mendoza once again is staged as the perfect royal representative here, granting pardon to the Araucanians but minimizing his power over them by extending this forgiveness

> en el nombre del rey
> . . . . . . .
> en quien, sobre su poder
> siempre la piedad se halla
>
> (*EC* III.3135–39)
>
> (in the name of the King, whose power is always mitigated by mercy)

This scene does contain all the attributes of a fawning *obra de encargo* as it lionizes a viceroy who is effective in battle, generous with defeated enemies, restrained in his deployment of power, and loyal to his monarch, but the minimal role assigned to the Marquis and the war effort limits the impact of the few hagiographic scenes. More important, the political reconciliation does not close the play; it is immediately followed by potential personal tragedy in the style of the *drama de honor*. Pedro enters brandishing a dagger and threatening to kill his sister, Juana, to restore the family's honor (*EC* III.3140–42). In the closing lines, the Marquis is reduced to a puppet who approves the solutions proposed by other characters: Diego recognizes his debt to Juana, then renounces his claim to Fresia and grants her to Tucapel. In a final instance of innovative gender dynamics, Juana claims the right, as a former rival, to bestow Gualeva to Rengo. Mosquete, like many comic *graciosos*, laments that he alone lacks a spouse: "¿Falta una china / con quien darme la pedrada?" (Isn't there anyone I can be hooked up with?) (*EC* III.3198–99). This complaint can be seen as yet another element of metadrama, as it emphasizes the convention of multiple marriages as a vehicle for staging all-encompassing reconciliation.

The Marquis's final exhortation that everyone follow him to church closes the play on a note of religious and ideological harmony. The polyphony of genres in the final scenes and the profusion of different forms of reconciliation, however, undercut the play's celebration of Spanish conquest. Through its ideologically complex, self-conscious, "anatomic" exploration of historical and dramatic inscription, González de Bustos's *Los españoles en*

*Chile* goes far beyond a sycophantic glorification of the Hurtado de Mendoza family. This late baroque history play constitutes an experiment in dramatic, historical, and epic writing, exploring, like the *nouveau roman*, the potentials and limits and minimum essences of each genre as a transmitter of the era's most engaging aesthetic and ideological issues.

In the novelistic history plays of Rojas Zorrilla and González de Bustos, generic juxtapositions marginalize the epic dimension of military-centered narratives and provide both aesthetic and ideological innovation. These works incorporate the profusion of genres and exaggerated deployments of Golden Age literary conventions typical of the less popular late baroque style as well as meditations on the process of historical inscription, and they serve to mediate the conflicting discourses concerning militant imperialism that circulated in the waning years of aggressive Spanish empire building.

## "War and Lechery"

*La gatomaquia* and the Burlesque Epic

According to Gregory Colomb, the parody of epic literary conventions functions as "propaganda" for discrediting aristocratic privilege, which is often grounded in the glorification of military heroism associated with epic literature (*Designs on Truth*, xv). Although Colomb's remarks refer to Augustan English mock-heroic literature, his observation is relevant to a "sociology of genres" approach to the early modern Spanish burlesque epic (Bennett, *Outside Literature*, 112). This chapter will analyze the burlesque epic as a specific form of counter-epic poetics characterized by the combination of an aesthetic strategy—the parody of epic conventions—and ideological commentary expressed as deprecatory representations of military heroism and battles. Here, I will focus on Quevedo's short poems, "Imitación de Virgilio en lo que Dido dijo a Eneas queriendo dejarla" ("What Dido Said to Aeneas as He Abandoned Her, in the Style of Virgil") and "Pavura de los condes de Carrión" ("The Cowardly Counts of Carrión"), and Lope de Vega's full-length epic, *La gatomaquia (The Battle of the Cats)*. Launching a sustained critique of heroic discourses deployed by an aristocracy whose role in the military arena is waning, these works combine deflationary descriptions of iconic epic figures with metafictive commentaries on the limitations of idealizing texts. They all convey the notion that the emergent sense of a chasm between "les mots et les choses" is linked to the lack of correspondence between medieval heroic ideals and the material achievements of the early modern aristocratic class, a class that continued to deploy epic discourse as the justification for its power and privilege despite its decreasing military participation and despite skepticism about the value of imperialist warfare. These counter-generic texts also provide one form of discursive mediation concerning the aristocracy's role in a post-feudal world, serving as a potentially oppositional discourse through the critique of aristocrats' use of epic values in order to maintain their dominant position in the hierarchies of power.

## Parody and Burlesque Poetics

Linda Hutcheon draws upon Victor Šklovsky's work to define parody as a mode that lays bare "the essential conventionality of literary form."[1] While Hutcheon focuses on postmodern forms of parody, her observations are also relevant for early modern burlesque texts. Although she incorrectly characterizes earlier forms of parody as lacking in "distantiation" and as offering a primarily "nostalgic" perspective, her view of parody as "a model for the process of transfer and reorganization of the past" is useful for examining Lope's and Quevedo's parodic poetics (4–10). Hutcheon astutely identifies the paradox at the heart of parodic (and burlesque) writing: "Even in mocking, parody reinforces; in formal terms, it inscribes the mocked conventions onto itself, thereby guaranteeing their continued existence" (75). This paradox has both aesthetic and ideological ramifications, for parody not only revives outdated genres but also gives new strength to waning belief systems. Hutcheon points out that for contemporary audiences, parody elicits critical denigration as an "overcoded discourse" (ibid.). This observation may help explain the relative marginality of parodic or burlesque epic within current canons of early modern masterworks.

Parody occupies a unique place within Renaissance poetics, for literary theorists and writers alike devoted considerable attention to the norms and techniques of *imitatio*—the rewriting of classical models. Robert Ball argues that such imitations are marked by "conflicting pressures of filial piety and

---

1. Linda Hutcheon, *A Theory of Parody: The Teachings of Twentieth-Century Art Forms* (New York: Methuen, 1985), 3; Victor Šklovsky, "Sterne's *Tristram Shandy:* Stylistic Commentary," in *Russian Formalist Criticism: Four Essays*, ed. Lee T. Lemon and Marion J. Reiss (Lincoln: University of Nebraska Press), 30–31.

Oedipal defiance."[2] Clearly, parody provides a form of rewriting in which defiance is maximized and filial respect plays a more limited role. Although parody of epic forms was common throughout western Europe, the humorous and irreverent tone violated the period's norms of literary decorum. Parodic epics were thus excluded from the canon of contemporary works that received respect and attention in early modern theoretical treatises.

The analysis of generic function in this chapter is grounded in the "sociology of genres" described by Tony Bennett, who asserts that the task of genre study is not to define genres but rather "to examine the composition and functioning of generic systems" in order to trace the boundaries that separate these systems in terms of the close relationship between aesthetic practices and related social discourses (*Outside Literature*, 105, 112). Alastair Fowler's concepts of "mode" and "modal transformations" are also helpful for the study of epic characteristics in other literary forms. He defines a mode as a selection of a group of features from an earlier genre (Fowler prefers the term "kind" in order to distinguish his construct from mere pigeonholing). A mode, however, presents "an incomplete repertoire, a selection only of the corresponding kind's features, and one from which overall external structure is absent" (*Kinds of Literature*, 107). Fowler writes that a mode is often the final stage of a genre's development; after the genre has been "played out," certain of its characteristics "may remain lively . . . being able to enter into new commixtures and to continue in combination with kinds still evolving" (167). Quevedo's sonnets exemplify a modal deployment of the epic. Michael Murrin and Mary Barnard note that counter-genres, like parodies, actually prolong the life of exhausted genres by giving them a sort of "afterlife."[3] Thus, the counter-genre may function as a source of conservative nostalgia as well as opposition.

The texts under consideration in this chapter have not been widely studied and do not play a prominent role in literary canons, either for the epic as a genre or for Spanish literary histories. David Quint attributes the comparative neglect of one form of counter-text, the epic of the losers, to its "indefinite generic status" at the margins of epic, even though one early modern literary theorist, Pinciano, approvingly described *all* epic poetry as

2. Robert F. Ball, "Poetic Imitation in Góngora's *Romance de Angélica y Medoro*," *Bulletin of Hispanic Studies* 57 (1980): 33.

3. Michael Murrin, *History and Warfare in Renaissance Epic* (Chicago: University of Chicago Press, 1994), 16; Mary E. Barnard, "Myth in Quevedo: The Serious and the Burlesque in the Apollo and Daphne Poems," *Hispanic Review* 52, no. 4 (1984): 509.

encyclopedic—that is to say, of indeterminate generic status.[4] Despite the many defenses of generic hybridity that appeared during this period, however, generic indeterminacy often produces a sense of instability that even postmodern critics of early modern texts seem reluctant to confront. Diana Conchado identifies a similar scholarly marginalization of burlesque epics, such as *La gatomaquia*, which are considered not only indeterminate but also derivative or subgeneric ("Género y poética," 174). She also notes that the parodic injection of levity into a sacrosanct genre elicits critical contempt. Conchado points out that critics of the burlesque epic focus on the limits rather than the possibilities of tertiary genres. The current marginalization of the burlesque epic as a parodic counter-genre may arise from the residual influence of the Romantics, who glorified artistic originality (even though post-structuralism's emphasis on the unavoidable intertextuality of all discourse has rendered this doctrine questionable).

Michael Murrin argues that the marginalization of martial heroism is not limited to counter-epic texts, for conventional English epics such as Spenser's *Fairie Queene*, Sydney's *Arcadia*, and even Drayton's *The Civile Wars* demonstrated a marked reduction in the narration of battle scenes. Murrin's *History and Warfare in Renaissance Epic* provides the most detailed examination to date of specific technological and tactical innovations of the fifteenth and sixteenth centuries. In his introduction, Murrin describes a pattern in which increasingly technologized military strategies and practices ceased to correspond in any way to the activities described in classical epic narratives. In addition, he links these changes—which eliminated the face-to-face encounter upon which epic glory depends—to a decrease in aristocratic military service and in poetic representations of heroism.

A related phenomenon is the disdain for the dominant class expressed in much early modern Spanish literature ranging from *Don Quijote* to the "peasant plays" of Lope de Vega and Calderón de la Barca, in which aristocrats suffer punishment at the hands of plebian villagers, to Antonio de Guevara's essay, "Menosprecio de corte y alabanza de aldea" ("Contempt for Court and Praise for Rural Life"). Conchado notes that in the context of changing material conditions and changing attitudes toward the aristocracy, the emergence of counter-epic forms is not surprising: "parece inevitable que una forma literaria tan vinculada al *status quo* también entre en crisis y tome otro rumbo" (it seems inevitable that a literary form so

---

4. Diana Conchado, "Género y poética en *La gatomaquia* de Lope de Vega" (Ph.D. diss., Brown University, 1994), 132; Quint, *Epic and Empire*.

strongly linked to the status quo would also enter a crisis period and take on other dimensions) ("Género y poética," 171).

I hope that the present work will enable scholars to view these countergeneric, burlesque epic works in a new light by offering a materialist poetics that amplifies their dialogue with other antiaristocratic texts and discourses. This study does not seek to be exhaustive; for example, Cervantes's *Viaje al Parnaso (Voyage to Parnassus)* will not be considered. (As Rachel Schmidt indicates, the burlesque battle among the poets serves primarily to explore the process of literary canonization for individual authors rather than the relationship between canonical genres and imperial activity.[5]) This chapter will focus on three representative texts in which burlesque epic poetics are used to mediate ideologies of imperialist practice.

Homer's *Battle of the Frogs and Mice* is considered the first example of literary parody and it is also the first burlesque epic. Linda Hutcheon agrees with Mikhail Bakhtin that classical Greek parody sought to deflate social discourses that misused epic to glorify warriors rather than combat itself.[6] The deflationary aspect of Homer's poem derives from the contrast between the unheroic characters—small animals—and the exalted style used to describe their military activities (Conchado, "Género y poética," 178). Lope de Vega employs this type of burlesque technique in *La gatomaquia*, his representation of the *Iliad* as a feline war. By contrast, Quevedo's short poems represent traditional epic figures engaged in undignified activities. Many contemporary critics, following the lead of neoclassical theorists who had been horrified by the vulgarity of burlesque texts and who received the mock heroic favorably for aesthetic reasons, consider these two parodic approaches to the epic as distinct genres because of the difference in tone.[7] I concur with Conchado, however: there is no significant difference in the ideological or aesthetic implications of the burlesque and the mock epic. The popularity of counter-epic parody in these different forms demonstrates the importance of their persistent questioning of heroic discourses that is central to early modern meditations on empire (190–91).

---

5. Rachel Schmidt, "Maps, Figures, and Canons in the *Viaje del Parnaso*," *Cervantes* 16, no. 2 (1996): 30–31.
6. Hutcheon, *Theory of Parody*, 77; M. M. Bakhtin, *The Dialogic Imagination: Four Essays*, ed. Michael Holquist and trans. Caryl Emerson and Michael Holquist (Austin: University of Texas Press, 1981), 52.
7. Ulrich Broich, *The Eighteenth-Century Mock-Heroic Poem*, trans. David Henry Wilson (Cambridge: Cambridge University Press, 1990), 11–12.

Conchado refers to a number of parodic epics of both types written in Spain during the late sixteenth and early seventeenth centuries (210–29). One noteworthy example is a miniature burlesque epic, a battle between cats and rats, that functions as an interpolated story within Luis Zapata's "straight" epic from 1560, *Carlos Famoso (Charles the Great)*. Conchado points out that Zapata's digression constitutes a deflation of the very text in which it appears (217). These forms of counter-epic share a "family resemblance" as they deploy literary parody and social satire to take aim at epic texts and the aristocratic value system those texts extol (see Fowler, *Kinds of Literature*, 40–44). Thus, I use "burlesque epic" to refer to all texts that parody epic literature's glorification of military achievements.

The term "burlesque" has a conflicted critical history. Quevedo labeled his poetry as burlesque *and* satiric—implying agreement with both seventeenth-century and contemporary critics who argue that burlesque entails parody and humor but not social criticism, which falls under the separate rubric of satire.[8] Lope, on the other hand, completely avoided traditional generic nomenclature. He described his story of warring cats as "gracioso" (amusing). As I have argued in an article on the function of the "problem comedy," the distinction between conventional and experimental humorous genres is meaningful because of the ideological differences in their deployment ("Dramatic and Discursive Genres," 192–95). And Northrop Frye has noted that traditional comedy conveys an optimistic sense of a world in which opposing forces are ultimately reconcilable. By contrast, the burlesque is a "dialogic" entity whose "double voiced" revisioning of an orthodox form is inherently skeptical of the status quo celebrated by that form (Hutcheon, *Theory of Parody*, 19; Cronk, "Défense du dialogisme," 335–37).

## QUEVEDO'S BURLESQUE EPICS

Francisco de Quevedo offers a compelling parody of epic conventions through his rewriting of one of Virgil's most famous episodes: the

---

8. Jean Rohu, "Le Burlesque et les avatars de l'écriture discordante (1635–1655)," and Nicholas Cronk, "La Défense du dialogisme: Vers une poétique du burlesque," both in *Burlesque et formes parodiques dans la littérature et les arts*, ed. Isabelle Landy-Houillon and Maurice Menard (Seattle: Papers on French Seventeenth-Century Literature, 1987), 349 and 324–28, respectively; William Woodhouse, "Hacia una terminología coherente para la poesía del Siglo de Oro," in *Actas del VIII Congreso*, ed. Kossoff et al., 750.

encounter between Aeneas and Dido. In the sonnet "Imitación de Virgilio en lo que Dido dijo a Eneas queriendo dejarla," Quevedo focuses on the demystification of the Trojan prince whose royal blood is the basis of Roman grandeur. The poem deflates Aeneas by emphasizing his youth and the pathetic circumstances of his first encounter with Dido as well as criticizing his dishonorable departure.

The queen addresses her lover in the diminutive form, as "Eneíllas," and describes him as a "pimpollo"—a sapling tree, and also a colloquial term for a "pretty boy" (l. 1). Dido compares Aeneas arriving on her shores to flotsam washed up on a beach, and she remembers him as a vagabond, near death from cold and hunger (ll. 5–6). His weak cries for help remind her of the peeping of a young chicken (ll. 7–8). These reductions of Aeneas stand in sharp contrast to the Roman poem, in which Virgil dedicates four lines to a description of his beauty as Dido sees him for the first time, the result of an "aura" that Venus had placed about her son so that he would make a favorable first impression upon the ruler of Carthage. Depicting Aeneas as a weakling rather than an emblematic Roman hero is particularly significant because of Spain's deployment of epic iconography (particularly in texts that address the Roman conquest of Numancia) to represent itself as the early modern inheritor of imperial Roman global hegemony.

The final two lines of Quevedo's sonnet assert that in seeking to reconstruct his father's flame-engulfed kingdom in Italy, Aeneas abandons Dido to the pain of the flames he awoke in her. This critique does not differ much from the lines given to Dido by Virgil, but here, the prince is given no voice with which to defend himself. This poem thus inverts pastoral poetry in which shepherds, in an endless parade, condemn the harsh treatment they receive from silent, absent "mujeres esquivas" (disdainful women).[9] Of course, there is a limit to how much can be expressed in a fourteen-line sonnet. Nonetheless, in light of the treatment of women in other burlesque epics, Quevedo's decision to target Aeneas rather than Dido is noteworthy. Here, the burlesque epic offers a counterpoint to its classical predecessors: Roman epic served as "a repository of culturally valued *exempla*," and Roman tutors used epic poetry to teach male students not only grammar, rhetoric, and oratory but also "Roman conventions of

---

9. Yvonne Jehenson, "The Pastoral Episode in *Don Quijote:* Marcela Once Again," *Cervantes* 10, no. 2 (1990): 17; Ruth El Saffar, "In Praise of What Is Left Unsaid: Thoughts on Women and Lack in *Don Quijote,*" *Modern Language Notes* 103, no. 2 (1988): 207.

manliness."[10] The burlesque epic overturns this tradition, representing a key icon for early modern European epic values as both unmanly and dishonorable.

Quevedo's "Pavura de los condes de Carrión" departs from the burlesque epic norm in that its *hypotexte* is the Spanish national epic, *Cantar del mío Cid (Song of the Cid)*, rather than a classical pagan epic. The early modern *hypertexte* targets all of the characters in the poem as objects of degradation. Even the Cid receives less-than-respectful treatment. In the opening lines of "Pavura," Spain's national hero is taking his afternoon siesta. The monumental figure at rest is described as "boquiabierto" (with his mouth hanging open), "roncando como una vaca" (snoring like an ox). Members of his entourage stand by to brush flies from his neck; rather than the elegant "cuello," the term "pescuezo," which signifies the scruff of an animal, is used to designate the hero's neck (l. 12). When the Cid awakens, he must rub his eyes to clean them, for they are "empedrados de lagañas" (crusted over with dried mucus) (l. 48). The ostensible hero is demystified through this emphasis on the unattractive elements of human corporeality.

Quevedo's poem revises the famous episode in which a lion appears during this period of slumber, and it greatly expands the narration of the unheroic reactions of the Infantes of Carrión, the Cid's two sons-in-law. Where the original epic text dedicated a mere 6 lines to their cowardice, Quevedo provides 160, embellishing the tale through a multisensory extravaganza of vulgarity. Surely this representation of all the grotesque physical consequences of cowardice produces a much stronger negative impression than the original poem. Particularly in an age of mercenaries and chivalric jousts with shielded lances, the failure to demonstrate physical valor signifies not merely a defect in isolated individuals from a rival province and from a challenged social "estado," as was the case in the medieval version,[11] but also a critique of the new and supposedly inferior genus of early modern courtier nobility.

As the poem opens, the entering lion ignores the Infantes because he thinks they are corpses, due to the bodily odor their fear has produced (ll. 25–28). Descriptions of the retreat and subsequent humiliation of the younger son emphasize the grotesque and childlike dimension of the physical

10. Alison M. Keith, *Engendering Rome: Women in Latin Epic* (Cambridge: Cambridge University Press, 2000), 10–11.
11. Michael Harney, "Class Conflict and Primitive Rebellion in the *Poema de mio Cid*," *Olifant: A Publication of the Société Roncesvals, American-Canadian Branch* 12, no. 3–4 (1987): 171–72.

indignities produced by hiding from an enemy. Fernán's posture in his hiding place is described through sewing metaphors: he is "devanado" (wound up) and "hecho ovillo" (like a skein) (ll. 63–64). The Cid and his followers identify his hiding spot by the "vapores" (odors) that rise to their noses, because terror has caused Fernán's "yantares" (guts) to go straight to his "ancas" (rump) (ll. 79–80). A masterly play on words concludes this section as Fernán is advised to brandish Tizona, the famous sword given to him by his father-in-law, in order to protect himself; a colloquial meaning of *tizón* is "stain," which in this context reminds the reader of Fernán's inability to control his bowels (ll. 81–84).

Gross physiological references multiply in the next section of the poem, for the elder brother takes refuge in the latrine pit. The squire who drags Diego back does so with one hand, while the other is used to hold his nose. The detritus that clings to him is "bascas"—nauseatingly odiferous (l. 88). The Cid uses another scatological metaphor in asserting that the Infantes have now shown their true selves: "descubierto habéis la caca" (they have revealed their excrement) (l. 112). He employs antithesis and *conceptismo* in addition to physical imagery in pointing out that while danger strengthens the worthy knight, "face . . . de las tripas corazón" (creates heart out of guts), it has weakened these inferior courtiers as it "facéis del corazón tripas" (reduces their hearts to guts) (ll. 123, 127). The name of the sword, Colada, is also employed as an insulting pun as the Cid tells Diego to clean himself: "Echaos, buen conde, en colada" (Clean yourself up, Count) (l. 132).

Diego's defense of his action directly criticizes the conventional heroic ethic. He asserts,

> Si non fice valentía,
> fice cosa necesaria
> . . . . . . . . .
> Más ánimo es menester
> para echarse en la privada,
> que para vencer a Búcar,
> ni a mil leones que salgan
>
> (ll. 139–45)

> (If what I did was not brave, it was necessary. . . . More courage is needed to throw oneself in a privy than to conquer Bucar or a thousand stalking lions.)

This redefinition of bravery foregrounds the growing gap between courtiers and warriors that was denounced in *menosprecio de corte* writings of all genres.

The conclusion of Quevedo's poem does not validate Diego's argument; it concludes with the Cid continuing to chastise his sons-in-law. The burlesque tone of the entire poem, however, with its emphasis on the gross physical bodies of the hero and of the traditional antagonists, demystifies medieval aristocratic and heroic discourse for the seventeenth-century reader. Diego's rationalization of the pragmatic quality of his escape further highlights the chasm between the epic ideals of a bygone era and the realities of contemporary early modern military circumstance. As we have seen, this connection between technological advancement and the decline of knightly skill and valor is also underscored in the Numantian response to Scipio's military strategies in Cervantes's and Rojas Zorrilla's dramatizations of the siege of Numancia.

### Feline Combat

*La gatomaquia* is Lope de Vega's parodic revision of a Greek epic, the *Iliad*. This poem offers a significant departure from the Homeric *hypotexte* in that two of the three members of the love triangle are—or pretend to be— unfaithful lovers. Like the late baroque dramas of Rojas Zorrilla and González de Bustos, the first four *silvas* owe nearly as much to the Renaissance chivalric epic as to the classical Athenian epic. The narrator contributes to that impression by comparing the lovers to Angelica and Orlando as well as to Helen and Paris (*G* III, 43; IV, 50; IV, 51; VI, 64; VI, 66).[12] Zapaquilda, the Helen figure, is being courted by Marramaquiz as the first *silva* opens. Her interest shifts when a new male, Mizifuf, arrives on the scene, but by the end of the first *silva* Zapaquilda has succumbed to Marramaquiz's jealous remonstrances and promises "te guardo la fe como tu esposa" (I pledge my faith to you as a wife) (*G* I, 14). In the beginning of *Silva* II, however, she is waiting for word from Mizifuf and accepts the note and food he sends her via a page. Marramaquiz, who has observed this interchange, accepts the advice of a friend that he pretend to be interested in Mizilda to arouse Zapaquilda's jealousy. He does so successfully, and the *silva* ends with a literal catfight between the two females. In the third *silva*, Zapaquilda's

---

12. Arabic numerals refer to the page numbers in the Ibáñez edition of *La gatomaquia*; Roman numerals indicate the *silva*.

interest shifts again to Mizifuf, and from this point on, Zapaquilda remains loyal to him. In the fourth *silva*, a marriage contract is signed; Zapaquilda is kidnapped by Marramaquiz on her way to the altar in the fifth *silva;* she is "más dura que marmol" (harder than marble) during the remaining two *silvas* in which she is Marramaquiz's prisoner (*G* VI, 70). (Here, the narrator's observation that Marramaquiz had read Garcilaso's *Eglogas* limits readerly sympathy for the rejected suitor's plight.) The mixture of classical and chivalric plot events in the first four *silvas*—infidelity, jealousy, and emblematic loyalty—is a key component in *La gatomaquia*'s deflation of epic grandeur.

In *La gatomaquia*, although martial aristocracy is a significant object of mockery, much of Lope's critique of aristocratic behavior is aimed at the female characters. One prominent demystificatory strategy of early modern burlesque epic texts, including Scarron's *Virgile travesti* and Shakespeare's *Troilus and Cressida* as well as *La gatomaquia,* is an emphasis on the grotesque nature of bodily functions. In these works, the female characters' morals and physical bodies are most often the primary targets of deforming scrutiny, because they are identified as the cause of a temporary rupture in the patriarchal order. The thematic and linguistic prominence of negative representations of women significantly revises the original texts that these works parody. Alison Keith's study of women in classical epic, *Engendering Rome,* identifies pervasive misogyny in epic depictions of women as fickle, weak, and driven by their passions, or as dehumanized figures of fertility (26–28, 36–40). The burlesque epic amplifies and alters misogynist discourse by scapegoating women and deforming the desirable female body. This denigration of the feminine serves multiple purposes directly related to early modern Spanish negotiations of hierarchies of gender as well as *estado* (caste).[13]

Lope's narrative of a war caused by the kidnapping of a female (cat) makes a major departure from the Greco-Trojan triangle: the "lady" was originally engaged to the Paris figure before jilting him to marry another. Thus when the "heroine," Zapaquilda, first takes note of the new suitor, Mizifuf, the narrator accuses the female sex as a whole of fickleness:

> Siempre las novedades son gustosas:
> No hay que fiar de gatas melindrosas. . . .
> ¿En qué mujer habrá firmeza alguna?

---

13. Amy Williamsen, "Death Becomes Her: Fatal Beauty in María de Zayas's 'Mal presagio casar lejos,'" *Romance Language Annual* 6 (1994): 622.

> ¿Quién tendrá confianza,
> Si quien dijo *mujer,* dijo *mudanza?*
>
> (*G* I, 11–12)
>
> (Novelty is always attractive; we should never trust fickle female cats.... When has a woman ever been loyal? Who could be trusting, since to say "woman" is to say "unfaithful"?)

When Marramaquiz confronts Zapaquilda in a courtly fashion, the less gallant narrator declares "fuera harto mejor pegarla un chiro" (it would have been better to slap her around) (*G* I, 12). The narrator attributes the inappropriately polite behavior of cuckolded males to a combination of masculine gullibility and feminine artifice, for "una lagrimilla" (one tiny tear) from a woman's eye induces a man to believe "mil mentiras" (a thousand lies) (*G* II, 20). When Marramaquiz feigns interest in a new female, Zapaquilda's jealousy provides the narrator with the opportunity to condemn a whole class of women, for he categorizes her as one of those "mujeres de modo / que aunque no han de querer, / lo quieren todo" (women who don't fall in love, but want all the men to love them) (*G* II, 28).

By *Silva* III, Zapaquilda has made a firm commitment to Mizifuf, yet she continues to pose a threat to social harmony. Concerned because Mizifuf did not fare well in his first martial encounter with Marramaquiz, she suggests that he resort to a dishonest, indirect—and thus nonheroic—method of eliminating his rival: poison. Zapaquilda's infidelity is blamed for the jealousy that launches a duel between the two males at the end of the third *silva,* leading to their incarceration. A parallel battle between the two females occurs as they visit their lovers in jail. The narrator, however, dismisses the women's jealousy as lacking "fundamento" (cause) and as "bajeza" (baseness) and launches into a pseudo-epic parade of mythological, historical, and literary examples of this phenomenon in order to characterize unfounded destructive jealousy as an essentially female quality (*G* IV, 45–46). Throughout the first three *silvas* of the poem, gender-specific "feminine" defects of one sort or another constitute the source of every conflict. Even when both male and female characters display the same behavior, such as jealousy, it is judged differently. Gender essentialism dominates the representation of male and female in this text, so that when a servant wishes to insult the aristocratic characters in the text, he uses the phrase quintessentially associated with women: "fácil . . . en la mudanza" (he is fickle and faithless) (*G* IV, 50).

Because of the timing of Zapaquilda's switch in loyalty, both of the male figures combine elements of Paris and Menelaus. Both received promises of marriage from her and each of them stole her away from the rival, literally or figuratively. The narrator casts Mizifuf in the role of Menelaus, for he refers to Zapaquilda as Mizifuf's Helen, calls Marramaquiz a "gato troyano" (a Trojan cat), and uses the adjective "mizigriego" (Greek Mizi) (*G* VI, 66; VII, 97). The validity of Marramaquiz's claim is also treated seriously, however. When Mizifuf seeks help in order to free Zapaquilda from Marramaquiz's tower, he feels compelled to defend his theft: he declares that he fell in love with Zapaquilda without knowing of Marramaquiz's prior claim and adds that his conquest was accomplished with gallantry, "sin violencia alguna" (without a hint of force) (*G* VI, 73). The lack of a clear distinction between the offending and offended character is similar to the dialogic representation of imperialist warfare in early modern Spanish iterations of the Numantian and Araucanian conquests, which have been pointed to by some critics as examples of antimilitary discourse.

Although Lope's text focuses on a humorous rather than serious critique of martial behavior, particularly in the first four *silvas*, the final pages of the poem do point to the harsh consequences of battle. Jupiter decides to put an end to the war out of fear that the cat as a species will be wiped out; this concern may echo Bartolomé de Las Casas's critique of the genocide of indigenous peoples. The god also describes the suffering of the victims of siege warfare, which the Spaniards practiced in the Netherlands: "a Zapaquilda desfigura / la hambre la hermosura: / Vueltas las rosas nieve" (Hunger has robbed Zapaquilda of her beauty, and has blanched her rosy cheeks) (*G* VII, 89–90). The narrator concludes the fifth *silva* with the observation, "quien más en los principios fía, / no sabe donde ha de acabar el día" (those who most closely adhere to the rules do not have good luck) (*G* V, 66). Here, the obsolescence of heroic military conventions, or "principios"—not the inhumanity of warfare—is the focus of counter-epic discourse.

For the most part, though, Lope ridicules martial endeavors and their participants rather than condemning them. In his work, emphasis on vulgar corporeality plays a key role. Lope's choice of cats, notorious as the "índice" (index) of physical passion as well as inherently "golosas" (greedy), guarantees that the hero's debasement will include the representation of bodily functions and of the unmentionable portions of the body (*G* I, 18; IV, 43). The first description that the narrator provides of each of the female cats catches them in the base physical act of grooming themselves (*G* I, 5; II, 26). The cats' tails receive the most attention. The narrator specifies that Zapaquilda's initial grooming includes licking her tail (*G* I, 5), and the text juxtaposes the heroic and the vulgar in describing Mizifuf as being famous for "gala, cola, y gallardía" (finery, tail, grace) (*G* I, 11). When Marramaquiz condemns Zapaquilda for paying attention to Mizifuf, the tail appears to cause a sort of phallic anxiety, for he asks if Mizifuf has "mejor cola" (a bigger tail) (*G* I, 12). After they agree to wed, the intimacy between the two is sealed by a farewell gesture: "se hicieron reverencia con las colas" (they saluted each other with their tails) (*G* I, 15). And to signal that Marramaquiz and Mizilda's initial encounter is going well, the narrator notes that "andaban de los dos las colas / más turbulentas que del mar las olas" (their two tails were waving more turbulently than the ocean's waves) (*G* II, 27). Here, the amorous encounter is characterized as primarily physical, not idealized as a Platonic dialogue of souls.

Food also plays a prominent role in Lope's use of the physical to demystify aristocratic pretensions. In one instance, eating and sex are linked: like Scarron's Dido, whose mouth watered during her first encounter with Aeneas, Zapaquilda licks her lips at the sight of Marramaquiz (*G* I, 7). Gifts of food, rather than jewels or flowers, are crucial to courtship as well. In the opening scene, Zapaquilda receives scraps of bacon and sausage as a tribute (*G* I, 12). When Mizifuf's page brings a bundle of gifts wrapped in a decorative shawl, Zapaquilda takes no notice of the aesthetic object; she wants to know if there is anything to eat inside. The narrator describes the "señas de la verdad del amor" (signs of true love): a nicely sized wedge of cheese and a breakfast sandwich (*G* I, 18). Cheese is also a featured item in Zapaquilda's dowry (*G* IV, 49). This emphasis upon booty that provides personal enjoyment may reflect a Lascasian critique of military encounters whose primary benefits are economic.

Because food is represented as a prized gift, the kitchen becomes the site of burlesque battles where unheroic trophies are won. When Marramaquiz lists the attributes that should make Zapaquilda choose him rather than Mizifuf, he reminds her of the many kitchens he has invaded in order to bring her fish, fowl, cake, and sausage (*G* I, 13). This speech parodies the representation of the courageous, generous, chivalrous lover. Mizifuf denigrates this form of warfare; he refuses to resort to poisoning a rival who is "valiente en la cocina" (brave in the kitchen) but probably "cobarde en el campo" (cowardly on the battlefield) (*G* III, 35). Marramaquiz asserts that he has won many other victories in the Holy War against "gatos moros" (Moorish cats) (*G* III, 38), but when the news of Zapaquilda's wedding to Mizifuf reaches him, his "demencias y furores" (rage and fury) are manifested by his making a huge mess in his own kitchen (*G* IV, 51). This degraded space for aggressive activity may be viewed as an allegory for Spanish doubts about the worth of the American territories they sought to dominate. In the final three *silvas*, where more formal warfare dominates the action, Lope shifts his focus to the conventional mock-epic conventions of demystifying the opposing forces' armaments and strategies. Once Mizifuf's forces achieve victory, however, the poem immediately reverts to the approach employed in the earlier *silvas* as the hero distributes fish and cheese, rather than horses and swords, to his loyal followers as booty (*G* VII, 90).

Although Lope's title is a clear imitation of Homer's *Battle of the Mice and Frogs*, the influence of this mock epic is most obvious in the final three *silvas*, where Lope shifts from a parodic treatment of the *Iliad*, a serious work, to a respectful imitation of a comic epic. Lope's interest in Renaissance norms of self-authorization through *imitatio* is evident in this display of mastery over two distinct precedents (Ball, "Poetic Imitation," 34). Like the Greek poet, Lope degrades warfare through the choice of protagonists whose diminutive size creates a space for humorous and demystifying descriptions of arms, steeds, and military strategy. The early encounter between the two males and both encounters between the females resemble plebian brawls rather than polite duels, because the only weapons used in the impromptu battles are the cats' natural ones—their claws (*G* I, 12; II, 28; IV, 45). In the duel that closes *Silva* III, swords are drawn, but Marramaquiz's rusty weapon is drawn from a moldy scabbard (*G* III, 38). The narrator interrupts his account of the match immediately, comparing swordsmanship to singing and playing an instrument. His assurance that there are indeed significant differences is nearly as insulting as if he had asserted little difference, for aristocratic privilege rests on the assumption that martial activity is extremely specialized and heroic (*G* III, 38). The two rivals are arrested before they have a chance to display their prowess. This encounter thus falls into the realm of the burlesque in the sense that the narrator provides the drama of drawn swords but no significant action.

In the opening lines of the final *silva*, mockery of epic heroism reaches its peak through Lope's description of the not-terribly-frightening armies. The feline soldiers use hairpins for swords, frying pans as helmets, ladles instead of halberds, and animal bones in place of cannons and arcabusses (*G* VII, 79–80, 85). Mizifuf himself uses a tortoise shell as his coat of mail. The cats do not blow a trumpet but rather panpipes for the call to arms (85). Marramaquiz had been mounted on an ape in the first *silva*, but the armies now possess miniature winged horses. In case the reader doubts the existence of such animals, the narrator reminds us of the pygmy humans and beasts described in Pliny's *History* and elsewhere (81–82). To further undermine the gravity of the situation, the narrator observes that the great variety of combatants' uniforms produces the effect of a garden filled with colorful April wildflowers (80). Mizifuf then gives a speech to rally the troops in which he likens himself to Alexander, Hannibal, and Scipio; his pretensions are particularly ridiculous in this context (86–87). After noting admiringly that Mizifuf has killed seven enemies in his first foray, the narrator concedes that the seventh victim had never shown any aptitude for warfare (87). The juxtaposition of inflated rhetoric and debased reality in this *silva* points to the equally large gaps between the aristocratic order's heroic discourse and the actual function of the early modern "service" courtier—as well as to the gap between idealized epic battles and early modern military practices. Employing parodic epic as a deflationary tool is particularly effective, because it exemplifies "dismantling the master's house with the master's tools."[14]

Lope's burlesque revisions of clichéd epic stylistic devices are also notably successful. Parodies of the extended simile include the comparisons of dueling with making music (noted above), of Marramaquiz as he waits for the right moment to attack Mizifuf with cats stalking birds (*G* III, 33), and of Mizifuf's forces laying siege to Marramaquiz's tower with the chaos of neighbors who try to help a friend save the possessions in his burning house (*G* VII, 88). The epic inventory is also parodied in two instances. Zapaquilda's dowry contains the aforementioned aged cheeses as well as a wicker basket for outdoor naps, handkerchiefs to serve as sheets, and some scraps from a cast-off coat of arms to use as carpeting (*G* IV, 48). The hall where the wedding will take place is adorned with portraits of Mizifuf's bellicose ancestors, whose names signify "tumorous," "hornless," "de-tailed," and "pig-snout" (*G* V, 56). This list is immediately followed by the "parade" of wedding guests. Here, the poem deflates the male guests by providing details of clothing that belong to the world of feminized, bourgeois novelistic discourse. These burlesque elements are particularly significant in that they place moments of martial confrontation on the same level as mundane events, thereby blurring class-specific activities and eliminating the justification for hierarchical social relations. This transgression of boundaries functions in much the same way as Scarron's burlesque epic poem,

---

14. This is a variation on Audre Lorde's famous dictum: see her *Sister Outsider* (New York: Crossing Press, 1994), 112.

*Virgile travesti*, which demystifies social hierarchy by linking epic characters and bourgeois economic concerns.[15]

The narrator deflates his own rhetorical techniques as well, which constitutes another significant source of parody and counter-epic commentary in Lope's poem. In naming and characterizing the illustrious collection of ladies who attend the ill-fated wedding, the narrator includes Zarandilla, "la gata más golosa de Castilla" (the greediest female cat in Castile), and a beauty named Laura who is loved as much as Petrarch loved his Laura (*G* V, 57–58). The narrator's self-referential comments about naming a cat after a Petrarchan heroine (as well as his defense of the tiny horses' existence) is typical of the way in which meta-artistry contributes to the antiheroic atmosphere of Lope's poem. In addition to the many instances in which the narrator compares the feline protagonists to literary figures of both epic and chivalric romance genres, references to the poem's own artistic devices foreground poetic practice and distance the reader from the events narrated.[16] In an aside to the patron to whom the entire poem is dedicated, the narrator defends his satiric treatment of warfare by noting prior examples of this phenomenon in Virgil, Ariosto, Plutarch, and Homer (*G* V, 53–55). The wedding itself is bracketed by self-reflexive elements: just after Mizifuf learns of the kidnapping, the narrator explains that the bridegroom was held up by a delay at the shoemaker, and then chastises himself for including novelistic details in "tan funestos casos" (such tragic circumstances) (*G* VI, 67). The most effective self-reflexive moment directly links artistic and martial activity. Marramaquiz's despair at the small force and inadequate rations with which he will have to defend himself is compared to that of a "poeta afligido / que ha parecido mal comedia suya / o bien la de su cómico enemigo" (a poet, saddened at the negative reception of his work, or the success of a rival author) (*G* VII, 84). Like the other parodic similes described above, this conflation of poetic rivalry and armed combat demystifies the role of the warrior and refocuses the reader's attention on the "battle" among writers, which was equally compelling for many members of early modern Spanish court society. Each of the meta-artistic moments described here occurs at the beginning of a major event—such as a battle or the wedding—and interrupts the narrative at precisely those

---

15. Jean-Yves Boriaud, "L'Image des dieux dans le *Virgile travesti*," and Bernard Gicquel, "Pour une sociopsychanalyse de la réception burlesque," both in *Burlesque et formes parodiques*, ed. Landy-Houillon and Menard, 411 and 370–73, respectively.

16. See my "Generic Dimension" for an exploration of early modern reader/spectator reception of meta-artistry.

points where the rupture of the reader's illusion is most likely to reinforce the poem's mockery of epic values. This foregrounding of literary convention emphasizes the artifice that underlies both the epic genre and the aristocratic practices grounded in that literary form.

## HEGEMONY AND RECEPTION

There is no critical consensus about the ideological status of burlesque epic texts. Jean-Yves Boriaud seems to imply that the oppositional possibilities of burlesque texts were limited, and he asserts that "true" comprehension of a travesty depends upon familiarity with the elite classical text to which it refers ("L'Image des dieux," 413). I would argue that it was not necessary for the early modern Spanish reader to have read classical epics in order to appreciate the oppositional nature of the deflationary text. The widespread circulation of heroic discourses in early modern Spain is amply documented in the interactions between the deluded protagonist and deluding characters in the best-known text that incorporates burlesque epic elements, *Don Quijote*.

Critical studies of the texts under consideration here express considerable disagreement over the function of the parodic and satiric elements in burlesque. Kimberly Contag's study of "burlesque mockery" in *Don Quijote* offers the closest approximation to my own sense of the burlesque as a mode that simultaneously satirizes "those who follow inappropriate or ridiculous social norms" and parodies a particular outdated literary form that encourages adherence to antiquated belief systems. By contrast, Mary Barnard and Diana Conchado view the social critique in Quevedo and Lope in an ahistorical manner, as a generalized ridicule of human folly rather than a specific commentary on local conditions.[17] A few scholars argue that burlesque writings offer no ideological content at all, affirming the claims of such seventeenth-century French writers as Gabriel Naudé, Cyrano de Bergerac, and Molière that the purpose of the burlesque is merely to produce laughter (Cronk, "Défense du dialogisme," 328; Rohu, "Burlesque," 349). As Ignacio Arellano Ayuso notes in his study of Quevedo and the burlesque, however, most early modern and contemporary studies

---

17. See Kimberly Contag, *Mockery in Spanish Golden Age Literature: Analysis of Burlesque Representation* (Lanham, Md.: University Press of America, 1996), 3–6; Barnard, "Myth in Quevedo," 522; Conchado, "Género y poética," 196.

assert that these texts are inherently political representations: of a reactionary desire to restore the glory of feudal aristocracy (Maravall, Miller), of a conservative appeal to reform the status quo (Pinciano), or of emergent counter-hegemonic thought (Jammes).[18] In Quevedo's burlesque sonnets and in *La gatomaquia,* the literary protocols that form the idealizing basis of early modern Spanish imperialist activity are evoked to reveal the chasm between the ideal and the reality of those imperialist practices. In these texts, counter-generic parody and self-referentiality contribute directly to a far-reaching scrutiny of the ideological underpinnings of a social group already under pressure as a result of unprecedented social mobility. This critique may be seen as a conservative clarion call, urging the restoration of the values of a prior age, stable and hierarchical. Alternatively, it may manifest an embryonic stage of a new hegemony, one based upon economic rather than military success, or it may be polyphonic—relying on the reception of the (early) modern reader for its meaning. These burlesque, counter-epic texts of contestatory ideology and indeterminate genre constitute a significant element within the matrix of early modern Spanish cultural and political discourses that mediated the negotiation of international power relations and the representation of that power.

18. Ignacio Arellano Ayuso, *Poesía satírica burlesca de Quevedo* (Pamplona: Universidad de Navarra, 1984), 20–32.

# 7

## Conclusions

This final chapter investigates the place of early modern Spanish counter-epic literature within European literary and social history. The first section points to significant similarities in the counter-epic poetics of Spanish, French, and British literature through the analysis of two representative texts: Scarron's burlesque epic poem, *Virgile travesti (Virgil Travestied)*, and the Shakespearean "problem play" *Troilus and Cressida*. The second section provides a summary of the many forms of counter-epic poetics found in *Don Quijote*—an exhaustive study of this topic would require another book—and begins to explore counter-epic poetics both as the final, modal phase of an exhausted narrative genre and as an overlooked contributor to the rise of the novel, the subsequent dominant narrative genre. The third part of this chapter continues to develop the notion of counter-epic literature as the bridge between the epic poem, which commemorates and celebrates aristocratic military activity, and the novel, which helps to foster, mediate, and question the rise of the new dominant social class whose victories take place on a balance sheet rather than a battlefield.

## The Counter-Epic in France and England

Jean Rohu identifies the deaths of Louis XIII and Richelieu and the unpopular Regency guided by Anne of Austria and Cardinal Mazarin as the specific context from which the burlesque epic emerges in France ("Burlesque," 357–60). Rohu cites a *mazarinade*, a burlesque political pamphlet, that laments, "les fats remplaçent les héros" (the fops are replacing the heroes) (357). The burlesque epic's popularity coincides with the years of the Fronde uprisings against the Regency.[1] The negative attitude toward heroic values expressed in the travesties, however, could be directed against the members of the Fronde, who represented feudal aristocratic privilege, as well as against the monarchy. Paul Bénichou documents the growing influence of Jansenist thought during the seventeenth century, which is significant because the Jansenists' radical pessimism and conception of the *honnête homme* were completely antithetical to the celebration of an idealized aristocracy.[2] It is also worth noting that parodic representations of martial values did not disappear with the ascension of Louis XIV. Instead, the mock epic replaced the burlesque, satisfying classicist tastes with its more dignified tone. In *Virgile travesti*, both Aeneas and Dido (Enée and Didon) are targets of Scarron's caustic pen. Scarron reduces the status of all the characters and situations through his use of vulgar diction, descriptions of "unmentionable" body parts and functions, and a consistent metaphorical pattern in which he compares heroes, gods, battles, and the founding of cities to the everyday events of bourgeois life (Boriaud, "L'Image des dieux," 411; Gicquel, "Sociopsychanalyse," 370, 373). In addition, Scarron employs a self-reflective, meta-poetic narrator who criticizes and corrects Virgil. All of these devices reinforce the negative representation of the primary standard-bearers of epic and aristocratic values.

One striking example of demystification is Scarron's treatment of the goddess Juno. Referring to Paris's judgment, the narrator states that Paris did not choose Juno because of her sagging "udders" and long underarm "fur" (*VT* I.103–4).[3] Her "guerre terrible" (terrible war) against the

---

1. Jean Serroy, "Prolegomènes à une édition du *Virgile travesti*," in *Burlesque et formes parodiques*, ed. Landy-Houillon and Menard, 144; Georges Forestier, "Le théâtre dans la Fronde, la Fronde dans le théâtre," in *La Fronde en questions: Actes du dix-huitième Colloque du Centre meridional de rencontres sur le XVIIème siècle, Marseille 28–29, Cassis 30–31 janvier 1988*, ed. Roger Duchêne et Pierre Ronzeaud (Aix-en-Provence: Publications de l'Université de Provence, 1989), 241.
2. Paul Bénichou, *Morales du grand siècle* (Paris: Gallimard, 1948), 155.
3. References to *Virgile travesti* (abbreviated as *VT*) include book and line numbers.

Trojans is compared to lackeys kicking stray dogs (*VT* I.114–14). Juno worries that the defeat of Troy will result in a decrease in the quality of the sacrifices on her altars; rather than "boeuf, vache, mouton ou bélier," (bull, cow, sheep, or ram), she will have to settle for a rat, "qui n'est qu'un éxcrement" (which is nothing but excrement) (*VT* I.174–75). Scarron's irreverent depiction of the goddess in the opening lines of the poem sets the tone for the entire text (Boriaud, "L'Image des dieux," 415).

The French poet combines all of the burlesque techniques mentioned above in his portrait of Didon as well. Like Virgil, he provides the reader with background information concerning how she left her native land, but his account reads more like a gossip column than epic narrative. Scarron focuses on the queen's dishabille at the time of her flight: she was "contraignit de pliér toilette / et de déloger sans trompette, / un pied mal chaussé, l'autre nu" (compelled to throw together her belongings and sneak off, one foot badly shod and the other bare) (*VT* I.1131–33). Although Didon is characterized by the narrator as "charmante et belle" (charming and beautiful) (*VT* I.1724), her features resemble those of a hearty peasant. She is "une grosse dondon, / grasse, vigeureuse, bien saine, / un peu camuse, à l'africaine" (a plump turkey, corpulent, vigorous, healthy, a bit flat-nosed, in the African fashion) (*VT* I.2734–36).

Didon is reduced to a defensive, materialist hostess by Scarron's narration of the banquet given to welcome the Trojan refugees. Rather than listening in polite silence to the guests' recitation of their history, Didon assures them that her people are not stupid, that they keep informed about "ce qui se passe chez les autres" (what happens in other places) (*VT* I.2130–35). She emphasizes that her realm is not a backwater, that "le soleil reluit dessus nous, / aussi bien qu'il fait dessus vous" (the sun shines on us, just as on you) (*VT* I.2136–39). And she promises to provide the shipwrecked group with everything they need, including "quinze ou seize mil livres" (fifteen or sixteen thousand pounds) (*VT* I.2148). Here, hospitality is defined in modern, unheroic terminology as Didon offers a specific quantity of cash.

Falling in love with Enée does not elevate her character in this burlesque narrative. Unlike Virgil's figure, who still feels loyalty to her dead husband and battles her new emotions in grand style, Didon responds to Cupid's dart by musing that "le défunt ne le valait pas" (the dead guy wasn't worth much grief) and that she'd marry Enée right away if she did not fear the ensuing gossip (*VT* I.2722–27). The narrator notes that Didon displays her increasing interest by engaging Enée in a long, silly conversation in order to keep him at her side. She queries him about the mundane aspects of life in Troy, such as the details of Helen's wardrobe, the type of apple Paris bestowed, and the state of Hecuba's teeth (*VT* I.2852–79). This depiction of Didon amplifies and debases the misogynist but dignified tone of the Virgilian model (Keith, *Engendering Rome*, 23–26).

Scarron's first description of Enée serves to demystify the "aura" that Virgil's Venus bestowed upon her son. Here, the doting mother uses jasmine powder to tidy Enée's "chevelure frisé" (messy hair) and rouge to improve "son teint un peu fade" (his slightly pale complexion) (*VT* I.2206–8). Scarron uses an elaborate epic simile in order to compare Venus's efforts to commercial methods of enhancing appearance, such as polishing ivory tusks, in order to conclude that Enée, like the commodities, is "assez beau por être vendu" (handsome enough to be sold) (*VT* I.2211–19). At the banquet, Enée replicates Didon's modernization of the language of host and guest. His detailed descriptions of the food, furniture, and clothing he will give her in thanks for her aid covers three entire pages (*VT* I.2380–500). Throughout Book I, Scarron frequently makes use of economic language and imagery in his descriptions of noble or divine personages or events, emphasizing the highly porous and unstable nature of the barrier between economic and aristocratic activity. He thus undermines one of the primary tenets of the traditional social hierarchy.

In Book IV, Scarron's primary burlesque emphasis shifts from the economic to the corporeal sphere. The lovesick Didon is not merely unable to sleep; she tosses and turns because she cannot find a comfortable position (*VT* I.31–35). She is so captivated by Enée's "riche taille" (physical attributes) that her mouth waters (*VT* IV.68, 212). When Venus and Juno meet to discuss the terms under which they will allow their respective protégés to unite, their negotiations resemble a conversation between rival madams rather than goddesses. To describe the bond that will link Didon and Enée after their tryst in the cave, Juno uses the diction of the barn. The two will be "enchevêtrés" (chained together) like livestock, and their union will be as tenacious as an unwelcome insect—"un lien qui tient comme teigne" (a union that will stick like a tick) (*VT* IV.361–67). Scarron stops short of providing any graphic details of the first encounter, but assures the reader that it lasted a long while, that "tout alla bien" (everything went well), and that the new couple proceeded to spend entire days in bed "à faire des héretiers" (to create those who will inherit from us) (*VT* IV.762, 886). The choice of the term "héretiers" to indicate offspring emphasizes the economic dimension of family connections. The scorecard approach to physical intimacy serves the same purpose that a grotesque verbal portrait of the act would have performed, demystifying aristocratic discourses of courtly love, and it is similar to the tactic Shakespeare employs in *Troilus and Cressida*.

In the final scenes of Book IV, Scarron's vulgar and scatological language converts Didon's despair over being rejected and her subsequent suicide into a farcical rather than pathetic episode, partly via a debasement of clichéd epic stylistic devices such as the extended simile and the inventory. Didon's response to the news of her abandonment resembles Quevedo's sonnet, as she reminds her lover of the humiliating circumstances of their first encounter (*VT* IV.1643–46, 1697–713). Not only were Enée and his men on the brink of death, but they were also "sales magasines de vermine" (dirty carriers of vermin) (*VT* IV.1704). Didon compares the group to deceitful hotel guests who eat like wolves and then try to sneak off without paying their bills. In her inventory of the items that she wishes to burn on her funeral pyre, Dido includes several toiletries Enée left behind (*VT* IV.2293–98). And in her final denunciation of Enée, she wishes upon him "tic, scorbut, lèpre, diarrhée" (tics, scurvy, leprosy, diarrhea) (*VT* IV.2391). In this episode, as in the entire poem, the juxtaposition of grotesque corporeality and bourgeois economic detail contributes to the ultimate deflation of this "heroic" couple.

Meta-artistry adds to Scarron's demystifying treatment of epic heroism. In Book IV, Scarron interrupts Enée just as he begins to tell Didon about the visit he received from his father's ghost—and dedicates twenty lines to introspection about the role of rhyme in burlesque poetry. He concludes by justifying the interruption as "pour prendre haleine" (to take a break) and invites readers to complain if they wish (*VT* IV.1557–77). The rupture in the narration of such a dramatic event as a visit from the underworld disrupts what Timothy Reiss refers to as "dramatic illusion," the uncritical frame of mind that allows spectators to identify with seemingly real theatrical characters. This concept of illusion is equally relevant to describe the frame of mind for readers who identify with characters seen only in the mind's eye.[4] Scarron's foregrounding of both burlesque and classical epic poetic conventions lays bare the constructed nature of epic's social and literary norms.

Larry Clarke points out that in England, as in France (and Spain), advances in military technology during the fifteenth and sixteenth centuries led to a transformation of the function of the nobility from a feudal

---

4. Timothy Reiss, *Toward Dramatic Illusion: Theatrical Technique and Meaning from Hardy to Horace* (New Haven: Yale University Press, 1971), 130.

warrior class to a courtly "service" aristocracy. Moreover, the rise of Puritanism, whose notions of virtue were anathema to the aristocratic heroic vision, also contributed to the marginalization of the court in the early seventeenth century ("Mars," 211), and the merchant class competed for economic power as well (Lombardo, "Fragments and Scraps," 213). Debates about imperialist policy were common in the British court. The faction at the Isabelline court headed by Robert Cecil urged peace with Ireland and Spain, according to Eric Mallin, while the group headed by the more bellicose Earl of Essex favored continued aggression.[5] Factionalism played a unique role in this court, however. The core of Elizabeth's strategy for avoiding challenges to royal power was to encourage internal strife among the most powerful noble families (Mallin, "Emulous Factions," 147). Significantly, the Tudor monarchy deployed epic ideology in a more direct manner than other early modern states, using Geoffrey of Monmouth's mythography to emphasize the link between Britain and Troy (153). As in Spain and France, the continued glorification of martial activity in the ceremonial realm attracted negative attention. Moralists critiqued the Tudor revival of chivalric competition as "manslaughter" (158).

Over the past ten years, most issues related to parodic representation of the epic have been addressed in critical studies of *Troilus and Cressida*.[6] Here, I will bring together these disparate elements to explore the ways in which this text employs its counter-generic strategy. Like Lope, Shakespeare juxtaposes Trojan material with chivalric epic conventions in a manner that foregrounds their incompatibility; like Scarron's poem, Shakespeare's play employs vulgar diction and economic metaphors to demystify heroic characters. *Troilus and Cressida* also emphasizes the debasement of women and idealized notions of love.

---

5. Eric S. Mallin, "Emulous Factions and the Collapse of Chivalry: *Troilus and Cressida*," *Representations* 29 (Winter 1990): 146.

6. See Clarke, "'Mars His Heart Enflamed with Venus,'" 226; Mallin, "Emulous Factions," 148–58; Mihoko Suzuki, "'Truth Tired with Iteration': Myth and Fiction in Shakespeare's *Troilus and Cressida*," *Philological Quarterly* 66, no. 2 (1987): 153; Lorraine Helms, "'Still Wars and Lechery': Shakespeare and the Last Trojan Woman," in *Arms and the Woman: War, Gender, and Literary Representation*, ed. Helen M. Cooper (Chapel Hill: The University of North Carolina Press, 1989), 32; Harold Brooks, "*Troilus and Cressida*: Its Dramatic Unity and Genre," in *"Fanned and winnowed opinions": Shakespearean Essays Presented to Harold Jenkins*, ed. John Mahon and Thomas Pendleton (London: Methuen, 1987), 21; Maurice Hunt, "Shakespeare's *Troilus and Cressida* and Christian Epistemology," *Christianity and Literature* 42, no. 2 (1993): 243; Charles Boyle, "Bitter Fruit: *Troilus and Cressida* in Queen Elizabeth's Court," *The Elizabethan Review* 2, no. 2 (1994): 13; A. M. Potter, "*Troilus and Cressida*: Deconstructing the Middle Ages?" *Theoria* 72 (October 1988): 26–35; Lombardo, "Fragments and

The negative representation of women in this play centers on the infidelities of Helen and Cressida and on the demystification of idealized courtly love, which formed the basis for any positive notions of femininity in the early modern period. Thus, as in *La gatomaquia,* the juxtaposition of classical epic and chivalric romance is key in debasing aristocratic heroism. Cressida first undercuts the ideal of the chaste woman by using fencing terminology in her description of the various "lies," or defensive postures, that she needs in dealing with men:

> Upon my back, to defend my belly, upon my wit, to defend
> my wiles, upon my secrecy, to defend mine honesty, my mask,
> to defend my beauty, and you, to defend all these: and at all
> these wards I lie, at a thousand watches.
>
> (*TC* I.ii.262–66)

The vulgarization of courtship sets the tone for the bawdy and calculated nature of the relationship that will develop. Cressida shatters the myth of maidenly modesty when she reveals the reason why she is not immediately receptive to Troilus's advances, even though she admires him:

> Yet I hold off. Women are angels, wooing;
> Things won are done, joy's soul lies in the doing.
> . . . . . . . . . . . .
> Therefore this maxim out of love I teach:
> Achievement is command; ungain'd, beseech.
> Then though my heart's content firm love doth bear,
> Nothing of that from mine eyes shall appear.
>
> (*TC* I.ii.288–97)

It is particularly noteworthy that in this Shakespearean text, Cressida herself speaks many lines that reinforce negative stereotypes of female behavior.

The one occasion on which Cressida speaks as a faithful heroine is immediately undermined by subsequent plot events that are out of her control. She vows,

> I know no touch of consanguinity;
> No kin, no love, no blood, no soul so near me
> As the sweet Troilus. . . .
> . . . . . . .

---

Scraps," 205; Mary Beth Rose, *The Expense of Spirit: Love and Sexuality in English Renaissance Drama* (Ithaca: Cornell University Press, 1988), 195.

> ... Time, force, and death,
> Do to this body what extremes you can;
> But the strong base and building of my love
> Is as the very center of the earth,
> Drawing all things to it. I'll go in and weep—
>
> (*TC* IV.ii.98–106)

Cressida then repeats these vows of fidelity to Troilus and predicts that she will be "a woeful Cressid 'mongst the merry Greeks" (*TC* IV.iv.56). She appears quite untroubled upon her arrival at the other camp, however, where she kisses the leading generals and follows Patroclus's lead in mocking Menelaus for being a cuckold. Ulysses is moved by this encounter to decide that "her wanton spirits look out / at every joint and motive of her body" (*TC* IV.v.56–57). He reiterates this impression as he leads Troilus to where he can spy on Cressida and her new love: "she will sing any man at first sight" (*TC* V.ii.10).

Not only female characters suffer as a result of impossible ideals. Literary representations of idealized human behavior create unrealizable expectations for both genders. Chivalric and epic codes can thus be seen as the source of both idealized amorous and martial activity and their ultimate degradations, because of the impossibly elevated standards of behavior they impose. In *Troilus and Cressida,* Shakespeare's deconstructions of these literary codes have particularly subversive social implications, because epic and chivalric literary idealizations offered legitimization to the Elizabethan court structure.

The debasement of Platonic love goes beyond critiques of women to demystify the entire courtship process. In the first scene of the play, Cressida's uncle, Pandarus, introduces the subject of Troilus's pursuit of his niece, a process he compares metaphorically to the rather prosaic activity of making bread (*TC* I.i.14–15, 24–29). Troilus raises the tone to a conventionally exalted level, declaring that in comparison to his lady's hand, "all whites are ink" (*TC* I.i.58). Pandarus immediately undercuts this metaphor, pointing out that even if her hands are not so white, "she has the mends," or cosmetics, to produce the desired effect (*TC* I.i.70). Troilus then resorts to unconventional commercial metaphors to describe his relationship to Cressida, as mediated by Pandarus. He calls Cressida "a pearl" whose "bed is India," and then he refers to himself as a "merchant," with Pandarus as the ship that will convey the trader to his desired destination (*TC* I.i.102–5). Troilus's introduction of these economic or "secular" comparisons into the "sacred" realm of courtly love contradicts his previous effort to maintain the discussion of his pursuit of Cressida at an idealized level.

In his parody of the epic warrior ethos, Shakespeare has more in common with Scarron than with Lope, for the British author grounds his parody in the debasement of Homeric figures and of the motivation for the Trojan War. Although the Prologue describes the battle between Greece and Troy in appropriately epic terminology, Troilus asserts that the soldiers are "fools on both sides" (*TC* I.i.93). He lays bare the rhetoric of a noble war in declaring, "Helen must needs be fair, / when with your blood you daily paint her thus" (*TC* I.i.93–94). Diomedes goes even further in his rejection of Helen as the icon for whom the two sides fight, lamenting that "for every false drop in her bawdy veins, / a Grecian's life hath sunk; for every scruple / of her contaminated carrion weight, / a Trojan hath been slain" (*TC* IV.i.71–74). Ulysses' strategy for defeating the Trojans belies the ideal of high-minded and glorious military planning; he pragmatically suggests, "let us, like merchants, first show foul wares, / and think, perchance, they'll sell; if not, / the luster of the better shall exceed / by showing the worst first" (*TC* I.iii.358–61). Ulysses' economic imagery undermines idealizations of war just as Troilus's use of monetary metaphors debases the discourse of courtly love. Thersites links these corrupted ideals, proclaiming, "all the argument is a whore and a cuckold . . . war and lechery confound all!" (*TC* II.iii.71–74).

Achilles also reveals a lack of respect for the concept of fair and equal combat and dignified stratagems. Before the banquet at which he and Hector will dine together on the eve of their great battle, demonstrating their chivalry, he tells Patroclus that he plans to gain an advantage by giving Hector too much "Greekish wine" (*TC* V.i.1). Achilles' motives for meeting Hector have already been shown to be suspect. Ulysses torments him by describing the popularity Ajax is winning by agreeing to fight Hector, which moves Achilles to wonder, "are my deeds forgot?" (*TC* III.iii.144). He agrees to the confrontation out of vanity and the desire to repair a wounded ego: "I see my reputation is at stake; / my fame is shrewdly gor'd" (*TC* III.iii.27–28). These two scenes establish the tone of degraded warfare that culminates in Achilles' ignoble slaughter of Hector. The unfair ambush is premeditated. Achilles tells his men, the Myrmidons, "when I have the bloody Hector found, / empale him with your weapons round about" (*TC* V.vii.5). Despite Hector's plea for mercy, "I am unarm'd. Forego this vantage, Greek" (*TC* V.viii.9), Achilles orders his men to strike, and he then takes credit for their deed, instructing, "cry you all amain, /

'Achilles hath the mighty Hector slain'" (*TC* V.viii.13–14). In these scenes, Shakespeare questions the idealized representation of warfare, of its motivations, strategies, and modes of operation.

The characters on both sides show themselves ready to criticize their allies and opponents at every opportunity, which is in itself a critique of these idealized warriors. Gossip—warring with words, rather than with deeds—is generally associated with female characters and not considered masculine. When Ulysses criticizes Achilles and Patroclus, he describes Achilles as having grown "dainty" as a result of lying with Patroclus "upon a lazy bed the livelong day" and telling "scurrilous jests" (*TC* I.iii.148–50). The homoerotic implications of this accusation are borne out when Thersites tells Patroclus, "thou art said to be Achilles' male varlet" (*TC* V.i.14). Ulysses links Achilles' and Patroclus's practice of disrespectful imitations of Agamemnon and Nestor with the "sickness" that has imperiled the Greek martial efforts: their "slander" is part of a pattern in which the failure to "observe degree, priority, and place" is responsible for "this fever that keeps Troy on foot, / not her own sinews. . . . / Troy in our weakness stands, not in her strength" (*TC* I.iii.86, 135–37). The association of disrespectful speech with civil disorder can be an indication of the subversive power of theatrical parody, as well.

Self-referentiality, though less prominent in this play than in other burlesque epics, is present in one key scene. The morning after Troilus and Cressida consummate their love, as the lovers pledge their troth, Pandarus is present throughout, providing an ironic commentary to a potentially idealized interlude and distancing the spectators during one of the few conventional scenes of the play. After leaving the couple alone briefly, he returns to inquire, "Have you not done talking yet?" (*TC* III.ii.99–100). He then promises Troilus that the women in his family are loyal, using the basest of analogies: "they are burrs, I can tell you; / they'll stick where they are thrown" (*TC* III.ii.110–11). Pandarus interrupts again after Troilus has kissed Cressida, denying the audience the opportunity to indulge in sentimental pleasure, with his sardonic, "pretty, i'faith" (*TC* II.ii.134). At the conclusion of the scene, after the young people vow eternal constancy, Pandarus does not speak of marriage, the conventional romantic closure. He offers instead to lead them to a bed and urges them to "press it to death" (*TC* III.ii.206–7). Pandarus's parodic commentary, which reminds the audience of the gap between literary conventions of love and its real-life counterpart, contributes to the ultimate demystification of all forms of idealized and hierarchized behavior.

By debasing courtly love and military achievement, two of the linchpins of aristocratic privilege, and parodying the Virgilian epic (a primary source for idealizing discourse in early modern Europe), Scarron's *Virgile travesti* and Shakespeare's *Troilus and Cressida* offer a deflationary representation of both the aesthetics and the ideology that were used to validate early modern hierarchical values. As the analysis of *La gatomaquia* demonstrated, this form of critical representation may be interpreted as a conservative desire to reform yet maintain and defend the normative discourses by evoking an idealized past in which stability and glory were the result of uniform adherence to hierarchical values. The questioning of imperial and martial aristocratic discourses found in all the forms of counter-epic literatures studied here, however, also displays significant parallels to oppositional critiques of military discourses expressed in early modern political and theological debates.

## Counter-Epic Dimensions of Don Quijote

Considering Don Quijote's status as an "anatomy," or compendium, of all of the major genres of Renaissance literature, it is hardly surprising that most of the counter-epic elements identified throughout this essay can also be found in the Cervantine masterpiece.[7] The novel's two volumes incorporate a serious examination of imperial practice, discourses on freedom, meditations upon historiography, meta-artistic dialogues about classical epic texts, and scenes of aristocratic *furor* as well as the *harenga* about the relative merits of arms and letters. In addition, the ridiculous protagonist and his illusory adventures are quite similar to the military activity in *La gatomaquia*, while the negative portrayal of the upper nobility parallels Scarron's and Shakespeare's burlesque texts. Like those works, *Don Quijote* also demonstrates considerable fascination with the "bourgeois" and physical details of life, especially food, the sexual appetite, grotesque bodily functions, money, and clothing. The emphasis upon the amorous interests of a "warrior" protagonist also corresponds to the poetics of the novelistic history play. Many of the components of the novel studied in this section have been pointed out previously by Cervantine scholars in a variety of contexts; my primary interest here is to demonstrate the unremarked parallels to other burlesque epic texts. Thus, this section provides an overview of the

---

7. Parr, *Anatomy*, xv.

text's relevant counter-epic characteristics rather than a comprehensive explication.

The counter-epic scrutiny of aristocratic values can be expressed both through burlesque episodes and via serious critiques of idleness and decadence. The lampooning of the social order is manifested in Don Quijote's own excessive reading, subsequent madness, and ridiculous behaviors—not only in his imaginary battle situations but also in his reaction to the Cave of Montesinos episode and his gullibility in the face of deceptions perpetrated by his family and neighbors as well as those encountered in his travels. This deflation of the aristocratic, heroic protagonist is similar to Lope's literal diminution of warriors and weapons in *La gatomaquia,* to Scarron's demystification of Dido and Aeneas, and to Shakespeare's satirical treatment of Greek and Trojan leaders. Luis Andrés Murillo points to Don Quijote's sword and lance as key elements in this burlesque treatment of the hero, noting that in many of the early adventures, the protagonist uses his lance rather than his sword; on occasions when he does draw the sword, as in the case of the conflict with the Biscayans, he uses it as a bludgeon rather than employing the blade or the tip.[8] The related negative representation of aristocrats who do not even seek to serve their country—seen in the Numancia plays, where Scipio condemns the laziness of imperial military leaders and soldiers, and in the novelistic history plays, where noble characters often place personal concerns ahead of the needs of the *patria*—has a parallel in the lack of occupation that allows the Duke and Duchess, their retainers, and the nobility of Barcelona to dedicate (that is, waste) significant energies to the pranks they create to humiliate Don Quijote.

The representation of Don Quijote as a would-be chivalric hero is a gem of burlesque epic mockery. The evocations of Don Quijote's woefully inadequate armor, weapons, steed, and physical body, which are similar to those found among the feline protagonists of *La gatomaquia,* point to the fatally anachronistic appeal of both serious (classical) and chivalric epic texts and value systems. Rocinante, for example, is compared to Babieca and Bucephalus rather than to the mounts of Orlando or Amadís (*DQ* I, 76). Likewise, the series of ridiculous battles with nonhuman and nonheroic opponents, from the first encounter with the muleteer at the water trough to the episodes involving windmill, water mill, fulling mill, helmet of Mambrino, wineskins, flocks of sheep, Master Pedro's puppets, milk curds,

---

8. Luis Andrés Murillo, "La espada de Don Quijote (Cervantes y la poesía heroica)," in *Cervantes*, ed. Criado de Val, 667–680.

and so on, can be seen as an indictment of the excesses of all forms of military hyperbole, of Spain's pride stemming from the conquest of poorly armed indigenous peoples, and of the chagrin over Iberian failure to subdue small rebellious populations in the Netherlands and in Chile.[9] The questionable booty obtained from these battles, particularly the *baciyelmo* (barber's basin/helmet) and the provisions of food that Sancho steals from defeated groups, can be seen as a subtle reminder of debates over the costs—in human lives and actual funds—of winning small and often temporary victories in the Netherlands and Chile, as well as examples of the difficulty in distinguishing between legitimate spoils of war and illegitimate theft of the defeated peoples' personal property (Loftis, *Renaissance Drama*, 56–57).

One encounter that juxtaposes burlesque treatments of battle with serious explorations of military discourse is the conflict between the town of brayers and the town that mocks this skill in chapters 25 and 27 of Book II. On the one hand, Don Quijote repeats a litany of acceptable just war arguments, including defense of the faith and service to the king; he also indicates, however, that this particular battle is not defensible under any of those terms but is rather a case of seeking "venganza injusta . . . [que] va directamente contra la santa ley que profesamos" (to take an unjust revenge . . . [which] is directly opposed to the sacred law that we acknowledge) (*DQ* II, 254).[10] The latter comment may be seen as a critique of the *Requerimiento*, which employed a seriously flawed conversion procedure as the grounds upon which to attack an enemy for rejecting Catholic doctrine. This passage may also constitute a scrutiny of justifications of Spanish activity in Chile, which pointed to the supposed early acceptance of Spanish conquest by the Araucanian peoples as a covenant, and to the uprisings against Valdivia and subsequent governors as a treasonous violation of that accord (Lauer, "La conquista de Chile," 99–100).

Cervantes gives substantial consideration to the doctrine of natural liberty, a common feature of counter-epic texts and Lascasian thought. The presentation of the crimes that led to imprisonment provides a burlesque context, for the prisoners use the slang diction of convicts to describe their past activities in a humorous manner. Don Quijote's decision to free the captives is explained both as an ethical matter, "me parece duro caso hacer esclavos a los que Dios y naturaleza hizo libres" (it seems to me unjust to

---

9. Margaret Church, *Structure and Theme—Don Quixote to James Joyce* (Columbus: Ohio State University Press, 1983), 25.

10. All English translations are from the 1981 Norton critical edition of *Don Quixote*, ed. Joseph Jones and Kenneth Douglas (New York: Norton, 1981).

make slaves of those whom God and nature have made free), and as an inappropriate application of medieval, chivalric notions of personal honor to an early modern civil situation when he points out that "estos pobres no han cometido nada contra vosotros" (these poor fellows have done nothing to you [guards]).[11] The topic of natural liberty as it pertains to the sale and purchase of African slaves, a common practice in Caribbean parts of the Spanish empire, is raised when Sancho assuages the dismay he feels at the possibility of acquiring black-skinned vassals as governor of Micomicón. He decides that he will sell them off in exchange for gold or silver: "que por negros que sean, los he de volver blancos o amarillos" (no matter how black, I'll turn them into silver and gold") (*DQ* I, 366). In these episodes, Cervantes evokes the critiques of human enslavement and the *encomienda* system found in the Arauco and Numancia plays as well as reminders of the dangers posed by attempts at negotiated, peaceful coexistence.

Don Quijote's destructive *furor* scrutinizes Spanish conduct on the battlefield and treatment of indigenous laborers. In his slaughter of the sheep, his ferocious physical attacks against the animal herders at the inn's water trough and against the Biscayans, and his excessive reaction to Eugenio's critique of books of chivalry, Don Quijote's unprovoked violence merits the condemnation of Christian militancy put forth by Alonso López, whose leg was broken when Don Quijote attacked him as he accompanied the funeral party: "no sé como puede ser eso de enderezar tuertos, pues a mi de derecho me habéis vuelto tuerto" (I do not understand the part about straightening out wrongs ... for from straight you have made me crooked) (*DQ* I, 233). Don Quijote frequently initiates violence in order to right a perceived wrong, and his actions may serve as a Lascasian critique of the counterproductive Spanish practice of using military conquest to obtain indigenous converts and enslaving those for whom the Christian religion is described as freedom from idolatry (Díaz Balsera, "Araucanian Alterity," 31; Galbis, "Aspectos forenses," 700).

Don Quijote's inconsiderate treatment of his own squire may also be interpreted in the light of Lascasian discourse. In his failure to rescue Sancho from the *mantamiento* (tossing in a blanket), his insistence that Sancho get up from his sickbed immediately after he ceases regurgitating the loathsome balsam, and especially in the disenchantment of Dulcinea, Don Quijote completely ignores his servant's well-being. Don Quijote's

---

11. *DQ* I, 273; see also Ignacio R. M. Galbis, "Aspectos forenses de la obra cervantina: El *Quijote* a la luz del derecho natural," in *Cervantes*, ed. Criado de Val, 704.

focus upon his own worldview also dehumanizes Sancho: in his adherence to literary codes, he refuses to provide Sancho with any form of guaranteed earnings for his service, thus failing to ensure that his family's needs are met. Don Quijote's attempt to control Sancho's right to speak is also a blatant example of his abuse of his caste-based privileges. In these passages, Don Quijote's behaviors resemble, though in a less drastic form, the "othering" of the American labor force critiqued in Lascasian discourses and alluded to in the Numancia and Arauco plays and in *indiano* drama's evocations of the vast wealth brought back to Spain.

Sancho Panza's governorship has been pointed to as an additional example of New World discourse in Cervantes. Diana de Armas Wilson compares his motivations and less-than-ideal experiences to the dystopic adventures chronicled by the less fortunate conquistadors.

> Setting out for his governorship, Sancho, unlike Don Quixote, does not scorn the profit motive, as his letter to Teresa shows: "I go with a great desire to make money, which they tell me is the case with all new governors" *["voy con grandísimo deseo de hacer dineros porque me han dicho que todos los gobernadores nuevos van con este mesmo deseo"]* (II.36). Such a desire applied most pertinently to governors in the New World, and when Sancho finally gets what he wants—which is when his troubles begin—his sham governorship parodies, among other things, the dismal experiences chronicled by countless governors in Spain's colonies.[12]

Notably, the positive representation of Sancho's term as governor is grounded in his actual rejection of the profit motive associated with imperial ventures. He repeatedly emphasizes that he does not use his office for personal gain: "saliendo yo desnudo, como salgo, no hay otra señal para dar a entender que he gobernado como un ángel" (when I leave as naked as I do, there is no other proof needed to show that I have governed like an angel).[13] As an obvious counterpoint to the abuses of Spanish governors in America, the story of Sancho's restrained stewardship can be viewed as a counter-chronicle and also as an *espejo de gobernadores* (guide for governors) in the style of the popular guides for princes of the era.

12. Diana de Armas Wilson, "Rethinking Cervantine Utopias: Some No [Good] Places in Renaissance England and Spain," in *Echoes and Inscriptions,* ed. Simerka and Weimer, 202.
13. *DQ* II, 446; Ludovik Osterc, *El pensamiento social y político del Quijote* (Mexico City: Ediciones de Andrea, 1963), 286–89.

An interest in the problematics of historical inscription is a shared concern of the counter-epic history play, including Cervantes's own *Numancia*, as well as *Don Quijote*. The early references to the competing truths and gaps in information among the disparate oral legends and manuscripts concerning Don Quijote echo the concerns of Renaissance historiography. Similarly, the two chapters of the second volume, in which various narrators describe the events contained in those chapters as "apócrifos" (apocryphal), remind the early modern reader that problems in determining historical truth arise not only from disparities among sources but also from the differences in criteria that allowed previous generations of historians to mix truth and fiction.[14] Concern with historical truth is also expressed in the episode where Don Alvaro Tarfe is confronted with the two different versions of Don Quijote presented by the Arab historians deployed by Avellaneda and Cervantes (McKeon, *Origins*, 275–76). The frequent references in both volumes to the "absolute" truth of biblical history, voiced by a protagonist whose very essence is marked by the inability to distinguish between fiction and history, is also relevant.

Early in the second volume, the book that commemorates Don Quijote's initial sallies appears, which allows for a more complete examination of history and memory. The protagonist first raises this issue in the context of the older oral tradition when he asks his squire what the townspeople are *saying* about his accomplishments. His subsequent directives, telling Sancho how to relate what he hears, implies the objective standards of accuracy of the current era: "esto me has de decir sin añadir al bien ni quitar al mal" (you must tell me without adding to the good or taking anything away from the bad) (*DQ* II, 55). Cervantes also depicts Sancho's and Don Quijote's reactions to the news of a book containing their adventures, treating history writing from both serious and burlesque perspectives and often juxtaposing the two viewpoints. In Sancho's musing that "nunca hazañas de escuderos se escribieron" (the achievements of squires never were recorded), this early novel anticipates a key topic of postmodern historiography—namely, the validity of historical explanations that consider only the ruling class (*DQ* II, 58). Sancho later reveals his primary concern to be whether the inscription has cast doubt upon his status as "cristiano viejo" (an old Christian) (*DQ* II, 63), a concern that found parallels throughout all levels

---

14. Michael McKeon, *The Origins of the English Novel, 1600–1740* (Baltimore: The Johns Hopkins University Press, 1987), 279; André Brink, *The Novel: Language and Narrative from Cervantes to Calvino* (New York: New York University Press, 1998), 22.

of post-1492 Spanish society. Unlike the history plays in which characters seek to control the historical record but assume a unified reception of the narration of their expected triumphs, *Don Quijote* reveals the impossibility of truly controlling the historical record, a record that depends as much upon the idiosyncratic vagaries of differing levels of reading competency as upon commissioning and censoring activities that determine what is published. All of these episodes reveal a preoccupation with historical inscription as a fundamental but unstable and unreliable component of epistemology and the search for truth.

The exploration of physical and economic needs is an important component of the demystificatory and meta-artistic component of the counter-epic. In *Don Quijote*, this topic appears for the first time in the opening section of the first chapter, when the narrator reveals that Don Quijote must put his patrimony at risk by selling land in order to afford the chivalric texts with which he is obsessed (*DQ* I, 71). This issue arises again when the innkeeper points out to the protagonist that even though his favored tales do not mention the money or the clean clothing the heroes carried with them, he must not assume that literary *aporia* are the equivalent of material absence; this silence concerning daily necessities is also characteristic of the classical epic. Throughout the novel, the need for money—to pay for damages, for books, and for Dulcinea's loan in the Cave of Montesinos as well as to recompense Sancho Panza's service—and the hunger for substantial food in addition to herbs and flowers constitute a major component of Don Quijote's forced contact with material reality (Johnson, *Cervantes and the Material World*, 5–11). The emphasis upon the importance of liquid cash parallels that found in *indiano* dramas.

*Don Quijote* shares with Scarron's poem a fascination for detailed descriptions of food, from the protagonist's weekly menu provided in the first pages of the text to the enumeration of the delicacies offered at Camacho's wedding and at the tables of Don Diego and the Duke and Duchess. In addition, the scatological references found in Book I ground master and servant in the bodily realm, producing an effect similar to that evoked by Quevedo's detailed description of the Infantes' disgrace in the latrine. All of these episodes serve as parodies of the exalted, immaterial plane upon which the classical as well as the chivalric epic warrior exists.

Counter-epic poetics can also be seen in *Don Quijote*'s emphasis upon the amatory adventures of the military hero. Although sentimental plots are more common in chivalric romances such as *Orlando Furioso* than in classical epic, the debasement of the heroic protagonist through the depiction of a ridiculous romantic attachment can be seen as a parody of both genres. Unlike the Scarron and Shakespearean texts, which demystify idealized notions of the warrior/lover by emphasizing carnal desire, Cervantes depicts instead the ludicrous nature of a *truly* Platonic love, one that cannot seek physical fulfillment because the object of devotion is an impossible juxtaposition of an idealized noblewoman—a compendium of qualities inscribed in literary norms—and an attractive peasant woman from El Toboso. In addition to the Dulcinea subplot, most of the interpolated tales focus upon courtship rather than or in addition to warfare. This concern with the emotional, corporeal, and material world away from the battlefield is central to the novelization of epic themes found in *Don Quijote*. It is precisely the clash of the military and the mundane, along with the critique or satire of imperial values, that characterizes counter-epic literature as a transitional stage between heroic and bourgeois narratives. An indirect linkage of military pursuits and marriage can also be found in the *indiano* plays, for overseas conquest is the necessary prequel to the wealth that enables the *indiano*'s quest for social advancement through matrimony.

Through such techniques as the scrutiny of the military and aristocratic hero, the foregrounding of Don Quijote's amorous interests, the exploration of both the inscription of the hero and the reception of historical texts, the examination of practices of governorship, and the representation of the corporeal and material dimensions of life that even heroes cannot evade, *Don Quijote* incorporates nearly every type of counter-epic poetic practice described in this book. An appreciation of this dimension of the Cervantine masterpiece enriches the literary contexts in which we study this work and other counter-epic texts. In addition, identifying the counter-epic dimension of this important and influential narrative text, whether it is viewed as the "first modern novel" or merely as a key precursor, is significant for the study of the counter-epic's role in the emergence of the novel as the dominant modern narrative form.

## THE COUNTER-EPIC AND THE RISE OF THE NOVEL

Studies of the history of the novel have identified the early-eighteenth-century British mock-heroic poem as a significant component in the "rise" of the novel (and the concurrent "fall" of the epic) as the dominant form of narrative literature. According to Gregory Colomb, the mock-heroic poem functioned as "propaganda" for the emergent bourgeoisie in its effort to discredit the aristocracy (*Designs on Truth*, xv). However, the mock-heroic poem did not arise *ex nihilo* at the dawn of the eighteenth century. The previous century had also produced a significant body of parodic literature whose targets were epic conventions and the aristocratic classes deploying epic discourses as an ideological weapon. Michael Murrin has noted the decreasing importance of battle scenes even in the serious early modern epic, which parallels the phenomenon that has been documented here in the case of counter-epic texts. Diana de Armas Wilson relates these phenomena to the specific case of Spain, asserting that "Spanish imperial decline, the decline of the humanist heroic ethos, and the decline of epic were all imbricated."[15] She identifies the *Persiles*, rather than *Don Quijote*, as the Cervantine work that most strongly "gives the death knell to the prestigious imperialist epic" and that "signals . . . the disintegration of the epic system" (35–36). This shift away from epic values was also noted by thinkers of the period: Montesquieu asserted that by the end of the seventeenth century, imperial domination was grounded in commercial trade, not in military conquest (see Pagden, *Spanish Imperialism*, 7). And as the previous section indicated, examples of counter-epic poetics abound in *Don Quijote*, which most critics now recognize as playing a role of some importance for eighteenth-century British novelists.[16]

Critical frameworks for the emergence of novelistic narrative downplay the role of humor or marginalize the early modern burlesque as a relevant comic precursor. Mikhail Bakhtin notes that each emergence of the novel has been preceded by a "period of preparation" marked by significant parody of existent canonical genres.[17] Although he identifies "parodic-travestying forms" as an especially significant component of the history of the novel, he dismisses *Virgile travesti* and other early modern burlesque epic works as "impoverished, superficial, and historically [less] significant" than the parodic heroic works of the classical and medieval eras. This study has demonstrated that the attribute Bakhtin assigns to earlier travesties, the power "to provide the corrective of laughter and criticism to all existing

---

15. Diana de Armas Wilson, "Defending 'Poor Poetry': Sidney, Cervantes, and the Prestige of Epic," in *Ingeniosa Invención: Essays on Golden Age Spanish Literature for Geoffrey L. Stagg in Honor of His Eighty-fifth Birthday*, ed. Ellen M. Anderson and Amy R. Williamsen (Newark, Del.: Juan de la Cuesta, 1999), 35, 35–36.
16. See Ian P. Watt, *The Rise of the Novel: Studies in Defoe, Richardson, and Fielding* (Berkeley and Los Angeles: University of California Press, 1967); McKeon, *Origins*; Walter Reed, *An Exemplary History of the Novel: The Quixotic Versus the Picaresque* (Chicago: University of Chicago Press, 1981); Church, *Structure and Theme*.
17. Bakhtin, *Dialogic*, 6.

straightforward genres, languages, styles, voices; to force men to experience beneath these categories a different and contradictory reality," is also present in the early modern burlesque epic as well as in the parodic and meta-artistic passages of the novelistic history plays (52).

Many critics, most notably Ian Watt, have identified the shift of focus from military and aristocratic concerns to bourgeois ones—marriage and capital accumulation—as key elements in the rise of the novel as the dominant narrative genre.[18] Lukács contrasts the *agon* of epic and novel that are based, respectively, in the "struggle of national character" and the struggle of an individual within society, where economic and marital considerations dominate.[19] The social dynamic described by these critics is similar to that represented in *indiano* drama, where the epic deeds of previous generations form the unspoken background to the protagonist's current search for personal advancement within courtier society. George Mariscal traces a connection between the *indiano* and the protagonist of the early novel in his observation that "the thrifty *indiano*, always conscious of the hardships he has undergone in order to make his fortune, points toward a less generous figure only barely visible at this moment of European history—the calculating and prudent bourgeois" ("Figure," 57).

A related form of antiaristocratic, "bourgeois" discourse found in both the counter-epic and the early novel is a demystification of the idealizing tendencies found in epic literatures. Michael McKeon asserts that the dialectic between realism and "romance" is the base from which the novel emerges between 1600 and 1740; during this period, "the reigning narrative epistemology involves a dependence on received authority and a priori traditions" among which "romance idealism" dominates (*Origins*, 21). Ian Watt points to an additional dimension of bourgeois discourse found in the early novel, disapproval of the "immorality" of the aristocracy (*Rise of the Novel*, xv), which is central to *La gatomaquia* and other burlesque epic texts and is also found in *Don Quijote* as well as in *indiano* dramas that foreground the *menosprecio de corte* motif.

Georg Lukács, exploring the connections between epic and narrative, posits that in the classical era, drama arose out of the epic, while in the early modern world, the novel arises out of the history play. Shakespeare's *Henriad*, for instance, demonstrates "certain stylistic tendencies [that] take

---

18. Deirdre Lynch and William Warner, eds., *Cultural Institutions of the Novel* (Durham: Duke University Press, 1996), 1.
19. Georg Lukács, *The Theory of the Novel*, trans. Anna Bostock (Cambridge: The MIT Press, 1983), 148.

it in the direction of the novel" (*Theory of the Novel*, 90). In his view, these works encompass "the welter of contradictions which had filled the uneven but fatal path of feudal crisis over centuries" (153). The counter-epic history plays of Cervantes, Lope, Rojas Zorrilla, and González de Bustos, as well as the English and Spanish "journalistic" history plays studied by John Loftis, perform an equally important role in the rise of the novel as they deconstruct the inscription of triumph and heroism as well as mediate early modern nostalgia for an idealized version of medieval heroic culture. The demystification of the warrior found in the history plays, including both the critique of military practices and the marginalization of the protagonists' military deeds, are also important precursors to the emergence of a new type of protagonist and new forms of emplotment in novelistic narrative.

Early modern Spanish counter-epic literature, then, constitutes a significant subgenre or mode in the history of European and American literatures. Michael McKeon classifies the shift in narrative epistemology from romance to novel as "a change of attitude about how truth and virtue are most authentically signified," moving away from the heroicizing tendency of romance—and, I would add, of epic literatures (*Origins*, 20). Walter Reed writes that his goal in exploring the "exemplary history of the novel" is to identify "the historical moment when the past began to be read novelistically" rather than heroically (*Exemplary History*, 23). Sixteenth- and seventeenth-century counter-epic texts do not provide the new model of authentic bourgeois virtue asserted for the eighteenth-century novel, nor do they read the past from a totally new vantage point. As counter-generic works, however, they help demystify idealizing heroic and aristocratic literary and historical constructs—a demystification that is an essential precondition to novelistic discourse as characterized by Reed, McKeon, and many others. In his analysis of Ercilla's *Araucana* and other sixteenth-century "epics of losers," David Quint asserts that this unconventional epic mode makes a significant contribution to the shift of Western civilization's "master narrative" from the epic to the novel (*Epic and Empire*, 45). The early modern counter-epic also plays an important and overlooked role during the century prior to this transition. All of the counter-epic forms, including both serious and parodic explorations of the foundations of aristocratic and heroic ideologies, offer a profound meditation on the process of inscription through which dominant class and gender formations argue for the inevitability of their society's power relations. The counter-epic questions imperial practices and poetics and marks a transitional stage for narrative discourse and the representation of dominant aristocratic ideology and power relations. This hegemony was waning after an extensive period of discursive and societal empowerment such that civilization itself was associated with its particular manifestations of hierarchy. Counter-epic poetics constitutes one of the many stages in the movement from epic versification of a warrior nobility to the prose novels of the emergent commercial class. Early modern writers employed a wide variety of modal transformations of epic ideologies, themes, and aesthetic techniques in order to explore and shape the shifting terrain of imperialist discourses and practices. Counter-epic writing highlighted the symbiotic and even parasitic dynamics of the relationships among military activities, the power and privileges derived from armed conquest and the exploitation of colonized lands and peoples, and the cultural productions that mediated the power relations of their day through reinscriptions of the historical record and the literary treasures of previous imperial nations.

# Works Cited

*Primary Sources*

Cervantes, Miguel de. *The Siege of Numantia*. Translated by Roy Campbell. In *The Classic Theater: Six Spanish Plays*, vol. 3, edited by Eric Bentley. Garden City, N.Y.: Doubleday, 1959.
———. *Don Quixote*. Edited by Joseph Jones and Kenneth Douglas. New York: Norton, 1981.
———. *La destrucción de Numancia*. In *Teatro completo*, edited by Florencio Sevila Arroyo and Antonio Rey Hazas. Barcelona: Planeta, 1987.
———. *El ingenioso hidalgo Don Quijote de la Mancha*. Edited by Luis Andrés Murillo. Madrid: Clásicos Castalia, 1987.
González de Bustos. *Los españoles en Chile*. Edited by James T. Abraham. Online: http://www.coh.arizona.edu/chile. May 2001.
Guevara, Antonio de. *Menosprecio de corte y alabanza de aldea*. Edited by Asunción Rallo Gruss. Madrid: Cátedra, 1987.
Las Casas, Bartolomé de. *Brevísima relación de la destrucción de Indias*. Edited by Manuel Ballasteros Gaibrois. Madrid: Fundación Universitaria Española, 1977.
Molina, Tirso de. *Obras dramáticas completas*. Edited by Blanca de los Rios. Madrid: Aguilar, 1969.
———. *La celosa de si misma*. Edited by Serge Maurel. Poitiers: n.p., 1981.
Quevedo, Francisco de. *Obra poética*. Edited by José Manuel Blecua. Vol. 1. Madrid: Castalia, 1969.
Rojas Zorrilla, Francisco de. *Numancia cercada y Numancia destruida*. Edited and with an introduction by Raymond R. MacCurdy. Madrid: Ediciones José Porrua Turanzas, 1977.
Ruiz de Alarcón, Juan. *La verdad sospechosa*. Edited by Alva Ebersole. Madrid: Cátedra, 1992.
Scarron, Paul. *Virgile travesti*. Edited by Jean Serroy. Paris: Garnier, 1988.
Shakespeare, William. *Troilus and Cressida*. In *Complete Works*, edited by David Bevington. 3d ed. Glenview, Ill.: Scott, Foresman, 1980.
Vega y Carpio, Lope de. *Obras escogidas*. Edited by Federico Carlos Sainz de Robles. Vols. 1 and 3. Madrid: Aguilar, 1964.
———. *La gatomaquia*. Mexico City: Instituto Nacional de Bellas Artes, Departamento de Teatro, 1966.

———. *Arauco domado.* Edited by Antonio de Lezama. Santiago: Biblioteca Zig Zag, 1984.

## Secondary Sources

Abraham, James T. "The Other Speaks: Tirso de Molina's *Amazonas en las Indias.*" In *El arte nuevo de estudiar comedias: Literary Theory and Golden Age Spanish Drama,* edited by Barbara Simerka, 143–61. Lewisburg: Bucknell University Press, 1996.
Acereda, Alberto. "Hacia una revalorización de *La gatomaquia.*" *Anales de Filología Hispánica* 5 (1990): 183–90.
Alborg, Juan Luis. *Historia de la literatura española.* Vol. 1. Madrid: Gredos, 1966.
Albrecht, Jane White. "The Satiric Irony of *Marta la Piadosa.*" *Bulletin of the Comediantes* 39, no. 1 (1987): 37–45.
Alfonso Hernández, José Luis. "Claves para la lectura de la poesía satírica de Quevedo." In *Actas del X Congreso de la Asociación de Hispanistas,* edited by Antonio Vilanova, 743–53. Barcelona: Promociones y Publicaciones Universitarias, 1992.
Alter, Robert. *Partial Magic: The Novel as a Self-Conscious Genre.* Berkeley and Los Angeles: University of California Press, 1975.
Antonucci, Fausta. "El indio americano y la conquista de América en las comedias impresas de tema araucano (1616–1665)." In *Relaciones literarias entre España y América en los siglos XVI y XVII,* edited by Ysla Campbell, 21–46. Ciudad Juárez: Universidad Autónoma de Ciudad Juárez, 1992.
Aramburu Alana, Mercedes. "Del barroco español al 'burlesque' francés: Alonso de Castillo Solorzano y Paul Scarron." *Letras de Deusto* 19, no. 44 (1989): 39–53.
Arellano Ayuso, Ignacio. *Poesía satírica burlesca de Quevedo.* Pamplona: Universidad de Navarra, 1984.
Arenal, Electa, and Georgina Sabat de Rivers, eds. *Literatura conventual femenina.* Barcelona: Promociones y Publicaciones Universitarias, 1988.
Arenal, Electa, and Stacey Schlau, eds. *Untold Sisters: Hispanic Nuns in Their Own Words.* Translated by Amanda Powell. Albuquerque: University of New Mexico Press, 1989.
Bakhtin, M. M. *The Problems of Dostoevsky's Poetics.* Translated by Willard R. Trask. Ann Arbor, Mich.: Ardis, 1973.
———. *The Dialogic Imagination: Four Essays.* Edited by Michael Holquist. Translated by Caryl Emerson and Michael Holquist. Austin: University of Texas Press, 1981.
Ball, Robert F. "Poetic Imitation in Góngora's *Romance de Angélica y Medoro.*" *Bulletin of Hispanic Studies* 57 (1980): 33–54.
Barnard, Mary E. "Myth in Quevedo: The Serious and the Burlesque in the Apollo and Daphne Poems." *Hispanic Review* 52, no. 4 (1984): 499–522.
Bauer, Ralph. "Colonial Discourse and Early American Literary History: Ercilla, the Inca Garcilaso, and Joel Barlow's Conception of a New World Epic." *Early American Literature* 30, no. 3 (1995): 203–32.

Bell, Steven M. "The Book of Life and Death: Quevedo and the Printing Press." *Hispanic Journal* 5, no. 2 (1978): 7–15.
Belli, Angela. "Cervantes' *El cerco de Numancia* and Euripides' *The Trojan Women*." *Kentucky Romance Quarterly* 24 (1978): 121–28.
Bénichou, Paul. *Morales du grand siècle*. Paris: Gallimard, 1948.
Bennett, Tony. *Outside Literature*. New York: Routledge, 1990.
Bergmann, Emilie. "The Epic Vision of Cervantes' *Numancia*." *Theater Journal* 36 (1982): 85–96.
Beverly, John, Bridget Aldaraca, and Edward Baker, eds. *Texto y sociedad: Problemas de historia literaria*. Amsterdam and Atlanta, Ga.: Rodopi, 1990.
Blue, William R. *Spanish Comedies and Historical Contexts in the 1620s*. University Park: The Pennsylvania State University Press, 1996.
Boriaud, Jean-Yves. "L'Image des dieux dans le *Virgile travesti*." In *Burlesque et formes parodiques dans la littérature et les arts*, edited by Isabelle Landy-Houillon and Maurice Menard, 411–21. Seattle: Papers on French Seventeenth-Century Literature, 1987.
Boyden, James. *The Courtier and the King*. Berkeley and Los Angeles: University of California Press, 1995.
Boyle, Charles. "Bitter Fruit: *Troilus and Cressida* in Queen Elizabeth's Court." *The Elizabethan Review* 2, no. 2 (1994): 11–18.
Briesemeister, Dietrich. "El horror y su función en algunas tragedias de Francisco de Rojas Zorrilla." *Criticón* 23 (1983): 159–75.
Brink, André. *The Novel: Language and Narrative from Cervantes to Calvino*. New York: New York University Press, 1998.
Broich, Ulrich. *The Eighteenth-Century Mock-Heroic Poem*. Translated by David Henry Wilson. Cambridge: Cambridge University Press, 1990.
Brooks, Harold. "*Troilus and Cressida*: Its Dramatic Unity and Genre." In *"Fanned and winnowed opinions": Shakespearean Essays Presented to Harold Jenkins*, edited by John Mahon and Thomas Pendleton, 6–25. London: Methuen, 1987.
Brownlee, Marina, and Hans Ulrich Gumbrecht, eds. *Cultural Authority in Golden Age Spain*. Baltimore: The Johns Hopkins University Press, 1995.
Buffmam, Imbrie. *Studies in the Baroque from Montaigne to Rotrou*. New Haven: Yale University Press, 1975.
Canavaggio, Jean. *Cervantes dramaturge: Un théâtre à naître*. Paris: Presses Universitaires de France, 1977.
Casa, Frank P. "The Epic Intention of Cervantes' *La Numancia*." In *Studies in the Literature of Spain: Sixteenth and Seventeenth Centuries*, edited by Michael J. Ruggerio, 1–14. Brockport: State University of New York, 1977.
Casalduero, Joaquín. *Sentido y forma del teatro de Cervantes*. Madrid: Gredos, 1966.
Cascardi, Anthony J. *Ideologies of History in the Spanish Golden Age*. University Park: The Pennsylvania State University Press, 1997.
Case, Thomas E. "El indio y el moro en las comedias de Lope de Vega." In *Looking at the "Comedia" in the Year of the Quincentennial*, edited by Barbara Mujica, Sharon D. Voros, and Matthew D. Stroud, 13–21. Lanham, Md.: University Press of America, 1993.

Castillo Sandoval, Roberto. "'Una misma cosa con la vuestra'? Ercilla, Pedro de Oña y la apropiación post-colonial de la patria araucana." *Revista Iberoamericana* 61 (January–June 1995): 231–47.
Church, Margaret. *Structure and Theme—Don Quixote to James Joyce.* Columbus: Ohio State University Press, 1983.
Clarke, Larry. "'Mars His Heart Enflamed with Venus': Ideology and Eros in Shakespeare's *Troilus and Cressida.*" *Modern Language Quarterly* 50, no. 3 (1989): 209–26.
Cohen, Ralph. "Genre Theory, Literary History, and Historical Change." In *Theoretical Issues in Literary History,* edited by David Perkins, 85–113. Cambridge: Harvard University Press, 1991.
Cohen, Walter. *Drama of a Nation: Public Theater in Renaissance England and Spain.* Ithaca: Cornell University Press, 1985.
———. "The Uniqueness of the *Comedia.*" In *Echoes and Inscriptions: Comparative Approaches to Early Modern Spanish Literatures,* edited by Barbara Simerka and Christopher B. Weimer, 17–32. Lewisburg: Bucknell University Press, 2000.
Colie, Rosalie. *The Resources of Kind: Genre Theory in the Renaissance.* Berkeley and Los Angeles: University of California Press, 1973.
Colomb, Gregory G. *Designs on Truth: The Poetics of the Augustan Mock-Epic.* University Park: The Pennsylvania State University Press, 1992.
Conchado, Diana. "Género y poética en *La gatomaquia* de Lope de Vega." Ph.D. diss., Brown University, 1994. Abstract in *Dissertation Abstracts International* 55.7 (1995): 9433341.
Contag, Kimberly. *Mockery in Spanish Golden Age Literature: Analysis of Burlesque Representation.* Lanham, Md.: University Press of America, 1996.
Cook, Robert. "Charles Cotton: Scarron Travestied." In *Scholastic Midwifery,* edited by Eden Jan Peters et al., 67–84. Tubigen: Narr, 1989.
Corominas, Juan M. "Las fuentes literarias del *Arauco domado,* de Lope de Vega." In *Lope de Vega y los orígenes del teatro español: Actas del I Congreso internacional sobre Lope de Vega,* edited by Manuel Criado de Val, 161–70. Madrid: Edi-6, 1981.
Correa, Gustavo. "El concepto de la fama en el teatro de Cervantes." *Hispanic Review* 27 (1959): 280–302.
Cox, John D. "*3 Henry VI:* Dramatic Convention and the Shakespearean History Play." *Comparative Drama* 12 (1978): 42–60.
Cronk, Nicholas. "La Défense du dialogisme: Vers une poétique du burlesque." In *Burlesque et formes parodiques dans la littérature et les arts,* edited by Isabelle Landy-Houillon and Maurice Menard, 321–38. Seattle: Papers on French Seventeenth-Century Literature, 1987.
Culler, Jonathan. "Stanley Fish and the Righting of the Reader." *Diacritics* 5, no. 1 (1975): 26–33.
Daalder, Joost. "The Role of 'Senex' in Kyd's *The Spanish Tragedy.*" *Comparative Drama* 20, no. 3 (1986): 247–60.
Davies, Gareth A. "The Country Cousin at Court: A Study of Antonio de Mendoza's *Cada loco con su tema* and Manuel Brentón de los Herreros' *El pelo de la dehesa.*" In *Leeds Papers on Hispanic Drama,* edited by Margaret A. Rees, 43–60. Leeds: Trinity and All Saints College and Simbaprint, 1991.

de Armas, Frederick. "Classical Tragedy and Cervantes' *La Numancia.*" *Neophilologus* 58 (1974): 34–40.

———. "The Necromancy of Imitation: Lucan and Cervantes' *La Numancia.*" In *El arte nuevo de estudiar comedias: Literary Theory and Golden Age Spanish Drama,* edited by Barbara Simerka, 224–58. Lewisburg: Bucknell University Press, 1996.

———. *Cervantes, Raphael, and the Classics.* Cambridge: Cambridge University Press, 1998.

———. "Numancia as Ganymede: Conquest and Continence in Giulio Romano, Cervantes, and Rojas Zorrilla." In *Echoes and Inscriptions: Comparative Approaches to Early Modern Spanish Literatures,* edited by Barbara Simerka and Christopher B. Weimer, 250–70. Lewisburg: Bucknell University Press, 2000.

Derrida, Jacques. "The Law of Genre/La Loi du genre." *Glyph* 7 (1980): 202–32.

———. *Dissemination.* Translated by Barbara Johnson. Chicago: University of Chicago Press, 1981.

Díaz Balsera, Viviana. "Araucanian Alterity in Alonso de Ercilla and Lope de Vega." In *Looking at the "Comedia" in the Year of the Quincentennial,* edited by Barbara Mujica, Sharon D. Voros, and Matthew D. Stroud, 23–36. Lanham, Md.: University Press of America, 1993.

Dille, Glen F. "America Tamed: Lope's *Arauco domado.*" In *New Historicism and the Comedia: Poetics, Politics, and Praxis,* edited by José A. Madrigal, 111–28. Boulder: Society of Spanish and Spanish-American Studies, University of Colorado, 1997.

Di Salvo, Angelo J. "Spanish Guides to Princes and the Political Theories in *Don Quijote.*" *Cervantes* 9, no. 2 (1989): 43–60.

Dolfi, Laura. *Studio sulla commedia di Tirso de Molina* Por el sótano y el torno. Messina-Firenze: D'Anna, 1973.

Dollimore, Jonathan. "Subjectivity, Sexuality, and Transgressions: The Jacobean Connection." *Renaissance Drama* 17 (1986): 53–82.

———. *Radical Tragedy: Religion, Ideology, and Power in the Drama of Shakespeare and His Contemporaries.* 2d ed. London: Harvester Wheatsheaf, 1989.

Dollimore, Jonathan, and Alan Sinfield, eds. *Political Shakespeare: New Essays in Cultural Materialism.* Manchester: Manchester University Press, 1985.

Domínguez Ortiz, Antonio. *The Golden Age of Spain, 1516–1659.* Translated by James Casey. New York: Basic Books, 1971.

Easthope, Anthony. *Literary into Cultural Studies.* New York: Routledge, 1991.

Edwards, Gwynne. "La estructura de *Numancia* y el desarrollo de su ambiente trágico." In *Cervantes: Su obra y su mundo,* edited by Manuel Criado de Val, 293–301. Madrid: Edi-6, 1981.

Edwards, John. "Religious Faith and Doubt in Late Medieval Spain: Soria circa 1450–1500." *Past and Present* 120 (August 1988): 3–25.

Elliott, J. H. *Imperial Spain: 1469–1716.* New York: Pelican, 1963.

———. *Spain and Its World, 1500–1700.* New Haven: Yale University Press, 1989.

El Saffar, Ruth. "In Praise of What Is Left Unsaid: Thoughts on Women and Lack in *Don Quijote.*" *Modern Language Notes* 103, no. 2 (1988): 205–22.

Fish, Stanley. *Is There a Text in This Class?* Cambridge: Harvard University Press, 1980.

Fitcher, Andrew. *Poets Historical: Dynastic Epic in the Renaissance.* New Haven: Yale University Press, 1982.
Forestier, Georges. "Le théâtre dans la Fronde, la Fronde dans le théâtre." In *La Fronde en questions: Actes du dix-huitième Colloque du Centre meridional de rencontres sur le XVIIème siècle, Marseille 28–29, Cassis 30–31 janvier 1988,* edited by Roger Duchêne et Pierre Ronzeaud, 231–43. Aix-en-Provence: Publications de l'Université de Provence, 1989.
Foucault, Michel. *Les Mots et les choses: Une Archéologie des sciences humaines.* Paris: Gallimard, 1966.
Fowler, Alastair. *Kinds of Literature.* Cambridge: Harvard University Press, 1982.
Fra Molinero, Baltasar. *La imagen de los negros en el teatro del Siglo de Oro.* Madrid: Siglo XXI, 1995.
Freedman, Richard. "Sufficiently Decayed: Gerontophobia in English Literature." In *Aging and the Elderly: Humanistic Perspectives in Gerontology,* edited by Stuart F. Spicker et al., 49–65. Atlantic Highlands, N.J.: Humanities Press, 1978.
Friedman, Edward H. *The Unifying Concept: Approaches to the Structure of Cervantes' Comedias.* York, S.C.: Spanish Publications, 1981.
Frye, Northrop. *Anatomy of Criticism: Four Essays.* Princeton: Princeton University Press, 1957.
Galbis, Ignacio R. M. "Aspectos forenses de la obra cervantina: El *Quijote* a la luz del derecho natural." In *Cervantes: Su obra y su mundo,* edited by Manuel Criado de Val, 699–705. Madrid: Edi-6, 1981.
Galdames, Luis. *A History of Chile.* Translated and edited by Isaac Joslin Cox. New York: Russell and Russell, 1964.
Gallagher, Catherine. "Re-covering the Social in Recent Literary Theory." *Diacritics* 4, no. 2 (1982): 40–48.
Genette, Gerard. *Palimpsests: Literature in the Second Degree.* Translated by Channa Newman and Claude Doubinsky. Lincoln: University of Nebraska Press, 1997.
*Genre: Forms of Discourse and Culture* 15, no. 1–2 (1982). [Edited and with an introduction by Stephen Greenblatt.]
Gicquel, Bernard. "Pour une sociopsychanalyse de la réception burlesque." In *Burlesque et formes parodiques dans la littérature et les arts.* Edited by Isabelle Landy-Houillon and Maurice Menard, 367–77. Seattle: Papers on French Seventeenth-Century Literature, 1987.
Godzich, Wlad, and Nicholas Spadaccini. *Literature Among Discourses.* Minneapolis: University of Minnesota Press, 1986.
González, Aurelio. "Los Romances de la Conquista: Enfoques y perspectivas." In *Relaciones literarias entre España y América en los siglos XVI y XVII,* edited by Ysla Campbell, 211–24. Ciudad Juárez: Universidad Autónoma de Ciudad Juárez, 1992.
Gornall, J. F. G. "Gongora's *Soledades:* 'Alabanza de aldea' without 'Menosprecio de corte'?" *Bulletin of Hispanic Studies* 59, no. 1 (1982): 21–25.
Gough, J. W. *The Social Contract.* 2d ed. Oxford: Clarendon Press, 1957.
Green, Otis. *Spain and the Western Tradition.* Vol. 2. Madison: University of Wisconsin Press, 1964.
Greenblatt, Stephen. *Renaissance Self-Fashioning: From More to Shakespeare.* Chicago: University of Chicago Press, 1980.

———. *Shakespearean Negotiations: The Circulation of Social Energy in Renaissance England*. Berkeley and Los Angeles: University of California Press, 1989.
———. *Marvelous Possessions: The Wonder of the New World*. Oxford: Clarendon Press, 1991.
Greene, Thomas. *The Light in Troy: Imitation and Discovery in Renaissance Poetry*. New Haven: Yale University Press, 1982.
Greer, Margaret Rich. *The Play of Power: Mythological Court Dramas of Calderón de la Barca*. Princeton: Princeton University Press, 1991.
Guillén, Claudio. *Literature as System: Essays Towards the Theory of Literary History*. Princeton: Princeton University Press, 1971.
Guntert, Georges. "Arte y furor en *La Numancia*." In *Actas del VIII Congreso de la Asociación Internacional de Hispanistas*, vol. 1, edited by David A. Kossoff et al., 671–83. Madrid: Istmo, 1986.
Hamilton, Bernice. *Political Thought in Sixteenth-Century Spain*. Oxford: Oxford University Press, 1963.
Harney, Michael. "Class Conflict and Primitive Rebellion in the *Poema de mio Cid*." *Olifant: A Publication of the Société Roncesvals, American-Canadian Branch* 12, no. 3–4 (1987): 171–219.
Hegstrom, Valerie, and Amy Williamsen, eds. *Engendering the Early Modern Stage*. New Orleans: University Press of the South, 1999.
Heller, Scott. "The New Geography of Classical Spanish Literature." *Chronicle of Higher Education* 47, no. 21 (2 February 2001): A14–17.
Helms, Lorraine. "'Still Wars and Lechery': Shakespeare and the Last Trojan Woman." In *Arms and the Woman: War, Gender, and Literary Representation*, edited by Helen M. Cooper, 25–42. Chapel Hill: The University of North Carolina Press, 1989.
Hempel, Wido. "El viejo y el amor: Apuntes sobre un motivo en la literatura española de Cervantes a García Lorca." In *Actas del VIII Congreso de la Asociación Internacional de Hispanistas*, vol. 1, edited by David A. Kossoff et al., 693–702. Madrid: Istmo, 1986.
Hermenegildo, Alfredo. *La Numancia de Cervantes*. Madrid: Sociedad General Española de Librería, 1976.
Herrick, Marvin Theodore. *Tragicomedy: Its Origin and Development in Italy, France, and England*. Urbana: University of Illinois Press, 1955.
Hindson, Jean. "The Fernando-Dorotea-Cardenio-Luscinda Story: Cervantes' Deconstruction of Marriage." *Romance Language Annual* 4 (1992): 483–86.
Hirst, David L. *Tragicomedy*. New York: Methuen, 1984.
Holub, Robert C. *Reception Theory: A Critical Introduction*. New York: Methuen, 1984.
Hornby, Richard. *Drama, Metadrama, and Perception*. Cranbury, N.J.: Associated University Presses, 1986.
Hubert, Judd D. *Metatheater: The Example of Shakespeare*. Lincoln: University of Nebraska Press, 1991.
Hunt, Maurice. "Shakespeare's *Troilus and Cressida* and Christian Epistemology." *Christianity and Literature* 42, no. 2 (1993): 243–60.
Hutcheon, Linda. *A Theory of Parody: The Teachings of Twentieth-Century Art Forms*. New York: Methuen, 1985.

Iser, Wolfgang. *The Implied Reader: Patterns of Communication in Prose Fiction from Bunyan to Beckett.* Baltimore: The Johns Hopkins University Press, 1978.
Jameson, Fredric. *The Political Unconscious: Narrative as a Socially Symbolic Act.* Ithaca: Cornell University Press, 1981.
Jammes, Robert. "Elementos burlescos en las *Soledades* de Gongora." *Edad de Oro* 2 (1982–83): 99–117. [Madrid: Departamento de Literatura Española, Universidad Autónoma de Madrid.]
Jauss, Hans Robert. "Literary History as a Challenge to Literary Theory." In *New Directions in Literary History,* edited by Ralph Cohen, 11–42. Baltimore: The Johns Hopkins University Press, 1974.
Jehenson, Yvonne. "The Pastoral Episode in *Don Quijote:* Marcela Once Again." *Cervantes* 10, no. 2 (1990): 15–35.
Johnson, Carroll B. "*La Numancia* y la estructura de la ambigüedad cervantina." In *Cervantes: Su obra y su mundo,* edited by Manuel Criado de Val, 309–16. Madrid: Edi-6, 1981.
———. *Cervantes and the Material World.* Urbana: University of Illinois Press, 2000.
Kastan, David Scott. "The Shape of Time: Form and Value in the Shakespearean History Play." *Comparative Drama* 7 (1973–74): 259–77.
Keith, Alison M. *Engendering Rome: Women in Latin Epic.* Cambridge: Cambridge University Press, 2000.
Keun, Ricardo Ferrando. *Y así nació la frontera.* Santiago: Antártica, 1986.
King, Willard. "Cervantes' *Numancia* and Imperial Spain." *Modern Language Notes* 94 (1979): 200–221.
Kirschner, Teresa J. "Encounter and Assimilation of the Other in *Arauco domado* and *La Araucana* by Lope de Vega." In *Christian Encounters with the Other,* edited by John C. Hawley and Erik D. Langer, 33–43. New York: New York University Press, 1998.
LaCapra, Dominick. *History, Politics, and the Novel.* Ithaca: Cornell University Press, 1987.
Landy-Houillon, Isabelle, and Maurice Menard, eds. *Burlesque et formes parodiques dans la littérature et les arts.* Seattle: Papers on French Seventeenth-Century Literature, 1987.
Lanoue, David. "Calderón's Late Roman Plays and the Imperial Myth." In *Critical Perspectives on Calderón de la Barca,* edited by Frederick de Armas et al., 91–102. Lincoln, Neb.: Society of Spanish and Spanish-American Studies, 1981.
Larson, Catherine. "Labels and Lies: Names and Don García's World in *La verdad sospechosa.*" *Revista de Estudios Hispánicos* 20, no. 2 (1986): 95–112.
———. *Language and the Comedia: Theory and Practice.* Lewisburg: Bucknell University Press, 1991.
Lauer, A. Robert. "La conquista de Chile en el teatro español del Siglo de Oro." In *El escritor y la escena II: Actas del II Congreso de la Asociación Internacional de Teatro Español y Novohispano de los Siglos de Oro, 17–20 de marzo de 1993,* edited by Ysla Campbell, 95–103. Ciudad Juárez: Universidad Autónoma de Ciudad Juárez, 1994.
Loftis, John. *Renaissance Drama in England and Spain: Topical Allusion and History Plays.* Princeton: Princeton University Press, 1987.

Lombardo, Agostino. "Fragments and Scraps: Shakespeare's *Troilus and Cressida*." In *The European Tragedy of Troilus*, edited by Piero Boitani, 199–217. Oxford: Clarendon Press, 1989.
Lorde, Audre. *Sister Outsider.* New York: Crossing Press, 1994.
Lukács, Georg. *The Theory of the Novel.* Translated by Anna Bostock. Cambridge: The MIT Press, 1983.
Lynch, Deirdre, and William Warner, eds. *Cultural Institutions of the Novel.* Durham: Duke University Press, 1996.
Lynch, John. *Spain Under the Habsburgs.* 2d ed. 2 vols. Oxford: Oxford University Press, 1981.
MacCurdy, Raymond R. "The Numantian Plays of Cervantes and Rojas Zorrilla: The Shift from the Collective to Personal Tragedy." *Symposium* 14 (1960): 100–120.
———. *Francisco de Rojas Zorrilla.* New York: Twayne, 1968.
Magnan, Robert. "Sex and Senescence in Medieval Literature." In *Aging in Literature*, ed. Laurel Porter and Laurence M. Porter, 13–30. Troy, Mich.: International Book Publishers, 1984.
Maguire, Nancy Klein, ed. *Renaissance Tragicomedy.* New York: AMS Press, 1987.
Mallin, Eric S. "Emulous Factions and the Collapse of Chivalry: *Troilus and Cressida*." *Representations* 29 (Winter 1990): 145–79.
Maravall, José Antonio. *Teatro y literatura en la sociedad barroca.* Madrid: Seminarios y Ediciones, 1972.
Marinelli, Peter V. *Ariosto and Boiardo: The Origins of Orlando Furioso.* Columbia: University of Missouri Press, 1987.
Mariscal, George. *Contradictory Subjects.* Ithaca: Cornell University Press, 1991.
———. "Can Cultural Studies Speak Spanish?" In *English Studies/Culture Studies: Institutionalizing Dissent*, edited by Isaiah Smithson and Nancy Ruff, 59–75. Urbana: University of Illinois Press, 1994.
———. "The Figure of the *Indiano* in Early Modern Spanish Culture." *Journal of Spanish Cultural Studies* 2 (2001): 55–68.
Martín, Adrienne Laskier. *Cervantes and the Burlesque Sonnet.* Berkeley and Los Angeles: University of California Press, 1991.
Martínez Millán, José. "Familia real y grupos políticos: La princesa Doña Juana de Austria." In *La corte de Felipe II*, edited by José Martínez Millán, 73–105. Madrid: Alianza, 1984.
———, ed. *La corte de Felipe II.* Madrid: Alianza, 1984.
Mason, Philip. *A Matter of Honour: An Account of the Indian Army.* London: Cape, 1974.
McKendrick, Malveena. *Women and Society in the Spanish Drama of the Golden Age.* Cambridge: Cambridge University Press, 1984.
McKeon, Michael. *The Origins of the English Novel, 1600–1740.* Baltimore: The Johns Hopkins University Press, 1987.
McVeigh, Terrence A. "A Tragic Senex Amans: O'Neill's Ephraim Cabot." *Classical and Modern Literature: A Quarterly* 11, no. 1 (1990): 67–75.
Mejías López, William. "Testimonio jurídico de Alonso de Ercilla: Desafíos, poder temporal regio y estado araucano." *Revista de Estudios Hispánicos* 21 (1994): 149–69.

Millington, Mark, and Paul Julian Smith, eds. *New Hispanisms: Literature, Culture, Authority.* Ottawa, Canada: Dovehouse Editions, 1994.

Molloy, Sylvia. "Alteridad y reconocimiento en los *Naufragios* de Alvar Nuñez Cabeza de Vaca." *Nueva Revista de Filología Hispánica* 35, no. 2 (1987): 425–49.

Montrose, Louis. "Professing the Renaissance: The Poetics and Politics of Culture." In *The New Historicism,* edited by H. Aram Veeser, 15–36. New York: Routledge, 1989.

Morales, Carlos Javier de. "Francisco de Eraso y los Ebolistas." In *La corte de Felipe II,* edited by José Martínez Millán, 107–48. Madrid: Alianza, 1984.

Moretti, Franco. *Signs Taken for Wonders: Essays in the Sociology of Literary Forms.* London: Verso, 1983.

Murillo, Luis Andrés. "La espada de Don Quijote (Cervantes y la poesía heroica)." In *Cervantes: Su obra y su mundo,* edited by Manuel Criado de Val, 667–680. Madrid: Edi-6, 1981.

Murrin, Michael. *History and Warfare in Renaissance Epic.* Chicago: University of Chicago Press, 1994.

Nelson, Cary, and Lawrence Grossberg, eds. *Marxism and the Interpretation of Culture.* Urbana: University of Illinois Press, 1988.

Newton, Judith, and Deborah Rosenfelt, eds. *Feminist Criticism and Social Change.* New York: Methuen, 1985.

Niderst, Alain. "Scarron, les Scudery et le burlesque." In *Burlesque et formes parodiques dans la littérature et les arts,* ed. Isabelle Landy-Houillon and Maurice Menard, 139–46. Seattle: Papers on French Seventeenth-Century Literature, 1987.

Orgel, Stephen. *The Illusion of Power.* Berkeley and Los Angeles: University of California Press, 1975.

Oriel, Charles. *Writing and Inscription in Golden Age Spain.* West Lafayette: Purdue University Press, 1992.

———. "Cervantes' *Numancia:* A Speech Act Consideration." *Bulletin of the Comediantes* 47, no. 1 (1995): 105–19.

Osterc, Ludovik. *El pensamiento social y político del Quijote.* Mexico City: Ediciones de Andrea, 1963.

Pagden, Anthony. *Spanish Imperialism and the Political Imagination: Studies in European and Spanish-American Social and Political Theory, 1513–1830.* New Haven: Yale University Press, 1990.

———. *Lords of All the World: Ideologies of Empire in Spain, Britain, and France, c. 1500–c. 1800.* New Haven: Yale University Press, 1995.

Palomo, Dolores. "Chaucer, Cervantes, and the Birth of the Novel." *Mosaic: A Journal for the Interdisciplinary Study of Literature* 8, no. 4 (1975): 61–72.

Parr, James A. *Don Quixote: An Anatomy of Subversive Discourse.* Newark, Del.: Juan de la Cuesta, 1988.

———. *Confrontaciones calladas: El crítico frente al clásico.* Madrid: Orígenes, 1990.

———. *After Its Kind: Approaches to the Comedia.* Kassel: Reichenberger, 1991.

Pastor, Beatriz. *The Armature of Conquest: Spanish Accounts of the Discovery of America, 1492–1589.* Translated by Lydia Longstreth Hunt. Stanford: Stanford University Press, 1992.

Paterson, Alan K. G. "Reversal and Multiple Role-Playing in Alarcón's *La verdad sospechosa.*" *Bulletin of Hispanic Studies* 61, no. 1 (1984): 361–68.
Perelmuter-Pérez, Rosa. "El paisaje idealizado en *La Araucana.*" *Hispanic Review* 54, no. 2 (1986): 129–46.
Pieterse, Jan P. Nederveen. *Empire and Emancipation: Power and Liberation on a World Scale.* New York: Praeger, 1989.
Porter, Laurel, and Laurence M. Porter, eds. *Aging in Literature.* Troy, Mich.: International Book Publishers, 1984.
Porter, Laurence M. "Farce and Idealization: Dostoevsky's Ambivalence Toward Aging." In *Aging in Literature,* ed. Laurel Porter and Laurence M. Porter, 85–103. Troy, Mich.: International Book Publishers, 1984.
Potter, A. M. "*Troilus and Cressida:* Deconstructing the Middle Ages?" *Theoria* 72 (October 1988): 23–35.
Powers, Harriet B. "The Grotesque Vision of Rojas Zorrilla." *Bulletin of the Comediantes* 23 (1971): 1–6.
Puddu, Raffaele. *El soldado gentilhombre.* Barcelona: Argos Vergara, 1986.
Quint, David. *Epic and Empire.* Princeton: Princeton University Press, 1993.
Rabell, Carmen R. "'Menosprecio de corte y alabanza de aldea': ¿Crítica lascasiana, propaganda imperialista o 'Best-Seller'?" In *Actas Irvine-92, Asociación Internacional de Hispanistas,* vol. 3, edited by Juan Villegas, 245–53. Irvine: University of California, 1994.
Rackin, Phyllis. *Stages of History: Shakespeare's English Chronicles.* Ithaca: Cornell University Press, 1990.
Redondo, Augustin. "Du 'Beatus Ille' horacien au 'Mépris de la cour et éloge de la vie rustique d'Antonio Guevara." In *L'Humanisme dans les lettres espagnoles,* ed. Augustin Redondo, 251–65. Paris: Vrin, 1979.
Reed, Walter. *An Exemplary History of the Novel: The Quixotic Versus the Picaresque.* Chicago: University of Chicago Press, 1981.
Reichenberger, Arnold. "The Uniqueness of the 'Comedia.'" *Hispanic Review* 27 (1959): 303–16.
Reiss, Timothy J. *Toward Dramatic Illusion: Theatrical Technique and Meaning from Hardy to Horace.* New Haven: Yale University Press, 1971.
Rendall, Steven. "Argument and Persuasion in French Classical Drama." *Papers in Romance* 5, no. 1 (1983): 1–15.
Rodríguez, Mario. "Un caso de imaginación colonizada: *Arauco domado.*" *Acta Literaria* 6 (1981): 79–92.
Rohu, Jean. "Le Burlesque et les avatars de l'écriture discordante (1635–1655)." In *Burlesque et formes parodiques dans la littérature et les arts,* edited by Isabelle Landy-Houillon and Maurice Menard, 349–66. Seattle: Papers on French Seventeenth-Century Literature, 1987.
Romanos, Melchora. "La construcción del personaje de Caupolicán en el teatro del Siglo de Oro." *Filología* 26, no. 1–2 (1993): 183–204.
Rose, Mary Beth. *The Expense of Spirit: Love and Sexuality in English Renaissance Drama.* Ithaca: Cornell University Press, 1988.
Ruiz Ramón, Francisco. *Calderón y la tragedia.* Madrid: Alhambra, 1984.
———. *Historia del teatro español.* Madrid: Cátedra, 1988.

———. "El héroe americano en Lope de Vega y Tirso: De la guerra de los hombres a la guerra de los dioses." In *El mundo del teatro español en su siglo de oro: Ensayos dedicados a John E. Varey*, edited by J. M. Ruano de la Haza, 229–48. Ottawa Hispanic Studies 3. Ottawa, Canada: Dovehouse Editions, 1989.

———. "La voz de los vencidos en el teatro de los vencedores." In *Relaciones literarias entre España y América en los siglos XVI y XVII*, edited by Ysla Campbell, 1–19. Ciudad Juárez: Universidad Autónoma de Ciudad Juárez, 1992.

Said, Edward W. *Orientalism*. New York: Random House, 1979.

———. *Culture and Imperialism*. New York: Random House, 1993.

Sánchez y Escribano, Federico. *Preceptiva dramática española del Renacimiento y el Barroco*. Madrid: Gredos, 1972.

Schmidt, Rachel. "Maps, Figures, and Canons in the *Viaje del Parnaso*." *Cervantes* 16, no. 2 (1996): 29–46.

Schwartz Lerner, Lia. "Tradición literaria y heroinas indias en *La Araucana*." *Revista Iberoamericana* 38 (1972): 615–25.

Sedgwick, Eve Kosofsky. *Between Men*. New York: Columbia University Press, 1985.

Serroy, Jean. "Prolegomènes à une édition du *Virgile travesti*." In *Burlesque et formes parodiques dans la littérature et les arts*, ed. Isabelle Landy-Houillon and Maurice Menard, 339–48. Seattle: Papers on French Seventeenth-Century Literature, 1987.

Shannon, Robert. *Visions of the New World in the Drama of Lope de Vega*. New York: Peter Lang, 1989.

Shivers, George. "La historicidad de *El cerco de Numancia*." *Hispanófila* 39 (1970): 1–14.

Siegel, Paul. *Shakespearean Tragedy and the Elizabethan Compromise*. New York: New York University Press, 1957.

Simerka, Barbara. "The 'Efemination' of Flor: Satire and Sexuality in Ruiz de Alarcón's *Ganar amigos*." *Romance Language Annual* 4 (1992): 580–84.

———. "The Generic Dimension of Self-Referentiality: Calderón's *El médico de su honra* as *metadrama de honor*." *Bulletin of the Comediantes* 46, no. 1 (1994): 103–17.

———. "The *Indiano* as Liminal Figure in the Drama of Tirso and His Contemporaries." *Bulletin of the Comediantes* 47, no. 2 (1995): 311–20.

———. "Dramatic and Discursive Genres: *La verdad sospechosa* as Problem Comedy and Marriage Treatise." In *El arte nuevo de estudiar comedias*, edited by Barbara Simerka, 187–205. Lewisburg: Bucknell University Press, 1996.

———. "The Demystification of Providential Ideology: Skepticism and Unbelief in *El burlador de Sevilla*." *Gestos* 23 (April 1997): 38–66.

———. "'That the Rulers Should Sleep Without Bad Dreams': Anti-Epic Discourse in *La Numancia* and *Arauco domado*." *Cervantes* 18, no. 2 (1998): 46–70.

———. "The Indiano Senex as Subaltern Figure in Tirso's *Marta la piadosa* and *Por el sótano y el torno*." *Romance Language Annual* 11 (1999): 822–26.

———, ed. *El arte nuevo de estudiar comedias: Literary Theory and Golden Age Spanish Drama*. Lewisburg: Bucknell University Press, 1996.

Simerka, Barbara, and Christopher B. Weimer, eds. *Echoes and Inscriptions: Comparative Approaches to Early Modern Spanish Literatures*. Lewisburg: Bucknell University Press, 2000.

Sinfield, Alan. "Power and Ideology: An Outline Theory and Sydney's *Arcadia*." *English Literary History* 52, no. 2 (1985): 259–77.
Šklovsky, Victor. "Sterne's *Tristram Shandy:* Stylistic Commentary." In *Russian Formalist Criticism: Four Essays*, ed. Lee T. Lemon and Marion J. Reiss, 25–57. Lincoln: University of Nebraska Press.
Smith, Paul Lewis. "Cervantes' *Numancia* as Tragedy and as Tragicomedy." *Bulletin of Hispanic Studies* 64, no. 1 (1987): 15–26.
Snyder, John. *Prospects of Power: Tragedy, Satire, the Essay, and the Theory of Genre*. Lexington: The University Press of Kentucky, 1991.
Soufas, Teresa, ed. *Women's Acts: Plays by Women Dramatists of Spain's Golden Age*. Lexington: The University Press of Kentucky, 1997.
Spivak, Gayatri Chakravorty. "Can the Subaltern Speak?" In *Marxism and the Interpretation of Culture*, edited by Cary Nelson and Lawrence Grossberg, 271–313. Urbana: University of Illinois Press, 1988.
Stoll, Anita K. "The Dual Levels of Antonio Hurtado de Mendoza's *Cada loco con su tema*." *Bulletin of the Comediantes* 44, no. 1 (1992): 73–84.
Stoll, Anita K., and Dawn Smith, eds. *The Perception of Women in Spanish Theater of the Golden Age*. Lewisburg: Bucknell University Press, 1991.
Stroud, Matthew D. "*La Numancia* como auto secular." In *Cervantes: Su obra y su mundo*, edited by Manuel Criado de Val, 303–7. Madrid: Edi-6, 1981.
Suárez, José I. "Characterization of the Elderly in Vicentine Drama." *South Atlantic Review* 62, no. 1 (1996): 33–42.
Sullivan, Henry. *Tirso de Molina and the Drama of the Counter Reformation*. Amsterdam: Rodopi, 1976.
———. "Lacan and Calderón: Spanish Classical Drama in the Light of Psychoanalytic Theory." *Gestos* 5, no. 10 (1990): 39–55.
Suzuki, Mihoko. "'Truth Tired with Iteration': Myth and Fiction in Shakespeare's *Troilus and Cressida*." *Philological Quarterly* 66, no. 2 (1987): 153–74.
Tennenhouse, Leonard. *Power on Display: The Politics of Shakespeare's Genres*. New York: St. Martin's, 1996.
Terdiman, Richard. "Deconstructing Memory." *Diacritics* 15, no. 4 (1985): 13–36.
Todorov, Tzvetan. *The Conquest of America*. Translated by Richard Howard. New York: Harper and Row, 1984.
Turner, Victor. *The Ritual Process*. Chicago: Aldine, 1969.
Urtiaga, Alfonso. *El indiano en la dramática de Tirso de Molina*. Madrid: n.p., 1965.
Valbuena Prat, Angel. *Historia del teatro español*. Barcelona: Noguer, 1956.
Veeser, Harold A. "'That Dangerous Supplement': *La verdad sospechosa* and the Literary Speech Situation." In *Things Done with Words: Speech Acts in Hispanic Drama*, edited by Elias L. Rivers, 51–76. Newark, Del.: Juan de la Cuesta, 1986.
Villarino, Edith Marta. "*El indiano*, un entremés de Lope de Vega." *Signos* 25, no. 31–32 (1992): 227–33.
Wardropper, Bruce. "Cervantes's Theory of Drama." *Modern Philology* 52, no. 4 (1955): 217–21.
Warner, William B. "Formulating Fiction: Romancing the General Reader in Early Modern England." In *Cultural Institutions of the Novel*, edited by Deirdre Lynch and William Warner, 279–305. Durham: Duke University Press, 1996.

Watt, Ian P. *The Rise of the Novel: Studies in Defoe, Richardson, and Fielding.* Berkeley and Los Angeles: University of California Press, 1967.
Watt, Stephen. "Shaw's *St. Joan* and the Modern History Play." *Comparative Drama* 19, no. 1 (1985): 56–86.
Weiner, Jack. "La guerra y la paz espirituales en tres comedias de Lope de Vega." *Revista de Estudios Hispánicos* 17, no. 1 (1983): 65–79.
Whitby, William. "The Sacrifice Theme in Cervantes' *Numancia*." *Hispania* 45 (1962): 205–10.
Wicks, Ulrich. *Picaresque Narratives, Picaresque Fictions.* New York: Greenwood Press, 1989.
Wikander, Matthew H. "The Clock in Brutus' Orchards Strikes Again: Anachronism and Achronism in Historical Drama." In *The Delegated Intellect: Emersonian Essays on Literature, Science, and Art in Honor of Don Gifford,* edited by Donald E. Morse, 149–68. New York: Peter Lang, 1995.
Williams, Raymond. *Marxism and Literature.* New York: Oxford University Press, 1972.
———. *The Country and the City.* New York: Oxford University Press, 1973.
Williamsen, Amy. "Death Becomes Her: Fatal Beauty in María de Zayas's 'Mal presagio casar lejos.'" *Romance Language Annual* 6 (1994): 619–23.
Wilson, Diana de Armas. "Defending 'Poor Poetry': Sidney, Cervantes, and the Prestige of Epic." In *Ingeniosa Invención: Essays on Golden Age Spanish Literature for Geoffrey L. Stagg in Honor of His Eighty-fifth Birthday,* edited by Ellen M. Anderson and Amy R. Williamsen, 25–40. Newark, Del.: Juan de la Cuesta, 1999.
———. "Rethinking Cervantine Utopias: Some No [Good] Places in Renaissance England and Spain." In *Echoes and Inscriptions: Comparative Approaches to Early Modern Spanish Literatures,* edited by Barbara Simerka and Christopher B. Weimer, 191–209. Lewisburg: Bucknell University Press, 2000.
Woodhouse, William. "Hacia una terminología coherente para la poesía del Siglo de Oro." In *Actas del VIII Congreso de la Asociación Internacional de Hispanistas,* edited by David A. Kossoff et al., 749–53. Madrid: Istmo, 1986.
Yoch, James J. "The Renaissance Dramatization of Temperance: The Italian Revival of Tragicomedy." In *Renaissance Tragicomedy,* ed. Nancy Klein Maguire, 115–138. New York: AMS Press, 1987.
Zayas y Sotomayor, María de. *The Enchantments of Love.* Translated by H. Patsy Boyer. Berkeley and Los Angeles: University of California Press, 1990.
———. *The Disenchantments of Love.* Translated by H. Patsy Boyer. Albany: State University of New York Press, 1997.

# Index

Alba, duke of, 18, 35–36
Albrecht, Jane, 66–67
Alexander VI, 29
Alonso de Herrera, Gabriel, 47–48
*Amazonas en las Indias* (Tirso de Molina), 44–45
anachronisms, 116–17
*Anatomy of Criticism* (Frye), 8
Antonucci, Fausta, 94, 133, 137
Antwerp, sack of, 18
Araucana, 19–20
*La Araucana* (Ercilla), 14, 78, 120, 146, 201
*Arauco domado* (Lope de Vega)
   Biobío River boundary and, 22–23
   composition and performance of, 120
   cost of war in, 114
   critical attention to, 91–92, 93–95
   critique of military in, 96
   demonization of Other in, 123–24
   diplomacy in, 110–11
   historical inscription in, 84–86
   humanization of Other in, 119–21
   human suffering in, 113–15
   juxtaposition of genre in, 87, 88, 89, 96, 125, 127–28
   nostalgia in, 85–86
   perspectives on imperialism in, 106–9
   Providence in, 81
   representation of Spanish in, 108–9
*Arcadia* (Sydney), 164
Arellano Ayuso, Ignacio, 178–79
Arenal, Electa, 14
Ariosto, Ludovico, *Orlando Furioso*, 130, 197
aristocracy. *See* nobility
Armada, 19
*armas y letras* pamphlets, 34–35
assimilation, 32–33
Ávila, Gaspar de, 27

Bakhtin, Mikhail, 165, 199–200
Ball, Robert, 162–63
barbarians, beneficent civilization of, 25, 96
Barnard, Mary, 163, 178
*Battle of the Frogs and Mice* (Homer), 165, 175
Bénichou, Paul, 182
Bennett, Tony, 5, 9, 163
Bergmann, Emilie, 89
Black Legend, 83, 137
Boriaud, Jean-Yves, 178
bourgeois discourse, 200
Boyden, James, 35–36
Breda, capture of, 20
Brownlee, Marina, 3
burlesque epic. *See also Don Quijote* (Cervantes); *La gatomaquia* (Lope de Vega); Quevedo, Francisco de
   description of, 166
   in England, 185–91
   in France, 182–85
   gross physiological references in, 169, 171, 173–74, 184–85, 197
   hegemony and reception of, 178–79
   marginalization of, 164, 199–200
   overview of, 10, 161–62
   parody and, 165–66

Cabeza de Vaca, Alvar Núñez, 42
Calderón de la Barca, Pedro, 84, 93, 164
Canavaggio, Jean, 88
Cañete, marquis of, 22
cannibalism, 122, 123
Cano, Melchor, 27
*Cantar del mío Cid*, 168
*Carlos Famoso* (Zapata), 166
Cascardi, Anthony, 1–2, 5, 7, 79, 127
Cecil, Robert, 186

*La celosa de sí misma* (Tirso de Molina), 51–54, 70, 72, 73–74
Ceriol, Furió, 6, 35
Cervantes, Miguel de. See also *La destrucción de Numancia* (Cervantes); *Don Quijote* (Cervantes)
   *Persiles*, 199
   *Viaje al Parnaso*, 164
*Cervantes, Raphael, and the Classics* (de Armas), 88
Charles V, 24, 25, 36
Chile, 21–23. See also *Arauco domado* (Lope de Vega); *Los españoles en Chile* (González de Bustos)
Christianity and empire, 28, 108–9
*The Civile Wars* (Drayton), 164
Clarke, Larry, 185–86
Coe, Ada M., 132
Cohen, Ralph, 10, 15 n. 9
Colomb, Gregory, 6, 161, 198–99
*comedia de capa y espada*, 72–73, 146
comedias
   cross-dressed heroines in, 142
   location of, 43–44
   misunderstandings in, 57
   subplots typical of, 144–45
   *villano* and *cortesano* in, 46–47
Conchado, Diana, 164–66, 178
Contag, Kimberly, 178
*converso*, conflation of *indiano* and, 45, 70
*cortesano* character, 46, 53–54, 60
cost of war, portrayal of, 98–99, 114
counter-epic
   as denaturalization of power relations, 16
   emergence of, 164–65
   in France and England, 182–91
   marginalization of physical bravery in, 105
   materialist, "epochal" analysis of, 1–2, 4, 5–6, 13, 77–78
   meaning of term, 4
   novel and, 198–202
   strategies of, 129–30
counter-generic text and literary mimesis, 23
*The Country and the City* (Williams), 46–47
courtier, 2, 61
courtly system, critique of, 56–57
courtship, vulgarization and demystification of, 187–89

Covarrubias, Diego, 29
Cox, John, 80
*criollo*, 39–40
Culler, Jonathan, 13
*Culture and Imperialism* (Said), 40–41
Cyrano de Bergerac, 178

Daalder, Joost, 62
d'Aubigné, *Les Tragiques*, 14
Davies, Gareth, 43
de Armas, Frederick, 23, 88, 89, 90, 92–93, 122
defamiliarization model, 13–14
*La destrucción de Numancia* (Cervantes)
   classical views in, 23
   collective self-destruction in, 82–83, 113, 123
   cost of war in, 98–99
   critical attention to, 87–91
   critique of military in, 96, 99, 100–101
   demonization of Other in, 122–23
   diplomacy in, 110
   historical inscription in, 82–83
   historical writing in, 83–84
   humanization of Other in, 116–19
   human suffering in, 31, 101–2, 111–13
   ideology and closure in, 125–26
   imperialist discourses in, 92–93
   justification for rebellion in, 102–4
   juxtaposition of genre in, 87, 88, 89, 96, 126–28
   legitimacy of wars of imperialism theme in, 97–106
   links to Rome in, 79
   paradox in, 104–5
   perspective on Roman struggle in, 99–100
   Providence and history in, 81
   representation of siege warfare in, 105–6
   self-reflection in, 81–82
   as source for other works, 93
Díaz Balsera, Viviana
   on *Arauco domado* (Lope de Vega), 95, 97, 119–20, 121
   on Spain's justification of conquest, 115–16, 122, 124–25
Dille, Glen, 43–44, 93–94
diplomacy, scenes of, 110–11
discourses of empire, 1–2
discursive competition, 12

Dollimore, Jonathan, 8
*dominium*, 25–28
*Don Quijote* (Cervantes)
   amatory adventures in, 197–98
   aristocracy in, 192
   as burlesque epic, 178
   chivalry in, 154
   disdain for dominant class in, 164
   doctrine of natural liberty in, 193–94
   military in, 102, 192–93, 194
   overview of, 191–92, 198
   Sancho Panza's governorship in, 195
   treatment of squire by, 194–95
Drake, Francis, 19
dramaturgy, elements of, 108

"early modern," meaning of term, 3–4
economy of Spain. *See also encomienda* system; money
   merchant class, rise of, 2, 16, 186
   metal from colonies and, 21, 27–28, 29–30
   wealth and social status, 72, 198
Eguiluz, Martín de, 34
Elizabeth I, 18, 186
Elliott, J. H., 2, 3, 35, 48, 81, 110
emergent discourse, 6
*Empire and Emancipation* (Pieterse), 95–96, 116
*encomienda* system, 26–27, 31, 95–96, 103
*Engendering Rome* (Keith), 171
England
   counter-epic in, 185–91
   history play in, 79
   Spain and, 18–19, 21
epic, 23, 171. *See also* burlesque epic; counter-epic
*Epic and Empire* (Quint), 14
"epochal" analysis, 1–2, 4, 5–6, 13, 77–78
Eraso, Francisco de, 36
Ercilla, *La Araucana*, 14, 78, 120, 146, 201
*Los españoles en Chile* (González de Bustos)
   closure in, 157–59
   conflict in, 143–44
   critical evaluation of, 132–34
   deceptive honesty motif in, 148–49
   disguised identity in, 155–56
   dramatic convention in, 155–59
   dramatic emplotment in, 140–41, 147, 156–57

   farce in, 153–55
   historical inscription in, 137
   inscription and reinscription in, 157
   military in, 139, 149–51
   overview of, 129
   subplots in, 145–49
ethnicity, 95–96
*examen*, 152
Ezquerra, Ramón de, 33, 34

*Fairie Queene* (Spenser), 164
Farnese, Alexander, 18, 19, 36, 78
Ferdinand, 25, 29
Fish, Stanley, 11–12, 13
food theme, 112, 174–75, 197
Fowler, Alastair, 163
Fra Molinero, Baltasar, 3
France, counter-epic in, 182–85
Friedman, Edward, 89
Frye, Northrop, 8, 166

Galdames, Luis, *History of Chile*, 22
*La gatomaquia* (Lope de Vega)
   burlesque technique in, 165
   critique of aristocracy in, 175–76
   critique of military in, 173
   deflation of rhetorical techniques in, 177–78
   food and kitchen in, 174–75
   as *imitatio*, 175–76
   men in, 173
   overview of, 161–62
   plot of, 170–71
   stylistic devices in, 176–77
   vulgar corporeality in, 173–74
   women in, 171–72
gender study, 14. *See also* women
genre. *See also* novel; parody
   of *La destrucción de Numancia*, 88–91
   history play, early modern European, 78–86
   indeterminacy of, 163–64
   juxtaposition of in *La destrucción de Numancia* and *Arauco domado*, 87, 88, 89, 96, 125, 126–28
   juxtaposition of in *Los españoles en Chile* and *Numancia* diptych, 138
   materialist poetics of, 8–11
   "sociology of," 9, 161, 163
   violating boundaries of, 88

Geoffrey of Monmouth, 186
Godzich, Wlad, 8–9
Gómez de Silva, Ruy, 35–36
González de Bustos. See *Los españoles en Chile* (González de Bustos)
Greenblatt, Stephen, 8, 41–42, 45
Greene, Thomas, 23
Greer, Margaret, 3
Guerrero, Gonzalo, 42
Guevara, Antonio de, 47–48, 164
Guillén, Claudio, 4 n. 5
Gumbrecht, Hans Ulrich, 3

Hegstrom, Valerie, 14
Heller, Scott, 3–4
Hempel, Wido, 63
*Henriad* (Shakespeare), 78, 81, 200–201
Hermenegildo, Alfredo, 91
Hindson, Jean, 65
*historia*, 126–27
historical inscription
　in *Arauco domado* (Lope de Vega), 84–86
　in *La destrucción de Numancia* (Cervantes), 82–83
　in *Don Quijote* (Cervantes), 196–97
　in *Los españoles en Chile* (González de Bustos), 137
　in *Numancia cercada* (Rojas Zorrilla), 134
　in *Numancia destruida* (Rojas Zorrilla), 134–37
　role of, 82
historical periods as monolithic entities, 15–16
historiography
　printing press and, 79
　of Spanish Empire, 24
*History and Warfare in Renaissance Epic* (Murrin), 164
*History of Chile* (Galdames), 22
history play. See also *Arauco domado* (Lope de Vega); *La destrucción de Numancia* (Cervantes); *Los españoles en Chile* (González de Bustos); *Numancia cercada* (Rojas Zorrilla); *Numancia destruida* (Rojas Zorrilla)
　early modern European, 78–86, 127
　Elizabethan and Jacobean, 134
　late baroque, 138–44, 159
　novelization of, 129–30
　role of, 128
Homer, *Battle of the Frogs and Mice*, 165, 175

human suffering, portrayal of, 31, 101–2, 111–13, 113–15
Hurtado de Mendoza, García, 22, 78.
　See also *Arauco domado* (Lope de Vega)
Hutcheon, Linda, 162, 165

identity and status
　disguised, 155–56
　instability of, 7, 16, 41–46, 56–57, 72–76
"Imitación de Virgilio en lo que Dido dijo a Eneas queriendo dejarla" (Quevedo), 161–62, 166–68
*imitatio*, 162–63, 175
imperialism
　debate over, 2–3, 17, 24–30
　ideology of, 15
　juridical justifications of, 24–30
　Lascasian critiques of, 30–33
　overview of, 1559–1665, 17–23
　political factionalism and, 35–37
　professional soldier and, 33–35
　Rome in Spanish political *imaginaire*, 23–24
　urbanism and, 48
*Imperial Spain* (Elliott), 48
*indiano* drama
　as aspect of military conquest, 7
　characters in, 39–40
　critiques of, 43–44
　elements of, 48–49
　family honor in, 50
　pretenders in, 72–75
　*senex amans* conflation in, 62–69
　social dynamic in, 200
　stock characters and subjectivity, 46–48
　*villano* conflation in, 46–48, 50–51
*El indiano en la dramática de Tirso de Molina* (Urtiaga), 43
*El indiano* (Lope de Vega), 75
*indianos*
　ethnicity and identity of, 41–46
　liminal status of, 42–43, 44–46, 62, 69, 75
　meaning of term, 40
　money and, 69–72
　as naive and generous, 58–60, 61
　origins of, 40
　return of to Spain, 16
　silencing of, 44, 45, 65, 75–76
　wealth of, 27, 30, 198
Isaba, Marcos de, 34

Iser, Wolfgang, 11, 12, 13
Islam, 17
isolationism, 29

Jameson, Fredric, 8
Jansenist thought, 182
Jauss, Hans Robert, 11, 12, 13
Johnson, Carroll, 7–8, 88, 90–91, 92
Juana of Austria, 36
*juntas*, 24–25
"just war" theory, 28–29

Keith, Alison, 171
Keun, Ricardo Ferrando, *Y así nació la frontera*, 21–22
kind, 163
King, Willard, 90, 91, 92, 105
*King John* (Shakespeare), 80–81
Kirschner, Teresa, 95, 108

Larson, Catherine, 74
Las Casas, Bartolomé de, 3, 6, 30–33
Lauer, A. Robert, 133
Lerma, Duque de, 2, 19–20
Lindenberger, Herbert, 79–80
*Literature Among Discourses* (Godzich and Spadaccini), 8–9
Loftis, John, 84, 93, 102, 201
*Lords of All the World* (Pagden), 23–24
Lukács, Georg, 200–201
Lynch, John, 2, 18, 35

MacCurdy, Raymond, 131
Macherey, Pierre, 44
Madox, Richard, 45
Magnan, Robert, 62
Maguire, Nancy Klein, 88
Mallin, Eric, 186
Marañón, Gregorio, 35
Maravall, José Antonio, 15
Margaret of Parma, 18, 36
Mariana, Juan de, 79
Marinelli, Peter, 130
Mariscal, George
  on *indianos*, 40, 43, 45, 70, 200
  on Spain, 41
  studies by, 3
marriage
  courtship, vulgarization and demystification of, 187–89

*indiano* status and, 54
private, 65–66
*Marta la piadosa* (Tirso de Molina), 62–63, 66–69, 71
Martín, Adrienne Laskier, 106
Martínez Millán, José, 36
Marx, Karl, model of social and literary relations of, 4–6
*Marxism and Literature* (Williams), 5–6
Mason, Philip, 15
materialist, "epochal" analysis. See "epochal" analysis
materialist poetics
  burlesque epic and, 165
  of character and subjectivity, 7–8
  of genre, 8–11
  overview of, 4–6
  of reception, 11–14
McKendrick, Malveena, 14
McKeon, Michael, 200, 201
Medellín, Diego de, 32
Mejías López, William, 32
memoirs of soldiers, 34
Menchaca, Vázquez de, 26, 29, 40, 108
Mendoza, Bernardino de, 34–35
Mendoza, García de, 28
*menosprecio de corte y alabanza de aldea* discourse, 47–48, 51, 53, 55, 58, 61–62
"Menosprecio de corte y alabanza de aldea" (Guevara), 164
merchant class, rise of, 2, 16, 186
meta-artistry, manifestations of, 156, 177–78, 185
metahistorical reflections in historical drama, 85, 137
metal from New World, 21, 27–28, 29–30
Mexía, Pedro de, 79
military. *See also* siege warfare
  in *Arauco domado* (Lope de Vega), 96
  in *La destrucción de Numancia* (Cervantes), 96, 99, 100–101
  in *Don Quijote* (Cervantes), 102, 192–93, 194
  in *Los españoles en Chile* (Gonzalez de Bustos), 139, 149–51
  in *La gatomaquia* (Lope de Vega), 173
  *menosprecio de corte* writings and, 170
  in *Numancia cercada* (Rojas Zorrilla), 139, 149

military *(continued)*
    in *Numancia destruida* (Rojas Zorrilla), 139
    professional soldier in, 33–35
    in 1600s, 130–31
    in *Troilus and Cressida* (Shakespeare), 189–90
Millington, Mark, 3
mock-heroic poem, 198–99
mode, 163
Molière, 178
Molina, Luis, 28
Molina, Tirso de
    *Amazonas en las Indias*, 44–45
    *La celosa de sí misma*, 51–54, 70, 72, 73–74
    *indiano* characters of, 43
    *Marta la piadosa*, 62–63, 66–69, 71
    *Por el sótano y el torno*, 64–66, 71
    *La villana de Vallecas*, 54–57, 70–71, 72, 73
Molloy, Sylvia, 42
money
    in *Don Quijote* (Cervantes), 197
    in English burlesque epic, 188–89
    in French burlesque epic, 183, 184–85
    in *indiano* drama, 68
    *indianos* and, 69–72
Montesinos, Antonio de, 3, 25–26, 30
Montesquieu, 199
Montrose, Louis, 6
Morales, Ambrosio de, 79
Morales, Carlos, 36
Morcillo, Sebastián Fox, 28
Murillo, Luis Andrés, 192
Murrin, Michael, 78, 163, 164, 199

natural liberty, doctrine of, 193–94
Naude, Gabriel, 178
*Naufragios* (Cabeza de Vaca), 42
Netherlands, 18, 19, 78
New Historicist critics, 6 n. 9
nobility
    critique of, 161–62, 164–65, 168
    definition of, 43
    in *Don Quijote* (Cervantes), 192
    economic activity of, 184
    epic literature and, 200
    as feminized, 16
    in *La gatomaquia* (Lope de Vega), 175–76
    transformation of function of, 2, 16, 185–86
    wealth and, 74–75

*La noche de San Juan* (Lope de Vega), 46, 70
novel
    counter-epic and, 198–202
    *historia* compared to, 126–27
    history play compared to, 89
    picaresque, 4 n. 5
*El nuevo mundo* (Lope de Vega), 43–44
Numancia. See *La destrucción de Numancia* (Cervantes); *Numancia cercada* (Rojas Zorrilla); *Numancia destruida* (Rojas Zorrilla)
*Numancia cercada* (Rojas Zorrilla)
    Cervantine drama and, 129–30, 152–53
    conflict between personal and national goals in, 139, 140–41
    farce in, 151–53
    historical inscription in, 134
    hunger for power in, 106
    military chivalry ideal in, 149
    military issues in, 139
*Numancia destruida* (Rojas Zorrilla)
    Cervantine drama and, 129–30, 152–53
    conflict between personal and national goals in, 139, 141–43
    deception in, 144–45
    farce in, 153
    historical inscription in, 134–37
    military issues in, 139

Olivares, Conde de, 2, 20–21, 84
Oña, Pedro de, 14, 27
*Orientalism* (Said), 41
*Orlando Furioso* (Ariosto), 130, 197
Other
    demonization of, 122–25
    humanization of, 115–21
    returnees to Spain as, 41
*Outside Literature* (Bennett), 9
outsider
    *indianos* status as and marriage, 54
    values and, 52–53

Pagden, Anthony, 2, 23–24, 25–26, 29
Palacios Rubios, Juan López de, 25–26, 28
Papal Bulls of Donation, 27–28, 29
parody
    burlesque epic and, 165–66
    definition of, 162
    as deflationary tool, 176

of epic literary conventions, 161–62
in Renaissance poetics, 162–63
Pastor, Beatriz, 116, 120
Paterson, Alan, 74
"Pavura de los condes de Carrión" (Quevedo), 161–62, 168–70
Paz, Matías de, 25–26
Peña, Juan de la, 27
*Persiles* (Cervantes), 199
Philip II, 17–19, 24, 25, 33, 35–36
Philip III, 2, 19–20, 128
Philip IV, 2, 20–21, 43, 130
picaresque novel, 4 n. 5
Pieterse, Jan Nederveen, *Empire and Emancipation*, 95–96, 116
Pinciano, 163–64
Pinelo, Antonio León, 27–28
*Por el sótano y el torno* (Tirso de Molina), 64–66, 71
Porter, Laurence, 63
power relations, 16, 201–2
Powers, Harriet, 131
*El premio del bien hablar* (Lope de Vega), 48–51, 70, 72
Puddu, Raffaele, 2, 15, 33, 34–35
Puritanism, 186
"purity of blood," preoccupation with, 96

Quevedo, Francisco de
 genre and, 166
 "Imitación de Virgilio en lo que Dido dijo a Eneas queriendo dejarla," 161–62, 166–68
 Infantes de Carrión, 154, 168–69
 "Pavura de los condes de Carrión," 161–62, 168–70
 sonnets of, 163
Quint, David, 14, 89, 163, 201
Quiroga, Vasco de, 26–27

Rabell, Carmen, 48
Rackin, Phyllis, *Stages of History*, 79–81, 85, 116–17
Ranke, Leopold von, 35
reception theory, 11–14
Redondo, Augustín, 47–48, 54
Reed, Walter, 201
Reiss, Timothy, 185
*Renaissance Drama* (Loftis), 93
*Requerimiento*, 193
Requesens, Luis de, 18

residual discourse, 6, 28, 78
Ribera, Alonso de, 22
Riós, Gutiérrez de los, 33
Rojas Zorrilla, Francisco de, 131–32. See also
 *Numancia cercada* (Rojas Zorrilla);
 *Numancia destruida* (Rojas Zorrilla)
Romanos, Melchora, 93, 94, 119, 132–33
Rome
 *dominium*, legal theory of, 25–28
 epic iconography and, 167–68
 influence of thought of, 29
 in Spanish political *imaginaire*, 23–24
 Tudor history play and, 79
Ruiz Ramón, Francisco, 88–89, 90, 91–92, 120–21

Saavedra Fajardo, Diego, 29–30, 108
Said, Edward, 25, 30, 40–41, 44
Scarron, Paul, *Virgile travesti*, 171, 176–77, 182–85
Schlau, Stacey, 14
Schmidt, Rachel, 165
School of Salamanca, 26, 27
Schwartz Lerner, Lia, 146
self-reflexivity
 in burlesque epic, 177–78, 190
 in history play, 81–82, 155
*El sembrar en buena tierra* (Lope de Vega), 58–62, 71
*senex amans* character, 45, 62–69
Sepúlveda, Juan Ginés de, 26–27
Shakespeare, William
 *Henriad*, 78, 200–201
 history plays of, 80–81
 *King John*, 80–81
 *Troilus and Cressida*, 171, 186–91
Shannon, Robert, 90, 92
siege warfare, 78, 98, 105–6, 173
slavery, 194
Smith, Dawn, 14
Smith, Paul Julian, 3
Smith, Paul Lewis, 126
Snyder, John, 15 n. 9
"sociology of genres," 9, 161, 163
soldiers, memoirs of, 34
Soto, Domingo de, 26, 27, 28
Soufas, Teresa, 14
Spadaccini, Nicholas, 8–9
Spain. *See also* economy of Spain; imperialism

Spain *(continued)*
    England and, 18–19, 21
    justification for conquest by, 115–16, 122, 124–25
    military ventures of, 2–3, 20, 130
*Spanish Imperialism and the Political Imagination* (Pagden), 25–26
Spivak, Gayatri Chakravorty, 44
*Stages of History* (Rackin), 79–81, 116–17
status
    identity and, instability of, 7, 16, 41–46, 56–57, 72–76
    liminal, of *indianos*, 42–43, 44–46, 62, 69, 75
    outsider, of *indianos*, 54
    wealth and, 72, 198
Stoll, Anita, 14, 43, 74
Stroud, Matthew, 89
style, late baroque, 132–33
Suárez, Francisco, 28, 63–64
subalterns, 44, 57

taxation, 20
Tennenhouse, Leonard, 9
theater
    "dramatic illusion" and, 185
    eternal nature of, 92
    "willing suspension of disbelief" and, 156
Thirty Years' War, 20, 130
Thomist thinkers, 108
Tiepolo, Antonio, 36
Todorov, Tzvetan, 28, 122
*Les Tragiques* (d'Aubigné), 14
transformation, 42–43
*Troilus and Cressida* (Shakespeare), 171, 186–91

United Provinces, 18, 19, 20
urbanism
    imperialism and, 48
    negative stereotypes of, 51–52
    positive view of, 54–55
Urrea, Jerónimo de, 34
Urtiaga, Alfonso, 39, 43

Valbuena Prat, Angel, 89
Valdés, Francisco de, 34
Vatican and Spanish crown, 27–28, 29
Veeser, Harold, 74

Vega y Carpio, Lope de. See also *Arauco domado* (Lope de Vega); *La gatomaquia* (Lope de Vega)
    genre and, 166
    *El indiano*, 75
    *La noche de San Juan*, 46, 70
    *El nuevo mundo*, 43–44
    Olivares and, 84
    *El premio del bien hablar*, 48–51, 70, 72
    *El sembrar en buena tierra*, 58–62, 71
*La verdad sospechosa* (Ruit de Alarcón), 74–75
Verdugo, Francisco, 34
*La villana de Vallecas* (Tirso de Molina), 54–57, 70–71, 72, 73
*villano* character, 45, 46, 50–51
*El villano del Danubio* (Guevara), 47
Villarino, Edith, 7, 40
*Virgile travesti* (Scarron), 171, 176–77, 182–85
Vitoria, Francisco de, 25, 26, 27, 28
Vives, Juan Luis, 6, 16

war. See also cost of war, portrayal of; military; siege warfare
    "just war" theory, 28–29
    soldiers, memoirs of, 34
Wardropper, Bruce, 91
Watt, Ian, 200
Watt, Stephen, 80
wealth and social status, 72, 198
Weiner, Jack, 94
Williams, Raymond, 5–6, 12, 13, 46–47, 77–78
Williamsen, Amy, 14
Wilson, Diana de Armas, 195, 199
women
    as alien, 58
    in *La Araucana* (Ercilla), 146
    in *Arauco domado* (Lope de Vega), 113–14, 121, 124
    disrespect for, 50
    in *La gatomaquia* (Lope de Vega), 171–72
    in *Troilus and Cressida* (Shakespeare), 187–88
    of yesteryear, 60–61

*Y así nació la frontera* (Keun), 21–22

Zapata, Luis, *Carlos Famoso*, 166

www.ingramcontent.com/pod-product-compliance
Lightning Source LLC
Chambersburg PA
CBHW031549300426
44111CB00006BA/239